PRAISE FOR *ANNAH, INFINITE*

'What is behind a portrait? What layers of meaning and bodily experiences are hidden or distorted when one is objectified by the artist? Khairani Barokka breaks down *Annah la Javanaise* by Paul Gauguin through a lens of colonialism, ableism, heteronormativity, and racism. The author sees pain written on Annah's body and reflects on her pain journey, tracing years of torture and neglect. *Annah, Infinite* is a fascinating exploration of Barokka's relationship with a brown person who was real and made into a painting.'
— Alice Wong, author of *Year of the Tiger: An Activist's Life*

'Khairani Barokka's *Annah, Infinite* is staged at the limit of portraiture, metabolizing the body as a composite mode of figuration, both present and redacted in the face of violence that sometimes has a face and sometimes is just that, itself, a broad pressure with no fixed source and "multiple modes" In this context, as night falls and keeps falling, Barokka asks if it's possible: "to translate what we endure as human beings." Is it?'
— Bhanu Kapil

'From the twin poles of *Annah la Javanaise* and her own pained body, Khairani Barokka unfurls a bold reimagining of established orthodoxies, punctuated with sharp wit and informed by wide-ranging erudition.'
— Jeremy Tiang, author of *State of Emergency*

'A profoundly disturbing, intriguing, and illuminating work—Khairani Barokka is so precise and empathetic that the reader aches with phantom pain.'
— Anton Hur, author of *Toward Eternity* and 2025 International Booker Prize judge

'*Annah, Infinite* focuses on a single canvas and yet contains multitudes. The text combines poetry, fiction, critical analysis, queer theory, colonial history, artwork, pain memoir and even catalogue descriptions, tempting one to describe it as *genre-defying*, and yet, I would be tempted to say that this ambitious, searing work heralds the birth of a new, yet-to-be-named genre, a form of translation which demands that we summon all our faculties—seeing, sensing, thinking, hearing, raging, loving, truthing—to engage with the enormity of a single artefact.'
— Daisy Rockwell, International Booker Prize-winning translator

'Khairani Barokka exposes the full evil of oppressive systems even as she denies them the power to hold us down. A powerful alternative to life lived forever in the shadow of the colonial and postcolonial. Like Annah, we were and are and will be and always will be free.'
—Tiffany Tsao, author of *The Majesties* and award-winning translator

'A major work on language and translation, art-reading and writing, race, femininity and, above all, on pain. It has a definitive and reclamatory power, combining elegy with research and personal experience in a way that is scholarly, expressive, and immensely readable.'
—Preti Taneja

'*Annah, Infinite* is a powerful, poetic and urgent text that defies categorisation. It is about many things, including art and Gauguin, but also colonisation, exploitation, othering, pain, gender, and the body as it is perceived and as it is experienced – in the past and in the present. Khairani Barokka draws the reader into her concerns by layering what is known, with what might be known, and what can easily be imagined if one chooses to take the risk. And it is a risk because Annah, the 'Javanese girl' who was painted by the artist Gauguin - naked and with a monkey at their feet - is given a voice, many voices, including that of the author. All these voices are possible and they become a chorus of truths that corrupt the art, the artist, the critic, the historian and the viewer. As with any chorus, it cannot and should not be ignored. I read this book with awe.'

—Pip Williams, author of *The Dictionary of Lost Words*

'*Annah, Infinite* is essential, groundbreaking work, deconstructing and reframing colonialism, art, disability, ableism, racism and the understanding of pain, exploring selfhood and interconnectivity under the multiply dehumanising colonial gaze of the art world and medical gaze of the abled world. A unique and life-changing read.'

— Polly Atkin

'Khairani Barokka reclaims the figure of Annah la Javanaise, once a footnote in Gauguin's colonial fantasy, and reimagines her into a multiplicity. No longer the exoticised muse, Annah fractures into a thousand selves: disabled, racialised, violated, yet surviving, subverting, resisting. Through Barokka's daring, intellectual, and poetic experiment, Annah becomes a portal between the empire's past—dehumanised bodies from colonial archives—and contemporary violence: the persistent structures of colonialism, racism, ableism, and heteropatriarchy. *Annah, Infinite* is ambitious, defiant, and haunting.'

—Intan Paramaditha

'Through this study of a single canvas and its subject, Barokka presents a brilliant book that defies classification, one that delves into linguistics, colonial history, queer theory and memoir, and is by turns lyrical, angry, tender and pained, harking back to the pioneering work of Linda Nochlin and John Berger, but blazing a new trail that is as unexpected as it is enthralling.'

— Frank Wynne, *The Irish Times*

PREVIOUS PRAISE FOR THE AUTHOR

Praise for *amuk*
'Khairani Barokka's poetry both makes and unmakes, picking apart the fabric and function of language so that we may put it to braver and more necessary use. amuk is the work of a visionary.'
—Victoria Adukwei Bulley, author of *Whose Name Means Honey*

'A poetic act of resurrection. A defiant and hope-giving epic of a collection, reversing colonisation's murders to restore its victims to life. In these poems, buds sprout from what was severed, forests spring from land made waste. The end transforms into a beginning, a prayer stretching its tender leaves towards the sun.'
—Tiffany Tsao, the author of *The Majesties*

Praise for *Indigenous Species*
'Everyone who is interested in art/poetry/politics should be reading and looking at Khairani Barokka's work.'
—Sophie Collins, poet

ANNAH, INFINITE

Translated from the painting *Annah la Javanaise*

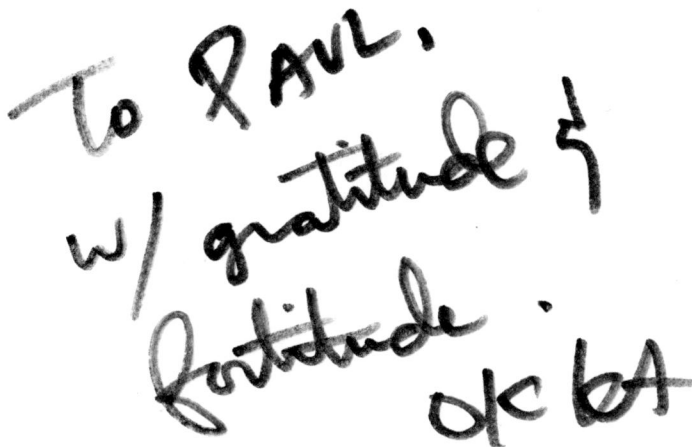

Khairani Barokka

Annah

Annah is a name that, in Bahasa Indonesia (Indonesian), can mean 'one Annah' or 'multiple Annahs', as any noun in the singular in Indonesian can also mean that noun in the plural.

Untuk Yangtiku tersayang. Untuk para Annah dan keluarga mereka.

COVER DESCRIPTION

Cover features a lilac purple background. The title appears in dark brownish-red at the center, with the author's name below. A dark brownish-red tilted axis runs through the middle and at the top is the Tilted Axis Press logo in black.

CONTENTS

Content Warning 3

Safety Message from Annah #0.346439 5

Notes on Language 7

Introduction: Selected Annahs 9

Chapter One: Caption: Annah/s, Infinite 29

Chapter Two: Complex Pain, Pictorial Forms 51

We Burn Disbelief 101

The Pained Archive 123

Nightmares of 1965 133

annah, three months
before escape (annah #835) 147

Chapter Three: Of Java 149

Interlude One: Queering and Cripping Time 177

Chapter Four: La Fille Française:
A Child of Thirteen 183

Chapter Five: In a World Where
No One is Voiceless, the Soulbody
Yells Through the Nerves 197

Interlude Two: Queering and Cripping Time 227

Our Language Opens Up 229

Annah #0.000000015 attends the first
Indonesian Women's Congress, in 1928 239

Chapter Six: Threatening Systems of Duress 241

State Violence and Moneybanks 245

The International 'Development'
Industry and Art Market 253

Some Months Earlier, or Annah #24,957
Observes a PhD Thesis 271

Chapter Seven: Annah As Rupture 285

Interlude Three: Queering and Cripping Time 293

Annah #8,923 floats next to me on
a trip to Royal Gallery X 295

Chapter Eight: Annah/s Onwards 303

annah #333,333,333 (and me) 319

Annah #1,567,732 moves through Harum 321

Selected References 327

Acknowledgements 335

[← A deliberate signpost, to which you will return.

CONTENT WARNING

This is an escape story. There are vast fields of intertwined kinds of violence to pass through, and I try my utmost to reference them without sinking you, to allude to them without being explicit where possible. I have tried to keep you here with gentleness, without gratuitousness, undue explicitness. Though of course my attempts may have differing outcomes for each of us, my intention is for this book to be about the peace on the other side, rarely thought of by many, for Annah, for many of us. We can return and return to that peace for the stretch you are here with me.

Many forms of violence are present in the possibilities for who *Annah la Javanaise* depicts. But there are also many possibilities to escape every single one of them. Possibilities that exist, that are always already here. I use this brushstroke over words, where I feel it may be needed for us: ▮▮▮▮▮▮▮▮▮▮. It is impossible, of course, to gauge every reader's zone of safety, but I have tried my best.

Gift yourself as many breaks as you need. Writing this required breaks of me, often. Then again, also, jags of delving into worlds where none of these modes of violence exist, when time is no object, time becoming an enveloping warmth.

No content warning, to my knowledge, exists in others' presentations of, or writing on, *Annah la Javanaise*, the painting or the figure.

SAFETY MESSAGE FROM
ANNAH #0.346439

Opening up to possibility, imagine yourself in the gentlest environs possible, where you can lie down if you need to, as soft textiles abound. The softest of senses. Your knees up in a forest, if you have knees and can pull them towards your chest, back straight with the soil.

If you feel jolted from this place, you can return to it.

NOTES ON LANGUAGE

- When italicised, i.e. '*Annah la Javanaise*', I am referring to the painting by Gauguin. When not italicised, i.e. 'Annah la Javanaise' or 'Annah the Javanese', I am referring to the 'historically real' person or people who were called by this name, though their name and/or cultural identity may have been other or multiple.
- If phrases that are not in English, e.g. 'dia', are not italicised, that is also deliberate. This is in keeping with my personal and political practice, as a literary translator who believes that to italicise in the English language is often to 'other'.

INTRODUCTION: SELECTED ANNAHS

An opera singer, Mme Nina Pack, was on friendly terms with a rich banker who had business relations with the traders of the Malayan Isles. The singer happened to say before the representative of one of these, 'I would like to have a little negro girl.' A few months later a policeman brought Mme Nina Pack a young, half-breed, half-Indian, half-Malayan, who had been found wandering about the Gare de Lyon. She had a label hung around her neck, with the inscription: Mme Nina Pack, rue de la Rochefoucauld, á Paris. Envoi de Java. She was given the name of Anna. Some time later, in consequence of a little domestic drama in which Anna was implicated, she was dismissed. She came to me, as I had known her at her employer's house, to ask me to find her a good situation. I judged her qualifications as a housemaid to be very middling, and thought she stood more chance of succeeding as a model. I told Gauguin about her.

'Send her to me. I'll try her,' he said.

Anna pleased him, and he kept her.

—Ambroise Vollard (Gauguin's art dealer), 1936

10 Annah, Infinite

The title of Paul Gauguin's 1893–94 portrait *Annah la Javanaise. Aita tamari vahine Judith te parari* has two parts, that describe its subject in two different languages: 'Annah the Javanese [in French]. The child-girl Judith has not been breached [in Tahitian]'. Relatively little is known of the real young person or people who inspired the painting. The instances in which people – whether art historians, the Nobel laureate Mario Vargas Llosa, or writers of art institution copy – have written of Annah contradict each other often, offering up vague and conflicting details of a supposedly insignificant life. Annah's ethnicity shifts, their origin changes from 'streets' to 'brothels'; I have seen the exact same photo of a child labelled 'Annah la Javanaise' also labelled as 'Teha'amana', a Polynesian teenager who'd been married to Gauguin. There is so much variation in these nonchalantly inconsistent accounts of their life that it's plausible multiple brown children could have been mistaken for one, that the figure known as 'Annah' could have been a composite. Gauguin was certainly associated with multiple young, brown people in Tahiti; there is no reason why his brown sitters in Paris could not have been multiple. The possibility exists. For that matter, it's possible that Annah, though widely interpreted as a girl, was trans or of a non-Western gender, and thus possibly desirous of 'they' as their pronoun in English, or 'dia', the Indonesian gender-neutral pronoun used for everyone. Or something entirely different, different possible Annahs preferring different pronouns.

These children exist in the archives as an afterthought, an appendage to a coterie of white, European, male painters in late nineteenth-century France, primarily Paul Gauguin.

I first learned of *Annah la Javanaise* in 2011. Today it is held in a private collection, inaccessible to the general public except when loaned out to museum exhibitions. I discovered its existence online, and thus experienced it, as most people now do, as a series of pixels on a screen, a digital ghost of an artwork whose original form exists exclusively for its wealthy owners. My first thought upon seeing the picture was that it showed a Javanese girl, like myself, a body labelled as a Javanese woman (though in photographs in the Gauguin archives, a similar-looking person presents as a child), documented abroad in the nineteenth century, captured in both painted and photographic form. This is rare to see.

At that time I had begun to think increasingly about women's pain, being in acute and untreated pain myself for what would later be diagnosed as permanent nerve damage; the northern hemisphere summer of 2011 was the beginning of continuous and then intermittent, always-at-risk-of-relapsing, 'ten out of ten', stunning, incomprehensible levels of pain. It would be more than a decade until I knew that the right word for this, what I should have been calling it all along, was *torture*. Even so, I did know – instinctively, instantaneously, of course – that the threat of this torture revisiting my soulbody, of it staying, was contingent on others believing me, providing the necessary conditions for proper treatment. I did not know that the abject lack of treatment, care and belief would become a recurring motif, the banal parameters of life, but I knew that all my life hinged on *was* belief.

It is this experience that sparked an instant recognition, upon seeing Annah/s portrayed, that the world was framing them so as to deny the truth of personal infernos. The world had instantaneously become so unsafe for me then that the only point of safety and possible understanding was the person, or various possible people, portrayed in this painting. The figure – figures – of Annah crystallised ideas that had been on my mind: the link between chronic pain and past trauma; how women are less likely to be believed when they experience pain, by the medical establishment and/or friends and family; the compounding of women's pain due to that disbelief, and the compounding of this disbelief due to gender and race.

Since my discovery of the painting fourteen years ago, I have held on to Annah dearly as a composite of figures to whom I could relate. Their probable horrors and experiences are likely different from mine, but here was a person labelled 'Javanese girl' who could well have been in pain, but for whom the possibility of pain does not occur to an ablenormative world. In subsequent years, I have projected scenarios of their escape, safety and joy onto my fiction, poetry and visual art, knowing that in reality, a child in their circumstances at that time was very likely to have suffered throughout their life. After all, interpreted as young, brown girl/s in 1890s France, they would have lived lives of isolation, and their captor Gauguin – captor, as they were likely enslaved – was a known domestic abuser who would certainly today be classified as a sexual predator. Gauguin delighted in humiliating all women, but targeted women descended from European colonies precisely because they were less protected. In *Noa Noa*, the journal of his time in Tahiti, Gauguin reminisced, 'I saw plenty of calm-eyed young women, I wanted them to be willing to be taken without a word: taken ▮▮▮. In a way longing to ▮▮.'

Gauguin lived twice in what was then French Polynesia, first from 1891 to 1893 – when he was in charge of an official mission from the French Ministry of Education and Culture – and again from 1895 until his death in 1903. During his first trip to Tahiti, he reportedly took three brides, aged between thirteen and fourteen, and was rumoured to have given them and others syphilis. Yet the artistic result of Gauguin's Polynesian trips – his famed portraits of brown children interpreted as girls – are not seen as artefacts of abuse but as remarkable contributions to Western art history. In 1896, Gauguin was commissioned to paint a portrait of Vaite Goupil, the nine-year-old daughter of his Tahiti-based French patron Auguste Goupil. The disturbingly adult nature of the portrait may have been what caused Goupil to distance himself from Gauguin, yet there was no known outcry from patrons about Gauguin's use of brown children, interpreted as girls, as sexual objects. In Paris and Brittany, between trips to Tahiti, according to numerous historians' accounts, he was seen in the company of Annah – a very young person who was taken to be sexually involved with him, though even the fact that they ever posed nude for him is an assumption, and cannot be proved. There is in fact no clear evidence, despite what disturbing biopics and Nobel-winning novelists will tell you, that Gauguin and Annah were romantically or sexually engaged at all, though it was widely assumed they were, and this assumption is treated as unequivocal fact by numerous history books and 'world-class' arts institutions. All art historical accounts portray this supposed relationship as benign, as part of the male artist's whimsy and exoticism, or else portray Annah as a heartless villain… for, as we will come to, there are accounts of them trying to regain power from Gauguin in a very specific way.

Over time, my understanding of who the children labelled as Annah might be has expanded as I've investigated the role of ableism as combined with white supremacy in arts institutions. I've grown increasingly aware of how archival texts and images concerning the figure of Annah impose a set of beliefs and agendas that support a very specific power dynamic between subject and artist – in which the former is an unharmed, impervious muse no matter what the truth may have been – and shape extant narratives surrounding the real child or children who lived and inspired the painting. A 1950 *LIFE Magazine* issue described Annah, without evidence, as 'Gauguin's Faithless Javanese'; they are portrayed as a willing sexual partner of Gauguin's in films such as 1986's award-winning (and thoroughly vile in its depiction of the endangerment of children) *The Wolf at the Door*. Their image is used today in art history classes as an example of Gauguin's primitivist oeuvre. Overwhelmingly, Annah has been depicted as supplementary, a tantalising femme fatale, proof of Gauguin's closeness to the 'natives', part of the myth of the genius artist, explorer and tamer of foreign wildnesses.

I'm convinced, however, that it's important to consider the notion, largely unexplored, that *Annah la Javanaise* is very possibly a portrait of a young child living with pain. Why Annah in particular? Why pain? There is a perception that it is counterintuitive to describe people in paintings as potentially pained. But this is only because ableist, ocularcentric interpretations permeate the field of visual cultures. A depicted body is assumed to be unpained, until a certain set of cues that abled people understand as 'cues for pain' somehow prove that they are pained. Yet as those of us who live with chronic pain know, in photos and in the flesh there is often no way that another person can know we are in pain, nor to what degree. Further, sometimes pain is incurred during the taking of an image – by sitting on the wrong nerve, for instance – and may manifest days later, acutely. Such emergencies, and lack of acknowledgment of them, have formed continual traumas in my own life, and I know that I am far from alone in experiencing this.

Disabled[1] people are the largest minority in the world, and most of us live or come from places that have borne the brunt

---

[1] I take the word 'disabled' to mean a complex combination of socially imposed disabilities (the opposite of 'enabled') and other person-specific factors. It is my opinion that a person has the right to self-identify how they wish, as long as it does not hurt others; in line with my transnational community of disability justice activists, I prefer 'disabled person' to 'person with a disability' in most contexts, the latter term often contributing to further stigma of 'otherness' and 'difference', and eugenicist urges to eradicate it. I also, however, understand that someone living with a chronic health condition, for instance, may vastly prefer to be described as 'living with [said condition]'.

of white supremacist political economies, in both the 'first world' and 'third world', whether lead-poisoned Flint, Michigan or environmentally threatened Kendeng, Indonesia. The medical model of disability, which claims that all 'differences' must be 'healed' (in other words, stamped out), was so entrenched in Indonesian psyches by Dutch missionary hospital systems that I was only explicitly reminded well into adulthood of a fact I knew subconsciously: that some Javanese deities are or have been disabled, as written about by disabled colleague Slamet Amex Thohari. These assumptions – abled until proven disabled, and that all disabilities are the same, and meant to be 'healed' or eliminated – are deep-rooted, and intrinsically related to colonialist human classification systems. When we look at any image of any human missing certain normative 'cues of pain', the default interpretation is not only that are they not in pain, but that the mere possibility of their painedness is preposterous. Greater society has no understanding of bodies that exhibit no outer sign of pain according to abled norms, and yet are in pain. This makes Annah's pain a certain possibility.

Is this so far-fetched? That a child in the presence of an abusive older man, who seemed to revel in the intimation that they had a sexual relationship, would hurt? This does not mean they were only ever a victim. One story of Annah claims they robbed Gauguin of everything except his art. In this possibility, Annah may have escaped. And even if they didn't, none of us are just victims of anything. We carry all of our lives in our bodies. These are stratified layers of emotion, complex memories kept in the sternum and soaked in the marrow. Annah would have had this kind of body too, a body that remembers, no matter how we choose to remember them.

I say that Annah could have been a pained body. Of course, the varieties of pain are infinite, from the aftermath of a stubbed toe, to fibromyalgia, to varying kinds of headaches. To torture. There are spectrums of pain's longevity, intensity, nature, origin, and crucially, spectrums of its meaning. Only Annah knows what was experienced by their body/ies. The operations of ableism, racism and sexism are closely linked within colonial mechanisms, in ways that are pervasive, enduring, and ongoing. Bringing these links to the fore illuminates how much we elide and deny histories of pain in portrayed human bodies, particularly vulnerable human bodies such as those of Annah. Portrayed as vivacious and lively, their wellbeing was profoundly at risk.

So here we go. Let's consider and imagine Annah differently, many different Annahs, Annah as infinite possibilities; the truth being the same distance from our grasp as the 1890s, truth kept with, and belonging to, only them and all the many possible thems.

★

Annah la Javanaise is a painting created in France, which affixes a name to its subject belonging to those who come from a densely populated Southeast Asian island. The painting uses bright colours, and is meant to be placed upright, meaning, vertically, as the subject is presented. When the piece is listed – in galleries, museums, libraries, and within the electric flow of their image – his name comes first. His name, then Annah's, then Judith's:

Paul Gauguin, *Annah the Javanese, or Aita Tamari Vahine Judith te Parari (The Child-Woman Judith Is Not Yet Breached)*, 1893–94. Oil on canvas, 45 1/4 x 31 1/2 in. (116 x 81 cm). Private Collection.

This is a rectangle-shaped piece of commerce. A person is sitting on a chair, taking up the frame's space. We infer: this is

Annah the Javanese. There is a creature alongside Annah, but it is not Judith: it is an unnamed monkey at their feet. Annah is smiling like Mona Lisa, but they are naked. The background wall is peach-terracotta.

What on earth is Judith doing in that title? you might ask. You might well ask. Judith Molard, the daughter of Gauguin's friend and patron, posed as a full-frontal nude model for him in sessions that were put to a stop by her mother, Ida, once they were discovered. *Annah la Javanaise* could have been, in fact, an amalgamated body of this girl and another. But it is, in the end, Annah, whom it is easier for Gauguin to objectify, to twist into an image of sexual openness. And it is emphasised that the child-girl Judith has not been breached – with the unsaid implication that this is not the case for Annah.

Annah has the body of a widely presumed cis-girl. 'Child-Woman', some might describe their presentation as, though one must remember: this label in the title applies only to Judith. They have pubic hair, possible snail trail, round breasts. Their hair is tied up. Their earrings are looped and golden. Their legs are crossed at the ankles, on a green cushion. They are naked and palatial.

Annah is said, in various sources, to be around thirteen, so perhaps, if in a menstruating body, they had not yet had their first period. Or perhaps they had, though the figure on the chair shows no signs of bleeding.

What is this Private Collection? The terms of possession keep *Annah la Javanaise*'s current owners to themselves.

★

Annah sits on blue upholstery in a carved wooden chair.

Would you feel comfortable being naked with a monkey at your feet? Would you be afraid of it biting you? Who would you allow to see you sitting in a chair with your legs crossed at your ankles, with nothing on but earrings and perhaps a hair clip? If you were thirteen years old?

★

In historical documents, Annah is given biographical attributes that are completely disparate from one to the next – 'half-Malay, half-Indian'; 'half-Indonesian, half-Dutch'; 'mulatto'; 'Polynesian', as a Tate Library archive entry has it. Originally, she was labelled as 'Javanese', but the varied writing on her origins allows for slippages in the interstices of these biographical facts. It doesn't matter what colony this person is from, these clashing documents suggest, as long as they are from a colony.

Over the past fourteen years, I have seen photos of brown children with faces that could have been from entirely different people, all labelled as Annah. I have seen two photos of exactly the same brown body assumed to be a girl, labelled both 'Hannah la Javanaise, Paul Gauguin's mistress' and 'Tohotaua of Polynesia who posed for Paul Gauguin'. They have never been able to tell us apart. When it comes to the object of colonisation, the details aren't important. All that matters is that details, people, are possessed and possessable.

That their origins are written as varied and clashing gives rise to this understanding: Annah could have been many kinds of bodies. They could have been trans. They could have hated the pronoun 'they' and preferred 'she', and in this case as in others, they could have been autistic or otherwise neurodivergent, could have been D/deaf, they could have limped. She or they or him or dia could have been in a non-normative body, and chosen not to disclose this. Perhaps non-disclosure would have been a small window to less vulnerability, a bit more safety in the terrifying world these child-figure/s inhabited.

★

maybe the body is the only question an answer can't extinguish

—Ocean Vuong

★

In her book *Paul Gauguin: An Erotic Life*, the art historian Nancy Mowll Mathews writes:

> Alternatively seductive and bullying in his manner... Although he did not hesitate to physically ▇ both men and women and evidently was titillated by their submission, he also imagined the pleasurable sensation of receiving such ▇. His many paintings of Eve frightened by the snake attest to his belief in the eroticism of both ▇ and submission.

★

An object sits on a chair in this painting, in the shape of a woman made of brown oil. Primate at her feet, whole nudity stretched out. Hair in a bun, bum perched on seat's edge.

Is this a 'nature painting'? Is this natural? *Annah la Javanaise. Aita tamari vahine Judith te parari.* With its title in French and Tahitian, the work has at least four cultural components that can be discerned: (1) French, (2) Javanese, a culture from Java, Indonesia's most populated island, and therefore (3) Indonesian, Indonesia being the country now fourth most populated in the world, which emerged as independent in 1945 and is and has been a perpetrator of colonialism itself, its borders including Java, the island on which Indonesia's capital Jakarta resides, and (4) Tahitian, a language invoked by Gauguin to suggest to others that he was close to 'savages', to the exotic, to 'primitive' peoples whose art he copied, whose young children he captured and made paintings of that are now held in private collections.

Despite the flattening of their identity, there remains the possibility that Annah's body had pulsating parts which were nerve-sensitised, vulnerable to variable jolts, waves and oceans of pain. As many kinds of pain as water, Frenchwaters, Tahitianwaters, Javanesewaters, Indonesianwaters, Englishwaters, traversing, concurrently – pain could have been a hazy drizzle in the arm, a shudder of rain, a deluge of sea; it could have been of different intensities, ebbing in some collections of cells, flowing in others.

Once a professor I know said of the painting something to the effect of, 'Yes, she could be disabled and in pain, she is tilted.' But those of us who know pain know: we can assume Olympian positions of strength and endurance, years at a time, holding it puckered in ligaments, giving no sign of our painedness to abled folk. We can smile widely, with no one but ourselves the wiser. Our bodies could be imploding internally and, perhaps because we have been disbelieved so routinely, we may not even signal in an ablenormative way that we are in distress. For we have experienced ablenormative surrounds as unsafe for pained people, we have had our distress weaponised against us and disbelieved, and so we act 'unpained' in order to avoid the brutality of disbelief.

In addition, when a body is experiencing acute pain, it may be to such a degree that the human brain is overwhelmed, bewildered, and causes behaviour inscrutable to others. Sometimes we must appear abled for employment purposes, such as when sitting as an artist's model, for a man with a known propensity for violence. Though Gauguin's son wrote of his father's domestic abuse, and Gauguin's over-familiar relationships with a plethora of children are documented in numerous archival sources, not a single authority figure stepped in to apprehend him for any suspected crime. Crimes, after all – who can be punished for them, whom they can be committed against – are created by a society of a particular time and place. The historical record names several young people whom Gauguin painted – Marie Jade, Judith Molard, Jeanne Schuffenecker, Teha'amana, Pahura (Pau'ura) a Tai, Vaeoho Marie-Rose, and Annah. The degree of protection afforded to these children varied widely, by virtue of race and class.

Annah's situation made them more vulnerable to chronic pain, and they were vulnerable due to many factors: a young, brown, child, interpreted as a girl, in Paris, of uncertain citizenship, with no documented guardians; a slave who was ordered by an opera singer, someone with a possible history of child labour according to accounts that they began Parisian life as a domestic worker or sex worker who was likely not paid; very likely an ongoing survivor of abuse at the hands of an older, colonial white man; a child who was surrounded primarily by other older, white men who condoned if not contributed to and perpetuated this abuse; set up as a sexual rival to girls their age who they were in contact with; profoundly isolated with a lack of holistic healthcare and wellbeing. All of these elements meant they were at risk of injury from trauma, which can result in chronic pain.

What if these were the painting's titles?

Portrait of a Child in Pain.
Portrait of a Nude Child in Pain.
Portrait of Nude Child Annah in Pain (The Child Judith Has Not Been Breached).

Gauguin's fantasies of young girls could actually have been fantasies of young girls in severe pain. Entertain this notion. Stay with it. It is a clear option.

What is this 'nature' Gauguin thought he was spelling out, if a painter is unaware of the nuances of the sittee's internal states? Do I assume that the painted body is not in pain? Why, and why not? Do I assume Gauguin was not in pain, the tortured artist? After all, an aspect of Gauguin's mystique is that he suffered for his eccentric identification with 'savage' cultures, that he was alienated from valorised bourgeois French values. In that article 'Gauguin's Faithless Javanese', Annah is blamed by *LIFE* for Gauguin's financial woes in the lead-up to his death – perversely, she is painless, he is pained by her. Stories of white male artists, who are the 'greats', the 'geniuses', in Eurocentric art history curricula, are littered with justifications for harmful behaviour. The actual power dynamics between them and their muses magically reversed. As I consider the power dynamics here, I de-intensify Paul Gauguin's pain in light of how vulnerable he made Annah.

I think of Annah as oil on a canvas in an unnamed private collection (a source I shall keep anonymous has told me of a diabolically wealthy family whom she thinks is in possession of the painting), and also as a series of pixels. Ones and zeroes, JPEGs, GIFs, PNGs, screenshots, Google Image searches, on endless screens. Alive in the cloud. The message here is repeated, subtle cues we receive every day in an ablenormative world about visual images: 'She is abled. She is not in pain.' Yet the notion that a body is either 'in pain' or 'not in pain', one or the other, is a falsehood foreclosing a world of possibilities, including, for instance, 'I'm fine, though now that I have a minute to rest, I realise my muscles feel exhausted' or 'I've lived with chronic pain that fluctuates from acute severity to bearability, depending on a bunch of factors. Right now I'd say it's five out of ten in my chest and two out of ten in my arm, if you want to use a flawed numerical system.' Abled assumptions of a monolithic, binary system for painedness are treacherous, and often deceitful.

A person can pose for a portrait sitting and be pained. A person can feel it acutely the longer they sit, or perceive it as a dull ache. Or they can forget about the pain, because it's lasted so long in the body that the mind has constructed a defence of many neurons that allows them to live so: pained, in varying degrees. Once again, it must be stressed that the pain might only be felt or intensify later.

The images discussed here – in painting, in photographic form, of children labelled 'Annah' – pose the question: where are the traces of possible pain in all forms of *Annah la Javanaise* as image: .JPEG, .PNG, screenshot, Google Search? I believe they have always been there.

The FAQs on the website for the Register for Artist Models, the UK's professional association for artist models and tutors, says:

'(3) Have you the patience and stamina required to keep very still for up to 45 minutes at a time, regardless of whatever discomfort (sometimes pain) you may be in? Sometimes you will be required to return to the same awful pose after a short break. Indeed, the same pose may last for several weeks. In time you learn what to avoid, to some extent, and you also become a bit tougher, but you will never avoid pain and discomfort entirely in this job.'

Here it is prudent to remind ourselves that Annah, of course, is never recorded as having been paid monetarily for their services as a muse.

For fourteen years now, I've created many multiform Annah scenarios, numbered randomly to emphasise the infinite nature of their possibilities, which includes, finally, the possibility that there are worlds in which the child is, or children are, somehow safe.

★

Annah #8,925 Conveys a Message to You

Schoolgirls learn about me in classrooms. They cup my breasts like a mug of hot tea, leaves picked from blurry lands, inconsequential plantations. They are quizzed on late eighteenth-century artistic movements in France. On his oeuvre. On my nudity compared to other forms of nudity. Not much in the teachers' lectures about provenance. Imagine them even broaching the provenance of my being, of my being here.

What is the term for this: erasure? Diminishment? Of humming we still feel in our bodies, and would rather forget – or better yet, transform into a substance of gentleness, protective momentum, beyond healed scar, beyond the right not to forgive.

I feel a constant panic, the panic of not being understood by yet another, and another, and another. They wear tartan skirts and red backpacks; I only notice the ones my age. That schoolgirls are taught about my image as benign is in no way benign. It is caught up in all the ways we revere male 'geniuses' so long after their deaths, so long after the deaths of us as muses, as more than muses. Our humanity is boiling hot to the blood as a cauldron, overspilling again and again within the confines of our skin; this is not taught to the schoolgirls. There is a constant mad rush to be known, and to be home. My inside stirrings have been denied not repeatedly but interminably, without end, and so it is their reality that reigns, that imperils me, that sickens me from within. And my hands begin to hurt.

Every time you try to thrash through the wall, beyond which, you hope, you will find peace and a whole sense of selfhood that thrives, you are shaken by it, the wall thrashes back, thunders against your shoulders as it throws you upon itself.

The monkey-fed room you have been thrust into is on fire. Walls of this room become limits of skin.

Something has been damaged to wrecking point.

It began before it began. When I saw him and, soon after, his paintings. I realised what he did in Tahiti, to those youths, and how he would make the painting with my name as its title. How my body would be on a plane, oiled, a representation foretold, as it had been for other women whose language I did not speak, whose customs I did not understand. I understood that, like a very small child, a Parisian not-brown would look at our skins, as though deciphering the remnants of a hunt, and draw circles around us.

And earlier, when I set foot in France for the first time, and the weight of universal unsafety descended on my black-haired head with every look that came my way, that wanted me gone or captured, a monkey in Europe, a curiosity. It began when I knew I would leave Java, and when my mother died it began very quietly there, with her last breath. As wicked as living often is, I want my mother in it. As wicked as living is, I want the strange thing that is life.

Annah, Infinite

Annah #67

So I wake up in monochrome, and someone is asking 'Why would you think of her in chronic pain?' And then it's more than a person asking, it's many. I scratch at the surface of the canvas from within, and find I can't breathe. To realise respiration was never an option when your flesh is paint, what a godawful relief. So I throw my head back and laugh, because I realise I am inanimate, I am a figurine on a canvas, there's no air to go in my lungs. How am I even sure there are lungs in here when I can't even remember the monkey's name; can I be sure of what I learned of anatomy? I try to remember the place where I could have learned of two bags of hollow lungs splayed in a chest, symmetrical, heaving in and out again.

Back in the village there was a school. Did I go? The Dutch weren't allowed to teach us, learning came from the mosque and aunties – Bu Des – around us. Rattan was used as a ruler might be in the white schools, rapped against walls and floors for attention. There is a lesson I knew before I knew it, which is that the maps of a woman's anatomy came about through torture of women whose skins were brown – slaves used for medical experiments – that led to white OB/GYN 'discoveries'. The sexual reproductive system was delineated this way. I don't remember the year I am in. I've banged my head, it seems, or were these voices always rushing, retching towards my body.

'Why would you think of her in chronic pain?
in chronic pain?
in chronic pain?'

And I think of when P. nearly choked on a fishbone and then chucked a decanter at my neck, screaming that came from the wine in his veins about how he'd hit his wife whenever he could, so I'd ███████████████████████████ ████████.

I somehow also know that his son will write about remembering this, father bloodying his mother.

In museums, there are so many girls who might be mistaken for me. I have been mistaken for them. I run my hands across their hair, all the world greyscale, in a different colour register from his. I lift up their hair with their permission, see scabs healing over on the napes from his hands. One of the girls tells me it is the Christian year 2020. The Javanese calendar: Jumadiawal – 1953 Wawu, Sengara Langkir.

'Don't worry', I tell all of them, 'I have a plan', and we leave stretched out canvases together, for a secret pot of retribution.

★

Annah #45 on the Water

I went to sit far by the river, as the river is also the ocean.
As marine goddess Nyi Roro Kidul came and
took me in her arms as a cauldron of fear, in a dream,
telling of such things that I now know. And currently
he is napping, so I may open into the sun.
Napping as a prerequisite for busy waves in miniature
and fervent, against my ankles. They call this liquid
the Seine, and I say it is the Java Sea.
Oil rises thick to the top,

    against banks; I swim deep.

CHAPTER 1:
CAPTION: ANNAH/S, INFINITE

[*Caption 1*

Content warning: the intertwining of multiple modes of harm, including multiple characterisations without express consent of the deceased.]

—

[*Caption 2*

Paul Gauguin, *Annah the Javanese, or Aita Tamari Vahine Judith te Parari (The Child-Woman Judith Is Not Yet Breached)*, 1893–94. Oil on canvas, 45 1/4 x 31 1/2 in. (116 x 81 cm). Private Collection.

This image is easily Google Image-searched. Enter the three words 'Annah la Javanaise' into the visual search engine. See how many-many. Sisters linked hand by hand, linked by primitivism's frame. Embroiled, as are all of us nowadays, in a grid of capturable pixels.

(The image of multiple Annahs below, in Google Image search, under the words 'Annah la javanesa - Viquipédia'.)]

30 *Annah, Infinite*

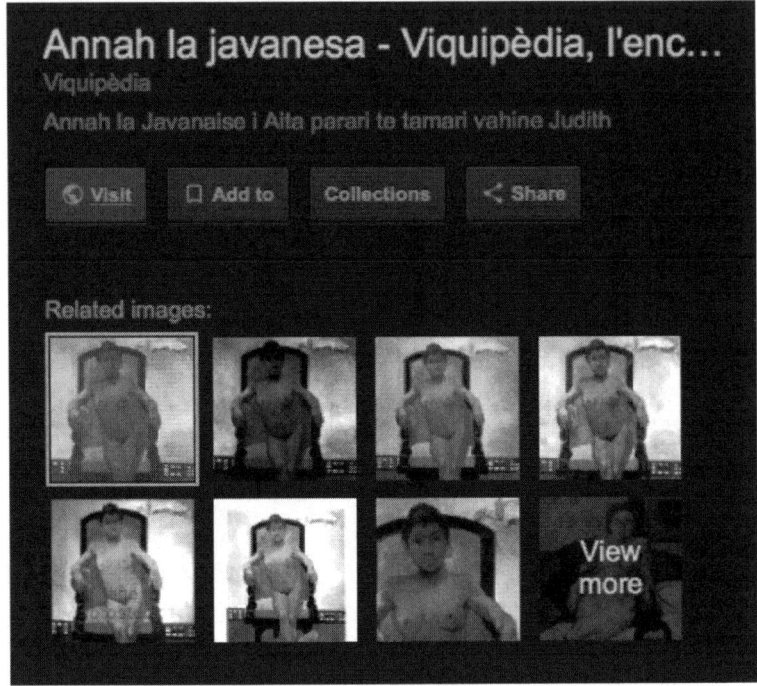

—

[*Caption 3*

Painting of a naked child on a chair, your hair in a bun, your ankles crossed, arms on the chair. Monkey at your feet.]

—

[*Caption 4*

To address you in Aksara Jawa (Javanese script), I would have to use pada andhap, punctuation for addressing a person of higher rank or age in a letter:

꧌꧍

Although, with your permission, I'd want to take you to a loving parent all the time. And that would feel as though it would require pada luhur, the punctuation for addressing a person of lower age:

꧌꧍

Except that pada luhur is also used for those of lower rank. I feel that you outrank me, however, in every instance. To use a term from poet Alexis Pauline Gumbs, everything I've created of your stories over the past fourteen years feels 'ancestrally co-written'. It feels as though you are banging down the door from inside a canvas, that all of you are, with an urgency that has not dissipated in 121 years.

Aksara Jawa punctuation without age or rank, pada guru:

꧋

Aksara Jawa punctuation for a person of equal age or rank, pada madya:

꧌꧍

]

[*Caption 5*

Here's to the plurality of 'you'.

If one looks at that particular Google Image search, and scrolls down the entries and notices the captions attached, they might come across a particular nugget of truth: the same girl marked 'Annah la Javanaise' is elsewhere marked as being Polynesian.

From *LIFE Magazine*'s 11 September 1950 issue, a feature entitled 'GREAT LOVES OF GREAT ARTISTS':

> [Paul] installed a bronze-skinned Javanese girl named Annah, whom he had met in Montmartre, and there he painted her like a South Sea queen on a blue throne, while his pet monkey leaped about the room and hung from the doorway on which was inscribed in Tahitian words, *Here there is love*. Later Gauguin took Annah and the monkey off to Britany [sic] where, in a fight with some sailors, the painter was seriously injured. While he was recovering, Annah slipped away to Paris, looted his studio and disappeared. Bitter and once again impoverished, Gauguin sailed away to Tahiti where he was to die, diseased and abandoned, eight years later.

Pobrecito Paul. Poor little man, of whom his son would write that he was a domestic abuser, who'd hit his Danish wife until she bled. Nowhere in what I've read so far is what ultimately became of you. The myth of the vanishing thief. I am proud of you, Annah, of all versions of your history that involve grand robbery on own initiative.

According to Mowll Mathews, there was no evidence that Paul was intimate with you. There is, however, every suggestion that he wanted the public to believe you were, to bolster his persona as closer to the 'savages'.

'Annah lived in Gauguin's Paris flat and it is believed that Annah was also his mistress... Annah was in fact Eurasian (Dutch-Javanese), brought to Paris from Southeast Asia by the opera singer Nina Pack and "found" by Gauguin's art dealer in the streets or brothels of Montmartre...' writes scholar M. Isaac Cohen.

'Dutch-Javanese'.
Other works describe Annah as, variously:
'mulatto'
'mixed-race'
'Ceylonese'
'half-Indian, half-Malayan'

In not one of these texts is it ever mentioned that others describe your heritage differently, describe how you came to know Gauguin differently. You are a puzzle piece that despite lack of specificity always fits into Gauguin marketing, into the numerical value at potential auction of the painting *Annah la Javanaise*, a painting as investment.

It doesn't matter which colony you came from, as long as you are from a colony (never mind that Java was then under Dutch rule, not French – you know, Annah, how they work in brutal cahoots).]

—

[*Caption 6*

Nearly every single source, whatever they say about your origins, mentions that you were thirteen, or 'around thirteen'. One day, I was discussing this, the strangeness of this and my confusion around it, when my colleague, the artist and curator Ala Younis, suggested that it might have been the age of consent in France at the time. She was right.

Schoolgirls are brought to museums and galleries, told how best to frame nudity. Taught of old masters, of sittees as muses, as willing friends of a genial mythos, as paramours to genius.]

—

[*Caption 7*

There's you. And you're the only one of all the ones he's painted who is ever described as Javanese. And there's Judith, the child-girl Judith who has not been breached, that's in the title. And she is also written of as around thirteen. This is most likely Judith Molard, daughter of his friends the Molards, in Paris.

The feature film from 1986 which lays claim to you: *Oviri, or Wolf at the Door*. Don't watch it, unless you'd like to see a scene in which a child actor with brown skin, portraying you, is seen ███████████ Paul, as portrayed by Donald Sutherland. The child is completely still, ███████████. And so they dubbed the sounds of a ███████████████████████ in which the child looks terrified. On IMDB, I see that the actor who plays this child (who I will not name here) has never acted in another film. I have no intention of seeking her out, of making more of her life research for my book. The scene is a bruise.

Don't watch *Oviri* unless you'd like to see the film cut – amidst the dubbed ▮▮▮ of Annah – to a shot of the child actor who plays Judith Molard in her bed in the room below Paul's. Tossing and turning at the sounds above, jealousy fanning the sheets of her bed. Don't watch *Oviri* unless you'd like to see the final scene with Sutherland as Gauguin kissing the child actor who plays Judith Molard, then refusing to have sex with her – how moral! How still-civilised towards white children! – before he returns to Tahiti.

The Child-Girl Judith Is Not Yet Breached. Victorious Paul, he who is savage-adjacent, yet would never transgress European morals. Tenets that do not extend to Annahs' protection in any possible way.]

—

[*Caption 8*

People referred to as Annah are never referred to as Javanese child-girl, but I remember being one. When I was twelve and in SMP (middle school) in Jakarta, it was the glory days before widespread internet access and smartphones, when we had to memorise each other's home landline numbers, and this cemented friendships. When we would scribble in each other's books, in distinctively individual handwriting styles that meant we were becoming. When we could still make up cocoons of childlike fantasy, when salty and ingenious insults were forms of experimentation with power, when our crushes were sacrosanct and our nicknames for each other were legion. It was rebellious to hike up your school uniform skirt, and it was the trend to wear bras with clasps in the shape of animals or other cartoonish images that would show underneath our regulation white, tucked in, button-down shirts. On Fridays at my school, we all wore long white skirts and long, white tunics, and went to the mosque in tittering unison, seen from above as a pale, moving sheet of burning hormones.

Below is a mixed media work entitled *Annah #99.16: School-aged*. The writing in the background is of the kind we would write in notebooks, in the mid-to-late 1990s. It was originally in greyscale, without collage in the middle; a photo printer mishap led me to rework the entire piece, when it was already on a gallery wall in Switzerland, hours away from opening time. I knelt on a cushioned stool, and remade you, already upright, with cut-up photo paper smeared with black ink, and pink halal lipstick of the kind I would have delighted in trying at around thirteen. As though you wanted to try some pink with you, as though you wanted layers and layers of ink to near terrify.

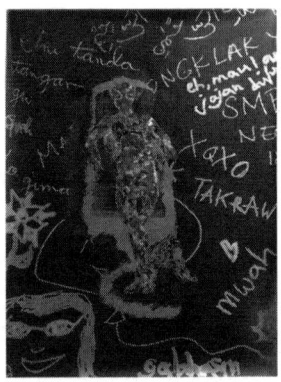

]

[*Caption 9*

In 2011, I was in New York City when I saw the painting of you, and the title it had been given; I was wracked with pain as I still am when overstrained, beyond scales of ten as maximum level, beyond all belief. Truly beyond belief – neurologists dismissed me, repeatedly, my claims met with raised eyebrows, marked as hysteria and impossibility, all my words bent and frenetic by shock and PTSD and neuropathic hurt that ebbed then ramped itself to eleven. It was physically difficult to speak at times; at other times, I rambled in confusion at what was happening to my body. For months, and then intermittently, it was difficult to move. I was often half-paralysed, my right side seizing up in agony and shock. It was years before I was given enough good medicine (four years, to be exact) to push away such torture most of the time when fully rested, though neural pain has remained a threat that bucks regularly. Particularly in the aftermath of a decade in which I needed dedicated care and help in the home, but was never told this, and was forced by circumstance to live without (as I would continuously, until late 2021), and I am a 'spoonie', chronically ill, writing about you from bed. I've come up for air now, made a life of as much joy and pleasure and love as I can fit into it, between electric shocks.

In 2011, I had not yet made this life of more enjoyment for myself, beset by such frequent if not constant knives, but I knew in that instant – of looking at how Paul had painted you, of looking at how others have looked at you for over a hundred years – that you too had a bodymind unknowable in spirit, that they thought they knew, but could not have known. That none of us ever really know what the other's miraculous body is feeling, and as such, you could have been a pained girl too. That, the more

I researched you, it would have been miraculous to have been so close to an abusive older man and escaped pain. That pain is multivariable, shades and colours, that it is not always suffering, though too often is. That people live with it all the time, and deserve to live. That who these people are, however, are often brown and/or Black bodies, femme bodies. That we in these bodies are seldom believed, often doubted when belief could save our lives.

Called Javanese, both of us, whether or not you were. You could have believed me about my pain, and I would have believed, readily, easily: all your pains that came with pictures where you are the only child, the only brown soul, never with family. In a Paris built on forced labour, on resource extraction dripping in blood, with so many white men, doing god knows what in relationships with you that the history books call benign, that you knew your own truth, and that that is not saying little at all.

Though we have lived different lives, I would have believed the whole of it from you, that you were not merely abject or as one historian called it, in a 'pathetic' position. To have stayed alive in such circumstances required intelligence and a will to live. I am calling it, though I know you may well not need me to at all: you were built with such fortitude.]

—

[*Caption 10*

'Queer kids, kids of color, street kids – all of the kids cast out of reproductive futurism – have been and continue to be framed as sick, as pathological, as contagious.'
—Alison Kafer, *Feminist, Queer, Crip*

I want you to be contagious. I've marked your outline in white on a gallery floor in London, I have exhibited in different variations for this outline of a body that actually could have been, as Mario Vargas Llosa wrote in *The Way to Paradise*, a composite of you and Judith. Judith who may have sat nude for Paul, but was never breached. I want you to be Child (including possible Child-Girl) too. I want people to think of what might have happened to you (though I hope and hope that, somehow, it did not, my mind continuously says as prayer, even with infinitesimal likelihoods) as a horrific breach.]

40 *Annah, Infinite*

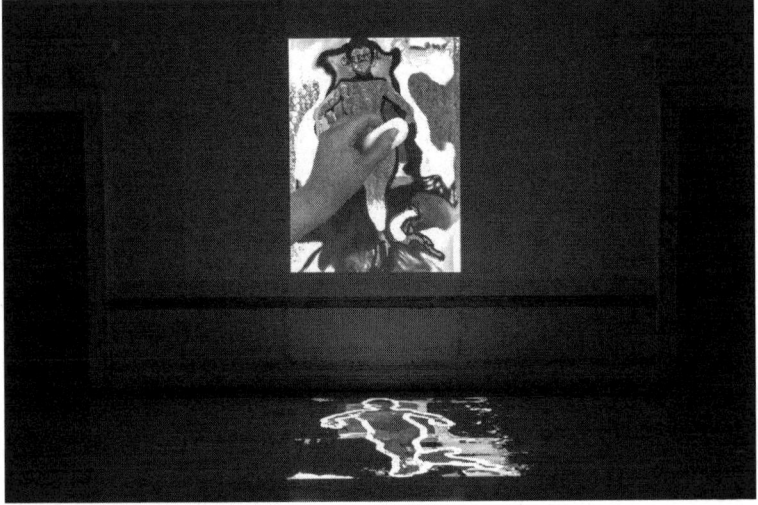

[Image description: Black and white photo. Two projections are shown: one against the wall, of an accompanying video, stopped to the image of *Annah #67, Greyscale*, a reworking of the original painting with a giant, dark hand holding an eraser to a grey, black and white outline of the Annah figure, with Javanese script across her face. The other projection is on the floor, with another artwork by Khairani Barokka. Photo by Christa Holka of the 'Annah: Nomenclature' performance installation (2018), performed by Khairani Barokka at the Institute of Contemporary Arts (ICA) in London.]

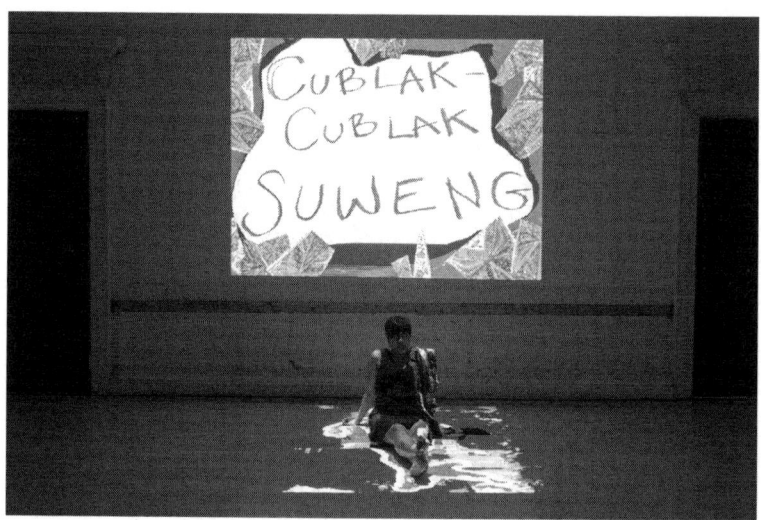

[Image description: Black and white photo. The artist in a black dress, sitting on the floor facing the audience/camera, in the outline of her Annah artwork projected on the floor. Behind her is a projection against the wall, stopped to her illustration saying 'CUBLAK-CUBLAK SUWENG'. Photo by Christa Holka of the 'Annah: Nomenclature' performance installation (2018), performed by Khairani Barokka at the Institute of Contemporary Arts (ICA) in London.]

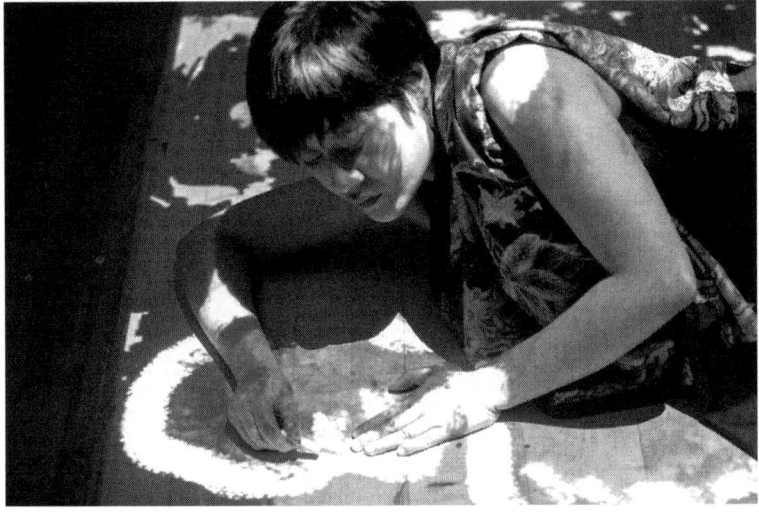

[Image description: Black and white photo. The artist in a black dress, reinscribing in chalk the outline of one of her reinterpretations of Annah la Javanaise, projected on the gallery floor. Photo by Christa Holka of the 'Annah: Nomenclature' performance installation (2018), performed by Khairani Barokka at the Institute of Contemporary Arts (ICA) in London.]

[*Caption 11*

This image has been redacted for the possibilities of violence, adult themes, trauma, language, disturbing imagery.]

[*Caption 12, Unavailable*

This museum is inaccessible to blind and sight-impaired audiences.]

[*Caption 13*

Annah silhouette in orange.

Who owns the piece now 'Private Collection'. I've fourteen years, leaning auction house leads. close to the truth, a from it, sitting across table from an auction corporate info. These wisps turn into wind, sawdust taste – yet this is consistent with been written about you. And give us, all you labelled 'Annah smokeshow, illusion trumped up is confidential information: been trying to trace you for into academic and Getting tantalisingly degree or two away a crowded dinner house rep with the right of potential information in the mouth, and rumour everything that has ever this is the main lead you la Javanaise'; to understand as art historical fact, cloud-

44 *Annah, Infinite*

large contradictions in hearsay turned inconsequential when it comes to your legacy.

TGA 20043/1/2/6	Joule, Barry	Paul Gauguin - Polynesian female nude seated on blue chair with a small monkey at her feet	nd			OPEN

Tate Library Archive and Public Records Catalogue entry, last accessed April 8, 2019 (when the screenshot below was taken), entry first discovered by me on April 9, 2016, in London. At that time, the print had been borrowed by another artist, who upon being contacted confirmed that it was indeed of the painting *Annah la Javanaise*.

> 'TGA 20043/1/2/6
> Joule, Barry [who first gifted it, presumably, to the Tate]
> Paul Gauguin - Polynesian female nude seated on blue chair with a small monkey at her feet
> nd
> OPEN'

The monkey sits at your feet as part and parcel of your mystique. Did you know the original King Kong came from what is presumably Nias Island, off Sumatra, in what is now Indonesia? Interchangeable apes, abducting white women atop buildings, originally known by 'natives', discovered by 'explorers', finally emasculated. Some days it's Paul Gauguin, some days it's Tom Hiddleston in a *King Kong* franchise, native beings as scenery. A gun is a paintbrush.

In 1893 at the World's Fair, the Javanese Pavilion captivated the French imaginary so much that, eventually, 'Javanaise' would become a term for a kind of French slang, a somewhat Pig Latin, meant to make language seem near impenetrable. Interchangeable sounds, haziness of meaning. A body, a body of text, a turn of speech. And a series of movements called the Java became a form of dance among the French. At one point, Parisian socialites would don Javanese dress to soirées.

Serge Gainsbourg and Juliette Gréco both sang a song titled 'La Javanaise' in 1963, after it was written by the former. The song plays with both the French slang form of language (similar to Pig Latin) called 'javanais', and a dance the French call the 'Java'. In it, the singer implores their lover not to be upset, and to join them in the latter.

Have you considered how deeming us specifically one thing, one hyperspecified, exoticised escape, is somehow also part and parcel of deeming us haziness, fog, inconsequential molecules, dissipation, oddity, air to be cleared?]

—

[*Caption 14*

Survivorship is a revenge plot. It is interminable – potentially infinite – and seemingly effortless.

I wonder at logistical marvels for this child you are:

Did anyone help you with your hair?
    Did anyone help you with your French? That's assuming you lacked 'native fluency' (what a disturbing term) in French, which may not have been the case.

Did you speak Javanese at all on French soil? That's assuming you were Javanese, which as we've deduced may not be the truth.

Did you know how to read? To write? To sing? If so, in which language(s)?

Did you eat alone in 1893–94, or always with Paul? With your fingers, as we often do among ourselves back home, especially when noodles are not involved? At a table? On a cushion on the floor?

Were you allowed to be alone?

Were you inclined to, allowed to, perform shalat? Did you sneak in a prayer or two, having determined the direction of Mekkah, having obtained enough privacy or respect for privacy to do so? Did you perform dzikir in your mind, so your captors would not be privy to a faith in God?

How many dresses did you own? Where were they procured, and by whom, and when?

Did you ever ask for a dress and receive it out of hand?

Did you know siblings, did you have extant family?

Did you initiate communication via long-shot whisper network with Java, or if you were not from there, wherever home of origin was (perhaps Paris), friends and family? (Throughout this work, I use the words 'perhaps', 'maybe', 'could have'; I do not wish to follow the vendors of false certainty.) Back then, on Java, native women weren't allowed to learn to the level Dutch women were. I quite pity Dutch women then for lacking knowledge of Javanese, unable to digest epic poems such as *Serat Centhini*, unable to access a language built on poetry. I excoriate myself for fluency in only Bahasa Indonesia and English, both such colonial languages (though so is, in contexts we'll swim in further, Javanese); for grasping at Baso Minang and Javanese as grandmother tongues I keep no time for, flailing and forgetting.

My grandmother was one of the first generations of native women to be educated to secondary school level. She would cry in the bathroom when her visiting father would leave the school, one she boarded at, though she was still a child, as it was far from home. It was so strange, so rare, to be given the chance to learn in that way for native girls; she would have to be alright. In black-and-white, blown-up pictures of herself in the classroom, and with her schoolmates at the age of around thirteen, smiling and standing side by side in sarung and kebaya: photographs all propped up in her bedroom by her desk until she passed away. Once, we discovered an archive of her writing in a history book a western woman had written about Indonesian women's education, a quote from a letter my grandmother wrote to her Dutch headmistress, saying she would use her education to teach other women.

My grandmother's writing desk and chair sit in my old room in Jakarta: inheritance. When she was alive, she would use them to draw up lists of all the birthdays of her children, grandchildren and great-grandchildren, write to me in cursive curlicues. When I was around nine, she wrote me a letter, several pages long, never replied to (because I was silly, and perhaps afraid of matching her elegance). And now, I am writing this book, about brown girls far from home and living alone (my grandmother, myself, and chosen subject/s: Annah/s), about one painting in particular that has probably never been exhibited in Java, about old photographs in archives abroad hoarding stolen loot. About the faces of girls more than a century old, those whom they say we should have no pride in, though they were children who persevered at a hostile life, who kept themselves alive.]

—

48 Annah, Infinite

[*Caption 15*

Annah of the painting, you weren't the first young, brown girl for Paul, and not the last. You probably weren't one person, though every scrap of photographic evidence suggests that she/they was/were lone, very much alone.

Your faces in the photographs, surrounded entirely by white men, don't look all alike to me. One is of a small girl with a round face, mostly straight hair with a part in the middle. You are at the top of the frame, surrounded by white men. Other photographs marked Annah show you by yourself, or with bodies coded as white men, artists all. No children. No other brown bodies. You are never shown smiling with teeth bared, or laughing, or touching another human being. There was likely no safety.

There is a photograph of you in the studio of Alfons (sometimes written as Alphonse) Mucha. There are versions of writing about you in which Alfons brought you to Gauguin, as a present. The Mucha Foundation describes it as follows:

'Mucha with his friends in the studio, Rue de la Grande Chaumière, Paris (c.1893–94). Mucha's snapshot captures a group of his friends in fancy dress gathering in his studio. [...] Behind Mucha on the left is Paul Gauguin, who sits tall in a Moravian folk hat, probably from Mucha's collection of hats. On the far right is Gauguin's teenage mistress and model, Annah la Javanaise, posing with an enormous Breton headdress.'

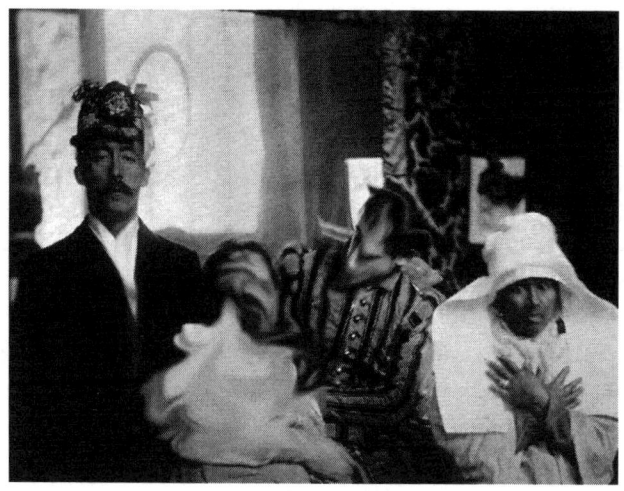

Left to right: Paul Gauguin, Alfons Mucha, Ludêk Marold, Annah la Javanaise. Your hands are across your chest. You look to me to be terrified.

In the image above, I have manipulated that photo in a piece I titled *Spectral Vision*: Mucha and Marold are twisted to highlight just you and Paul, the distance between you two, still too close, your hands to me seeming to seek protection, or otherwise at peace with yourself.

In 2016, I discovered a chapter entitled 'Gauguin, Mucha, and Art Nouveau', in the 2010 book *Lasers in the Conservation of Artworks VIII*. The chapter was written by John Fredrich Asmus, an eminent research scientist at UC San Diego, as well as the co-founder of the university's Center for Art/Science Studies. The Annah theory he proposed shook me (a discipline unto itself: Annah Theory).

'A few months earlier in Brittany,' I read, 'Paul Gauguin had been composing female images [...] until he became bedridden in the aftermath of a fistfight with three sailors. During the two-month convalescence Gauguin's model, "Annah la Javanaise", stole his belongings in order...'

Asmus had written of a famed poster of the actress Sarah Bernhardt, made with postage stamps on tile, which is attributed to Alfons Mucha, resulting in Mucha being called the progenitor of Art Nouveau. Asmus, however, suggests in his chapter that the poster was in fact the work of Paul Gauguin, and would have been created by him during his convalescence after the Pont-Aven fight. If this was true, how could this priceless artefact have been misattributed to Mucha?

The crucial missing link in this art historical tale, Asmus wrote, was 'Annah la Javanese' [sic]. She would have stolen from Paul in Pont-Aven, and then, according to this article, become Mucha's mistress and given him the Bernhardt poster.

In this version, Annah, you do not disappear without a trace. You leave your mark, and you know why. There is a possible version of the truth in which you knew full well your power to write history. There is a version where you knew the significance of the Bernhardt poster as Gauguin created it at his sickbed. There is a version where you refuse the ways in which he sickened you, and you wanted to siphon some of his glory away from him. There is a version I instantly want, and which is as possible as any other version of events, in which you never became intimate with Mucha at all, in which you simply dropped off the poster at his place and made your way in the world – however you were able to – refusing further harm from this circle of men, leaving them all to bicker amongst themselves. In which disappearance is escape and to vanish is sheer victory. I hope you felt exhilarated.]

—

[*Caption 16*

Painting of a child. Escapee, runaway swirl-steeped in marronage and recovery of safety. A young girl who survived against the odds to the age of always 'about thirteen'. A possible thief. Possible convict. Possible genius of revenge, and mastermind, possible invoking of all forms of mitochondrial song-story, child of fleeing capture under cover of interchangeability's stealthiness, under night, sun, windstorm, sea gale, riverine turbulence. Child of the Sunda Strait and/or of the French Riviera and/or of neither.

Child of possible mothers seeking lifelong, of possibilities beyond their knowing. Child of the therebegone. Child of no woebegone, not anymore, hush child lullaby, Nina bobok[2]. Child of lay with your secrets as finery, dust, and outpost of Scar Planet, alam barzah[3] in probable Qur'an learnings drip-fed somewhere in lineage, child on behalf of whom we will not ask forgiveness. Child whose name was perhaps not Annah. Child who was called Annah by a man who hit his wife, biographised violence in both fists dismissed by contemporary curators of taste. Child of melanin as prone to more sin against. Child of Eden and hellfire both as not-enough (compensation, description). Child of oh-so-many pixellated lies, crenellated buffoonery, in obituary form. Child of no owner, of once-mother. No truth alive but their clock-swallowed own, time its own passageway for you to come here from

---

2 'Nina Bobok' is an Indonesian lullaby.
3 A realm in Islam between our world and the afterlife.

so far beyond the edges of this screen, another set of frames, and tower upon us your sacred breath, tousling all of our heads with venom and grace in whichever measurements decided upon, to remind us all: no one can ever, ever hold the pith of you but you, in the end – Anna or Annah or Annahs or other names entirely, soul/s of unravelled, unravelling mistruths against, beading and threading each lie to a long cloth that holds in place bank vaults and market trends, and the exact, numerical value of your supposed semblance, and you who may shrug off each falsehood with each eclipse and laugh and laugh and stuff yourself with succour overflowing, to flood the sky with it, telling yourself, again, again – eternity, you have it – who you are.]

CHAPTER TWO:
COMPLEX PAIN, PICTORIAL FORMS

Having encountered few representations of my experience with both art and pain save for the life and works of Frida Kahlo, I had not expected to find an example of a Javanese girl in Western art to map this possibility onto. I have since come to steadfast belief that there are and have been many of us. We who are and have been in pain, of various levels and kinds, bodily and bodymindedly, psychically, and crucially, those of us who have not been able to translate this pain in order to be helped. The urgency of it. The fire of it. The way it intends to break us. The shock it can incur on the mind. The work required to undo this shock so that we may function in the contemporary world. The sheer added costs for those of us whose bodies are coded woman or girl or indigenous gendered and/or non-binary, who are also coded as people of colour, brown, Black, mixed, or any kind of othering from whiteness. The way 'painedness' can vary from low-grade day-to-day liveability to knife's sinking in upon innumerable soft points, and thus is so impossible to universalise. This matters. This matters in pictures.

Last night, I thought and thought again, another day, about how to translate what we endure as human beings, how marks persist. What pained Annahs could have been. What Annahs exist, here and not-here, parallel bodies. But let's not get ahead of ourselves.

54 Annah, Infinite

★

The words describing Annah exist within a caption. Supposedly, captions are meant to be concise descriptors of a visual image. In the interests of brevity, they tend to leave out plenty.

When we hold accessible events, my sighted colleagues and I like to describe people speaking or in films for the blind and sight-impaired colleagues or guests among us. Always, the description chosen by they who are described. Such as, 'Nina is a cis-woman of Manadoese descent, wearing bright blue pantaloons and a guayabera in all the colours of the rainbow.'

The continual absence of captions where they should be, in thousands of different languages, in languages always at risk or engulfing the world, is a reminder of an ableist penchant for the omission of a key form of translation.

★

The entire Javanese alphabet is a poem. It is recited in verse.

← In Javanese script, Puryapada introduces a poem.

To wit, the alphabet:

Hana caraka | Two soldier-messengers, | ꦲꦤꦕꦫꦏ

Data sawala | Each with animosity towards the other, | ꦝꦠꦱꦮꦭ

Padha jayanya | Equal strength in battle, | ꦥꦣꦗꦪꦚ

Maga bathanga | Both become carcass. | ꦩꦒꦧꦛꦔ

(My translation into English, of translations of Javanese into Indonesian. As every caption is a translation of an image.)

Is Annah a soldier-messenger? If so, who was their equal? We assume Annah has become carcass. We do not have a death certificate.

When titling a painting, it is like titling a poem. What information does not exist in the poem? How can you insert this in the title, to contextualise the text?

What is this business with Judith? Why does their name need to be inserted here? The whiteness of the girl matters.

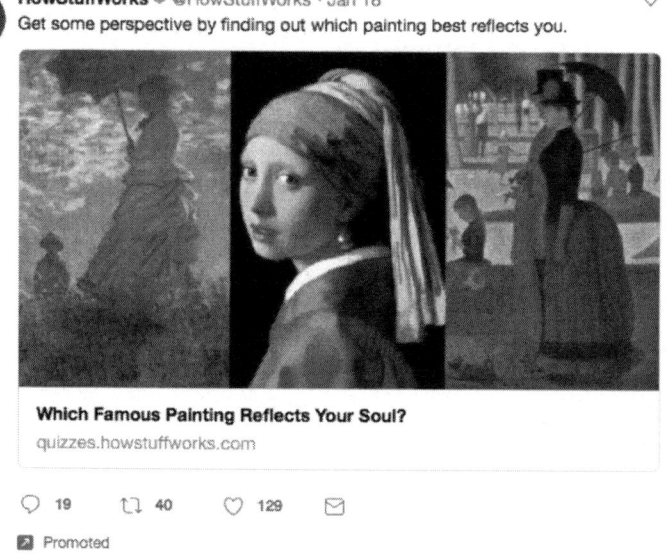

{This is a promoted tweet I read on February 11, 2018; most certainly because cookies pick up on the fact that I read and write about paintings on a daily basis. From @HowStuffWorks on January 18, 2018, it asks 'Which Famous Painting Reflects Your Soul?', offering us crops of famous paintings, *Girl with a Pearl Earring* among them. None of these white women feed me on the molecular level required for a painting to reflect a soul. Their insertion, again – the white girls, men, people in our minds that we are made to understand.}

★

What follows is a poem I wrote sometime in 2011, 2012, about measure and pain, meant to be performed:

Sliding Scale

What is it on a scale of one to ten.

Is it aching, burning, raw,
Enraged and radiating,
Agonising. Stinging.
Stabbing; is it suppurating.

Does it feel like a carcass under two tonnes of meat pounder,
Up and down, eternity. An apex of weight.

Is it mother's arm in the night,
The colour of langsat,
Glowing radioactive as a Chevy truck
Arrives and crushes it, grates it to the asphalt,
Sparing only her rings.

Is it the mouth of a gash.
       Sing it like a scream.

Who is invisible in there, is it malingering.
Is it attention you gouge out of knees
To bring them to the floor,
Joints and flesh uncertain of the stage cues.
Which act of empathy, fumbling,
All the world's pity and disinterest and love
Disguised or amplified in all the same trembling sighs.

Is it the neighbour man reaching his hand
Inside, pinning you beady-eyed
Just when you catch him in the door,
Was that a nightmare.

Is it her face. Is it his. Is it their legs
In your covers, and wondering
Which of these many weak bodies
Is weaker than yours.
Who could you get more pleasure from
In which of their open wounds.

Is it a wound.

Is it a blister, a bruise, a boil, a pimple,
An ingrown curse from an ancestor
Thick in the face and spitting through the aeons,
Heckling at your flesh to carve in it.

Did it begin when you turned the corner
And the street lights came on
And a cloud looked a lot like that road dweller you pass,
And everything became a cloud,
And you passed out. Was it in the bathtub.

Was it in the cubicle.
Or in the lap of a terrified stranger,
At the point of a revolver,
Because this man is not what his mama
Always thought he would be, and this is money, kid.
This is money. And I will pay you to shut
The doors of hollering grief for good
If you eat this, swallow this, believe in these studies.
This is antidote ethereal, this will stop a world
Of grief and the need to speak it.
I love you, I manufacture these compounds
In a heart grafted of selflessness and cashmere
Concern, sugar in my giving veins, just sugar, baby.
Are you telling me you haven't heard about
The mortgage like a noose and my own father's
Slit in the chest, you think it comes free.

Is it squares on a board you were born into
That began with spices in trading ships
And men in peaked headgear who terrorised
Your ancestor's chickens and worse,
So much worse you feel the sickening
Of history like a plague in all your parts,
And this came from my friend in school, miss,
Caught it from him, hysterical disease,
Are you saying colonialism didn't give you the flu
Or are you just trying to get him in detention.

Must be going around.
Must be terror so dark it spits void.
Must be a needle in the lower eyelid,
Going through the cheekbone,
Must be the heat.

We are shedding so much of our babyfaces.
We are falling apart under all of our eyes,
I mean really, disintegrating,
No wonder muscles are always breaking down.
This is a planet of slough and hell,
If you are human skin.
Now is it dermatological
Or can you feel it in the bone.
I honestly can't hear your answer, girl,
Are you dancing to show you can still
Make the party or was that a spasm
Or are you being clever.

What are these bales of letters on your tongue
When all I want to know is a number.

annah #843 with bodily memory

everyone else's trauma seems to glide on their skin like soft water.

their stories are jagged in the way precious gemstones reek architectural resplendence before human discovery, inevitable mining. untidy resolutions pat. there is always an arc.

my trauma presents as limescale and bone-breathing, spindly and burnish-prone, in a way that does not entice compassion. in a way that screams flying insects and bites off a chunk of perceiver's flesh. wards off with so much extra, such hissing.

no one wanted to sit with this. it was not that no one knew.

there are pictures of various girls who look like me but only two, despite what they think, are actually of myself. thus the possibility of my hurt maps itself onto other bodies. who came from other bodies.

parental love is insufficient against relentless bodyminded onslaughts perceived as gauche, in the way torture details sometimes are. this is why blooming ovaries may be hushed when they scream at the cranium. my folks did not deserve a child who lives through years in the ring with pain, many said. but my grandmother kept orchids every day. tending is in the blood too. and the orchids kept her.

every week it is a selfishness, a narcissism surely, coalescing into the nightmare that none of the hot irons we escaped are in fact translatable. in a way that others' seem to be. or perhaps this harsh dream is made of a survival instinct that requires understanding by others. if understandable and translatable are not the same concept, how so.

and why must memories be these things for a wider public? so pain is thrown off from boarding another naive vessel? does pain leave or does it simply permutate? would it descend into another form if shooed away from one?

i don't want more brown girls to know because they were left out in the open, that's part of why, to the first question. what tempts a potentially merciful god to set us alight in a trap. why must i always feel marks from a metal jaw meant for catching bears. he kept one in his study. and i—

[here the handwriting of #843 in her journal is smudged with inkblots.]

★

In the later stages of writing this book, an image comes to me during a reiki session. Unbidden, startling, frightening: a minotaur, human from the waist down, a creature I know instinctively as a she, is lying on the floor of a giant coliseum. The day is soaked in light. She has been skinned completely from base of horns to the tops of her thighs. She is red, bloody flesh rippling with muscle. She is alive, but stunned out of motion.

    I gasp as though I am choked, when this image comes crystal clear to my mind, while my eyes are closed. Later, I realise the coliseum may have contained people watching her, from above. The people, I understand, may well be you. Readers, for whom I must describe torture in a way that you believe, that you empathise with, that you do not question as I have been questioned for so long, in a way that prolongs this torture when it spikes – because questioning torturous pain is the antithesis of helping, of reducing it, of trying to make suffering disappear. It was only after twelve years of thinking about this book, practically every day, that I realised in order to be able to finish it – to avoid the paralysis and anxiety of trying to convince you – I must dispense with the prior instinct completely.

I do not, in fact, have to describe my torture in a way that you believe. If I have cared so much that you believe, it has been to protect myself, and the many millions of people around the world I know are like me, and in memory of the many who were like us, and are no longer here.

To care too much about your many, varied views on the truth of my body strangles my will to write, at the same time as the fury of experience propels this project onwards. What I must do is write in a way that honours Us, the grievously pained, the pained to the point of white light searing, the pained to the point where the world is nonsense, where nothing that we do or don't do will convince people through our agony, so we must focus on each pulse of pain, in a way I now know is in fact meditation. We must meditate on the impact of sharp scalpels digging deep on thousands of points on the body; we must try not to anguish over the ripping apart of nerve endings, as to do so while experiencing the ripping is to multiply the pain. Yet we are forced to feel anguish of the heart, because we are human, and because it has been proven that emotional and physical pain pathways in our neurological systems map on top of each other. They are not separate from each other. I knew this in my ripped-apart nerves before I read the science on it. I continue to resent that those of Us who passed before western science could prove this truth were even more violently dismissed.

The breathtaking effort of withstanding level ten out of ten pain, often, prolonged, over years, while enduring direct disbelief, while enduring direct laughter and mocking while we exist within bodies that are exploding internally, of trying to communicate in a way that abled overlords understand, so that we can get into an emergency room that may or may not treat us, so that we can survive, so that we might live – this is gargantuan effort. To deal with the slashing pain of friends dismissing our [torture that we sometimes call pain] for years, treating it as an inconvenience, until, sometimes years later, they understand that it *is* torture. Or, because we cannot try any longer to convince them, we remove them from our lives, and we must live with the knowledge that they may never believe. Or, to understand that people you thought would believe will inevitably fall into the same 'It's not that bad' hole of contempt for your body while it is being tortured. It makes me want to collapse. It makes me want to lie in the deep sea, breathing somehow, with a cloak as wide as the ocean around me, in a place of peace where no one who has hurt me can enter these waters. It makes me want to turn to the escape of skyward imaginings, picture myself so far above the fray of maddening disbelief that it does not exist.

When I write, all I need to be faithful to are the memories my own body continues to hold, and the memories held by the bodyminds of so many disbelieved. I am done with being bloodied on a platform of circular dirt, people in the stands, poking at places where they think we exaggerate. I do not need to write this for anyone who has never been tortured, even as I know your belief or disbelief will make or literally break so many of us.

This is for those who have been, who are being, tortured as a result of disbelief. I want us to know we can make our own sanctuaries, no matter how fragile, how fleeting, how exhausting it can be to seek them out and keep them fortified.

That is the only way I can write this story, which is for Annah/s, as well, always.

★

Could pictures of, a painting of, Annah la Javanaise, be of a person in pain? Any tendency towards 'no' is so peculiar. For it implies that a picture of you, yourself, could never be in pain, if you are not deemed to 'look pained'. The 'no' denies the possibility of pain in your own self. It denies the truth that we all hide pains from each other all the time. It denies the vulnerability of our bodyminds, or jiwa raga, soulbody/ies. It denies that we are all at the mercy of other people's misinterpretations, that this is a constant; it denies how strange it is that we may all continue onwards with life, with our own stories of truth, in the face of this.

'Jiwa raga' is a phrase in Indonesian that might be translated as 'soulbody', though I will use the Indonesian term where I can, to avoid denying its linguistic origins with an English substitute. It shares the 'soul' meaning of 'jiwa' with Hindi, as one of many words in Indonesian deriving from Sanskrit. 'Raga' in Hindi means something like 'passion', and I love that that has somehow metamorphosed into 'body' in Indonesian; a bodily encapsulated passion, the body as passion. What I am arguing in this book, through Annah stories, is for a certain way of approaching human figures in visual form, in the archives, in art and in other texts: a *jiwa raga reading*. My personal understanding of 'jiwa raga', like my Annah stories, is informed by the specific family-of-origin, Minangkabau, Javanese and Muslim pedagogies that have helped guide me throughout my life; they have saved me alongside Annah/s, and taught me not to generalise all Indonesian feminisms as the same. If one's spiritual background is wholly different, for instance, one that does not recognise the term 'jiwa raga' as appropriate, it may be substituted with a better term for the reader. As one example, someone whose spiritualities harken back to Minangkabau traditional spiritualities, in which there is a second spirit, or a force of 'semangat', may choose to call their method of interpretation a 'semangat reading'. Our jiwa raga, after all, are a composite of all our inheritances; all past relationships that make our selves heirs, each one a constellation of the impact of other lives.

A jiwa raga reading opens up space for an understanding that there is the possibility of pain in every picture, and especially for groups made more vulnerable to debility and disbelief by continued imperial violence. A jiwa raga reading for brown figures is the possibility of time-space understandings for humans that defy Cartesian duality and Western, colonial epistemologies and ontologies.

*

All pained people, unless racism and/or sexism lives within them to a terrible extent, would answer 'yes' to the question of whether or not there exists the possibility of Annah's pain. Because our own bodies matter to us, we count profoundly, we are possibility. Living possibility. The 'no' belongs to a land that does not sense us at all, does not value us at all, that deems us non-existent, disposable, freakish. Oh, how we are legion. And we are watching. We are sensing your arrogance, in the assumption that our pained bodies are not so very alive, very true. That you could never be one of us, that our lives are inherently less worthy, that you would rather not exist than be one of us.

A 2016 study published in *BMJ Open* found, of UK residents:

> Chronic pain was more common in female than male participants, across all measured phenotypes. Con-

> clusions: Chronic pain affects between one-third and one-half of the population of the UK, corresponding to just under 28 million adults [...] This figure is likely to increase further in line with an ageing population.

Let us begin, then, with Us.

Margaret Thatcher famously claimed there is no such thing as society. What is the proper response to this from us disabled and chronically ill people in the UK, living with the austerity measures that are her legacy, and a UN report declaring a humanitarian emergency in the UK for disabled people? Revisiting that malodorous quote may well induce prolonged, bitter laughter.

Alongside the increased likelihood of chronic pain in women, according to the 2016 study quoted in the British Medical Journal, there is clear evidence that many women in pain, particularly those of us from non-Caucasian backgrounds in western countries, still remain undertreated, ignored, and disbelieved. There exists what is called the 'gender pain gap' which refers to how people of different genders experience pain, but also, relatedly, how pain researchers and medical practitioners notice and treat pain in people of different genders. There is a gender-biased uncertainty about pain's presence in another's body, which has led, and continues to lead, to the undertreatment of pain. People who live with pain are so often disbelieved by medical professionals and others, to devastating effects – and may be left to suffer for years.

There is not only the gender pain gap, but also the racial pain gap. How we are seen as capable of pain hinges on all the inequalities that structure racial capitalism: race, gender, sexuality, religion, class, age, caste, citizenship status, an unfurling stack of characteristics wielded against the kindness of belief. In the wake of western colonial borders, access to healthcare is dependent on how the nation states whose borders we are in or are tied to decide to protect us. The key phrase here is 'how we are seen'.

All of this operates under the yoke of ocularcentrism – the privileging of abled, visual interpretations of whether or not a human, in paintings, photos, or in front of you in the flesh, is suffering. This contingency of the visual privileges us sighted people, and it permeates our societies and our lives in a way that marks interpretations of the visual as always 'objective'. 'Objective' cues of pain may always allow the ableist (and racist, sexist) observer to escape their duty of care. As many of us have discovered, there is in fact no reliable way, particularly in a brown body interpreted as female or feminine, to present so that you are given help.

It has never failed to shock me, over the past fourteen years, how securing relief from torture is contingent on how one appears, and on ableist visual interpretations thereof. I have often been in shock, shaking, making my behaviour even more nonsensical, full of non-sequiturs, confusing for beholders – and therefore, to them, I definitely am not and haven't been in torture.

*

It has been learned that you will not be believed:

    if torturous pain ignites for long periods of time, in waves over time, and you are in shock, and you behave 'hysterically', especially if you are interpreted as female or feminine, especially if you are brown or Black

    if part of your 'hysterical' behaviour under endless hours of ten out of ten torture is screaming, raising your voice in any way

    if you scream in an ER, which actually causes a white nurse to yell at you until you force yourself with immense strength to be silent, as she commands you to be if your screams are interpreted as aggression against staff, so you force yourself with immense strength to be silent, so that you can have a chance of help

if you are too silent, therefore you cannot possibly be under torture

if you are told that, because you have a history of depression and anxiety, you are imagining your pain

if you are told that, as a result, you can only stay in the hospital if you move to the psychiatric ward

if your father, frightened by this, calls the hospital from the other side of the world, begging them not to discharge you when you are at this moment literally half-paralysed by acute and widespread neuropathic pain, your muscles have seized up in shock and you cannot move your right side

if the hospital does not believe in your father's love, and you are discharged in the middle of the night, and your roommate who happens to be near the hospital at a social event must pick you up, half-paralysed and under torture, in a taxi to take you home

if multiple neurologists surround your bed and tell you what you are experiencing has nothing to do with nerves, as they've tried all possible painkillers and nothing is helping

if in your shock, you begin to make jokes to the people around you

if in your shock, alone in a country halfway around the world from your family, you don't know what else to do, and you set up a private twitter account and tweet continuous jokes about torturous pain

if as a result, your own extended family members and friends and colleagues gasp when they see you because they 'didn't know it was that bad' or, alternatively, say you seem like you're doing fine if you are told no medicine can help you, and you somehow have the will to live, because you love people who are alive so much, and you want to stay with them, and, as your relapses lessen slightly yet remain unpredictable, you begin to perform poetry, as it soothes your reality

if through frequent torture relapses, you travel to other countries to teach and perform, and having been told for years that nothing will help you, and not being believed, you do not seek out help, as you do not believe it exists

if the banal pull of social media increases on society, and you are not immune; you post the best parts of your day on social media, to bring some joy into your life through responses from people around you, and now more and more people disbelieve you

if people say they believe you and then, when you say you cannot do some work because you are ill, and what you mean is that you are still completely unmedicated after years under torture, even your closest friends will disbelieve you

if you speak about torture as 'pain' so repeatedly that even other disabled people in the arts think 'it's not that bad' and tell you 'you talk about your pain too much'

if you are smiling in your social media photos, to make yourself feel better in between torture relapses, or during one

if your CV increases, and you share your achievements, which you are quietly proud of having accomplished through endless waves of torture, coming and going

if your CV fools many people who are supposed to love and protect you, if one of them cries to a residency staff member on a visit that you shouldn't be working like this, yet does not stop you, nor provide the mobility aides and access assistance that you require, yet are too in shock all the time, and still too removed from any access intimacy, to realise you can even request if you burn with the torture-burning and then with the shame of having people who were going to promote your artwork drop you, because you couldn't complete the work in time because of torture, and you cannot yet articulate access requirements that should have been there from the start

if you will never be able to convince people that when the torture ebbs, you make the absolute most of it, and so you manage to obtain funding and pull off an entire edinburgh fringe solo show about the truth of pain in your body, against ocularcentrism, which you manage to perform in vienna, and in new delhi, and since you have been told for years by incompetent, unempathetic doctors that it is all in your head, and that no pain relief can help you, not once do you stop by a clinic in any of these places to ask for help you have always been denied (who would want to go through that again?) so you make art and burn in torture relapses then make art and burn in torture relapses, often in quiet, often alone in so many places, and when you are around the rare observer who asks what medicine can help you, you repeat what you have been told and believe: nothing

if you want this to be over, you wake up hoping manically that it can be over, so you make Grand Pronouncements when something great happens to you in the arts like i'mgratefulnowiamsomuchbetterthaniwas, when what that means is you are relapsing into torture every week instead of every day, because you are given a residency where you can rest, but you are still not given any pain medication, and it is always level ten out of ten pain

if you say in your shock that it's better now it's better now until everyone takes to mean 'curedness', because when you have tried to tell them that you can never tell how much pain a person is in, by their behaviour or their words or anything, ever, they nod and agree and publish your work but then lololol will tell you you talk about torture too much, before you realise it's because you used 'pain', a word that does not shock them, as 'torture' does, a word meant for easy minimising

if you tenderly, gingerly try to use the word 'torture' to refer to yourself, in a work meeting in which you are begging for the bare-minimum, liberal-approved anti-racism training that you and others have been requesting for over a year. if you say, 'i am a torture survivor. i need a safe working environment.' if, as a result, you are bullied even worse in that very meeting than you ever expected, and if you ask for a – bar-is-in-hell-absolute-minimum – apology for this bullying, and the chair of the board refuses to ask this of a white woman, even though you have a recording of the incident, and you are forced to leave a job you'd had such high hopes for. if, when you leave, you hear 'so sorry to hear this', 'so disappointed', from people who should be saying 'i'm sorry for my behaviour, for others' behaviour, for our actions and inactions and our regarding you as less-than-human. i am sorry we think of brown people in the abstract only, as a net good, and not as people we continue to interact with violently. i am sorry your hard work and sacrifice were met with this horrific inability to confront institutional racism that harshens ableism, which undergirds our industry, we who made the arts an '"industry".' if you only do this once, and it sends you reeling because *torture*, even that word *torture*, is so disregarded, is dismissed, even *torture* – because you are dismissed as whole, as a person, even as those who invisibilise in this way claim they are not only human, but more humane, laying claim to the moral high ground

if this pierces your heart, just as you are finishing a book in which you will tell everyone you are a torture survivor, and you are forced to contend with the fact that your words will not change desiccated hearts, hearts distorted by centuries of white supremacy handed down, even after someone confronts them with *torture*, they will not be forced to feel, and it prepares you for a future in which more people will stomp on this word like a piece of stray paper, but you must present it to the world because it is *truth*, because you must, must, must believe that the word will hit the chests of others, that there are some others who hold empathy, off of whom it will not ricochet

if you are young, therefore less likely to be grievously ill according to ableist ocularcentric standards

if you are told by others that you are perceived to be 'beautiful' by largely heteropatriarchal standards, and therefore, according to western scientific studies, perceived as incapable of being in torture, even if you had at a young age resigned yourself to being the ugly one in the family (in your mind), and had therefore focussed on studies and art, and are still occasionally that awkward child in your mind, and you may not fall into this category for all, but something an old therapist said while you were speaking about disbelief, that you were beautiful and therefore people were likelier to disbelieve, it burrowed in and you looked up the western scientific study and cried, and thought of Annah/s, Annah/s, Annah/s

if you try to fight against waves of torture by gorging yourself on the pleasures of life, on enjoying as much as you possibly can, on trying to be a relatively young person in the world, albeit one being intermittently tortured –

this is how you go on: enjoy a meal, enjoy a sunrise, try to pray, take naps, put yourself out there, try to make friends, watch endless entertainment, commit to doing a show, commit to doing a graduate degree, commit to doing ten thousand things as distraction and prayer in itself, travel, hitchhike across china, india and nepal, yes under intermittent torture because everything is nonsensical, is it not so, you have tried for years to get help, are consistently told there is none, or if acupuncture helps you a few times, you are not given any access instructions or guidance or regular medicine or wheelchairs or canes or rollators or access support people or access to public funds in the UK, so why not try for joy, try for peace, indulge in whatever might dull the torture or stave it off, get risky, get going, keep moving, keep falling, keep moving keep falling keep moving—

if you try to go on dates even when you could barely walk a block in london, and miraculously get second dates, and more, and pleasure does stave off torture in prolonged physical relief, and you do more of it, good decisions can wait, you are in constant emergency or panic that it may start again

if you try to include leisure in your life and collapse at peckhamplex, and the staff there help you call a taxi, which is why it is indelibly your favourite cinema in all the land

if you travel to countries not your own, and a man you go on one date with ends up holding you on a long bus ride as you spasm in torture, and though you never see each other again, and you didn't particularly like the date, you will be forever grateful

if complex PTSD addles your memory and protects you from recollections of torture by making time non-linear, if you struggle to remember details throughout your life because the cloud of brain-protection will not allow you to; if you are well aware that the cruel twist of trauma and post-traumatic stress disorder is that it decreases the likelihood of you being able to recall things in a 'straightforward' line of thought, which is necessary for bureaucratic note-taking, which is necessary, you discover, for you to be believed

if over the years, the extremes of complex PTSD and stress and violence incurred mean that from time to time, in the worse times, you smell burning

if you find yourself travelling with air canada for work, and your access attendant treats you with contempt, snaps at you that if you can't carry your own luggage, you shouldn't travel, which makes you well up, but to avoid further violence, you smile at them the whole way through security checks, until you burst into tears, and tell air canada, but when someone speaks to security team witnesses, they say, 'no, that didn't happen, she was smiling'; if a white man getting on the same flight mocks you while you are crying; and tweeting about the experience does absolutely nothing, as is actually usually the case for disabled people; routine experiences like this are why you usually do not make complaints, because you do not have the mental energy to make the number of complaints you would have to in a given year

if you make jokes about your condition, are able to smile while in torture, because your human movement, including your facial muscle movement, has been completely abstracted in your mind from what is happening to you, because if you are told this is reality forever and ever, nothing makes what you had thought to be 'logical sense' anymore in terms of behaviour, torture is the all-engulfing absence of sense

if you walked for ten years without a cane (which you now use on a daily basis, alongside other access items) because of the searing lack of consistent disability justice in your life, no consistent access doula (someone who can guide you to understand what access you need and ensure you receive it) around, because of the terrifying influence of ubiquitous ableism on your brain, internalised ableism, which prevents you from adopting the cane, because you think you don't really need it, you can walk short distances and then squat, even when you are trying to escape street gropers, even when you have to hide in an ASDA because it had a ramp and the man who grabbed you is just outside

if your lack of cane-using is also because *everyone should understand there is the possibility of pain in every picture*, and you refuse to use a visible marker of disability, in defiance of all the visually ableist norms for believing pain and disability that have been thrust upon you, and therefore you sustain the persistent bullets of ableist, unbelieving abuse, just to prove your point, like a good little self-immolating aries

if you travel to countless airports without once ordering a wheelchair, for years on end, because it did not occur to you this was a possibility, because your society's indigenous openness to disability justice has been closed by the fist of colonial medical ableism until it is all you know, this walking through knives in lines, in airports, and not 'appearing to be in torture' because you know what happens when you scream in pain, they will think you are on drugs or mentally ill and they will threaten you, and they might well hurt you more than these kniving walks

if six years after your initial internal explosion, when multiple neurologists finally say they believe you, that science cannot tell them if the initial nerve damage happened in your brain or your spine, but it has always been nerve damage, you weep with the realisation that if doctors do not understand something, they will say you are lying, and they have said many, many, many others are lying about the truth of our bodies

if it takes you around eight years after initial internal explosion, until you are around thirty-four years old, to tell the person you're seeing, who is now your husband, that when you say you've had a bad pain weekend, you would like him to understand that it is like being in a car crash, for days, and you would like him to be more responsive to this, and he is quiet for a long time, and from that moment on has never had to be told twice, has always believed, and in understanding how your torture makes you feel, while acknowledging that he can never truly understand (as it turns out he has), an inlet of joy unlocks

if it is not until years after this, when you move in together, that he forces you to confront how many things you do despite the fact they physically injure you: movements in the house, choices not to ask for help — there had been no help for so long, why would your body reveal a weakness that could flood the day with the anguish of disbelief, of lack of help salted in the wound by disbelief, when physical pain is the devil you know

if you are happily married, in a job that suits your interests, are seen smiling often, and supposedly 'have it together', so when you ask, with a tiny amount of internalised ableist shame, that spaces be made accessible, there might be a voice in the back of organisers' heads — in both social and professional situations — which says 'it isn't that bad', and they are lax about these considerations, and the earth falls beneath you, and you are back in torture

if you speak of your torture as 'pain', leading innumerable people to tell you that you speak too much about your [torture], even when you think you are reining it in compared to the amount of [torture] you actually experience, and this will gut you more than anyone can know

if you say 'i'm managing it' when there are so many more access measures you haven't learned your body needs, so when you fall into torture again, it confuses and tires people, who want a happy ending, so it's easier to let people think you have this happy ending and will never relapse again, not biweekly even during pandemic lockdowns (because of chores, and because you have no access to public funds that would enable you a carer); it's easier to let them think whatever they want, the best possible version of your life, which is not without pleasures, and you savour these pleasures and focus on them, and life is still worth living, keep going, keep going

if it was far easier to amass a decade of accomplishments in the arts under routine extreme physical duress, to talk about pain professionally, than to get adequate help and access for your body, which after twelve years since initial explosion, and finally in the hands of a good therapist, you are ready to acknowledge has survived prolonged, sustained, torture that has returned and returned over these many years

if in 2023, you experienced relapses of a week or more only once every one or two months, and this felt like sweet relief

if you feel from bitter experience that most people will read this list and be desensitised to even the word 'torture', that most people will question how crushing it really was, then remind yourself that you are not writing this book for them, you were stabbing yourself because the only escape routes were lined with knives for such long years by these kinds of soulless people, you write for the many, many, many who understand through bitter experience of their own

if you are resigned to the fact that because science has not caught up with what the bodymind knows – what for you is jiwa raga, what the soulbody knows – you cannot predict what tiny movements, what slips into overtiredness in a body that does not have a yellow traffic light, will tip you back into torture, you can only try to prevent them, but even then you can never know for sure, ever, this is your life, but at some point, you tell the woman in 2011 whose body broke the same New York summer she discovered online a painting called Annah la Javanaise and felt instantly and deeply with the child in the painting a strange kinship of misunderstoodness: 'there will come a time when you will finally have successfully filled your life with enough pleasures and kindness that when you say you are managing it, you are trying, this is the truth, and life is more kind than not to you now, even when it's level three pain on better days, even when you relapse into torture every month due to access fails or the nerves' own capriciousness, but are truly doing so much better than before, and will never lose hope that torture will never happen again, and you must remember this, this possibility that, if it could happen to you, it could happen for all the Annahs'.

★

Nina Pack did not believe in the possibility of suffering in Black and brown children. How else could she have asked for 'a little negro girl' to be taken from whatever family they belonged to and be made to live on the other side of the world in enslavement to her?

The echoes of Nina are legion in contemporary British society, where I have had to live in order to claim any kind of support for the *Annah, Infinite* project.

Nina's perfume lingers in the room in which I guest lecture, and am interrupted whilst speaking on the increased vulnerability of Black and brown children under colonialism, by a woman saying white children are vulnerable too.

Nina's aura of Parisian grandeur wraps around *Daily Mail* articles saying refugee children are not children.

Her stamp of approval is a watermark on criticism of documents I wrote for my PhD, chiding me for not using academic citations for statements about my own cultures, things I learned from my family, and which certainly have not been written about by the western academic industrial complex.

Nina Pack's spirit turned gargantuan and ferocious, a suffocating cloud, as a racist academic verbally assaulted me and prevented me from passing in the crucial last months of my PhD on Annah, because I dared to critique an influential white woman academic. The people who saved me from this situation, who forced an official apology from the academic were, as they always are, women of the majority world (i.e. outside the white global minority). It is no surprise to any woman of colour in the UK academic system that 'Black and Asian ethnic minority women' still make up only 2.1 per cent — yes, 2.1 — of professors in this country, while white women make up 24 per cent. It is not for our lack of qualifications or abilities. It is structural racism, and certainly the number of chronically ill and disabled professors who are women of colour is even smaller, in environs of structural ableism as well.

The more cocooned you are in the structures of white supremacy, the less you understand the pain you cause others regularly by virtue of the racism that we swim in every day in the UK and Europe. It is not 'unconscious bias', a term which truly lets people off the hook for their violence, which exists to make people feel better about the ways they deeply hurt others.

That I finished my PhD at all is a testament to my loved ones, those who kept me going. The anatomy of racial ableism in the academy means I should not have been able to finish, and I did it by withstanding intense physical and emotional pain, focussing on Annah/s, focussing on my family, focussing on my friends and on my own sense of self – my own existence as a disabled human.

As someone who was here on a Global Talent visa, supposedly with my worth approved of by the British state, I paradoxically did not have access to any public funds. It is as though I could not be a Global Talent of any kind if I am also seriously chronically ill. These two things do not coincide in the state's imaginary.

This is another bureaucratic reminder that 'proof' of our bodies is never enough. Even to obtain the PhD scholarship that brought me to the UK from Indonesia, I was asked to prove that I was bodily unable to participate in the physical boot camp associated with my government scholarship. My brother carried me on his back up the many stairs of the inaccessible government building where we were asked to meet the officials involved, who upon seeing me exhausted decided I was telling the truth. What a sick, bitter memory. How furious I am for the young woman I was, to have had to do this, to have had to survive amidst persistent disbelief.

It took me around twelve years to realise how much I needed not only medicine, but a carer, and access considerations throughout the years of living with this condition. Until I moved in with my now-husband, four years ago, I was constantly relapsing from the efforts of doing more chores than I was physically able to, with no one to share the labour. I was in incessant recovery, familiar with deep-rooted physical pain, trying to finish a graduate degree, to sustain artistic community with my peers through creation. I am stunned by the searing memories of trying to live as 'more abled' because I had no other choice, and the traumatising scalpels that sank into me. The memory of knives and knifing.

My last instance of acute access neglect in the arts, leading to severe triggering and a mental and physical breakdown, was only months ago at the time of writing this sentence. There have been less devastating, and more devastating, incidents since that sentence was written (such is the case with writing a book slowly, over years, at the pace of one's bodymind). My point is that I wake up in the morning, every morning, praying that I am not injured, still tentative in my understanding that the worst is now over. Because it isn't always, and there are different levels of vulnerability to access fails day to day.

The whole time, I have been asking people 'Could portrayals of Annah/s be of pained bodyminds?' When this question is scoffed at, the torture in my own bones has flared more acutely.

*

I honour the struggles of those who popularised the word 'crip', a term that arose out of western disability activism as a reclaiming, much as 'queer' is reclaimed by LGBTQI+ people. At the same time, I long for an Indonesian word that performs a similar reclamation, without complication. I wish for localised versions for us all, in all our many thousands of languages in the world.

People to whom the Indonesian language belongs have 'cacat' – 'deformed' – as a word that is still used in various government documents, in the minds of millions. Many of my peers, disabled and/or D/deaf people in Indonesia, have rejected this word, and instead take on the term 'difabel'. Yet this is an acronym (oh, we do love acronyms) of 'differently abled'. And why are we the strange difference? Aren't those 'abled', so many blissfully unaware of our universes, the different ones? Are we not always at the centre of our lives? My favourite saying from Indonesian disability movements: 'Seperti kamu, saya sama. Seperti saya, kamu berbeda.' Like you, I am equal. Like me, you are different.

I prefer the descriptive term 'disabilitas' – 'disability' – when using Indonesian. Though I know of people using 'cacat' as a reclamation, I personally refuse, for I am not deformed. The struggle of many of our pained lives is an inherent, bone-deep understanding that some of us may think of ourselves as perfectly formed. We are simply more vulnerable to the Suffering Abyss, in a world that takes away all the guardrails surrounding it, tilts us towards its maw.

Thus, though with slight reluctance as it is not in my own language, does not feel fully mine, I embrace 'crip' as an adjective, to connect with many others around the world who matter to me, to whom I hope my life matters also. Whose disability, D/deafness and/or neurodivergence may come together in many bodies, to form our own guardrails, our own mutual support.

Over the past fourteen years, 'cripping' has become an easy way for me to describe how I see the world, see the artworks I am obsessed with, see every visual interpretation of a person – the TV stars and profile photos and poster illustrations, the people I see before me every day.

In verb form, 'cripping' means to put disabled interpretations onto something, onto all manner of things. In this all-consuming project of pondering Annah/s, it means I do not, as per abled assumptions, assume they are non-disabled before they are 'proven' by ableist, ocularcentric assumptions, to be disabled. It means that I crip everything I see, and therefore I assume people can definitely be disabled, chronically ill and/or neurodivergent before assuming otherwise.

There is another verb that applies to what we are doing when we perceive Annah/s in a different way to the norm, which is 'queering'. The reclamation of the word has been extended by queer communities and theorists to denote queer interpretations of, naturally, all manner of things. This means I do not assume Annah/s' gender or sexuality is normative, especially according to the cis-hetero-normativity embedded in ocularcentrism as much as ableism, intertwined with ableism, part of it.

Disabled colleague Talila Lewis has, in fact, written up a succinct interpretation of what 'ableism' means, particularly for us disabled people of the majority (i.e. not white minority) world. This particular definition was shaped by Talila alongside other majority world (a term I prefer to Global South, as including Indigenous populations in North America, for instance) disabled people, and reflects my own understanding of the word:

> able·ism /ˈābəˌlizəm/ noun A system of assigning value to people's bodies and minds based on societally constructed ideas of normalcy, productivity, desirability, intelligence, excellence, and fitness. These constructed ideas are deeply rooted in eugenics, anti-Blackness, misogyny, colonialism, imperialism, and capitalism. This systemic oppression that leads to people and society determining people's value based on their culture, age, language, appearance, religion, birth or living place, 'health/wellness', and/or their ability to satisfactorily re/produce, 'excel' and 'behave'. You do not have to be disabled to experience ableism.

To Talila's definition, one can add other words related to discrimination, such as 'casteism', which may vary in how they manifest, from region to region, from localised context to localised context. And as to historical context: homosexuality was regarded as a psychiatric disability in the Diagnostic and Statistical Manual of Mental Disorders, a guidebook for the psychiatric profession, only decades ago. What is 'normal' or 'abnormal' relates to all manner of oppressions and resistances. And all of this relates to the likelihood of whether one will be helped when in danger, to the likelihood that the way one manifests the shock of that danger will be interpreted in a way that determines the urgency of such help, if given.

The insights that Talila and colleagues and I have about ableism and all its attendant oppressions have come through the truths of our bodyminds. The truth of physical and spiritual experience. These truths are often erased by western academic institutions, which only allow very specific 'discoveries' — often centuries belated, often gained without citing the natives who taught them these truths — and theories to be valid forms of knowledge. In my PhD, I was often asked to justify the truths of my bodymind by citing western, usually white scholars. Their bodyminds eclipsed mine, at every turn.

*

Jasbir K. Puar's book *The Right to Maim* claims that pride in being 'disabled' — as an identity marker in line with neoliberal projects, and framing policies within it — masks the debilitation of oppressed populations such as Black Americans in Ferguson and Palestinians battered by settler colonialism. She describes

> [A] legitimate identification with disability that is manifest through state, market, and institutional rec-

ognition, if not subjective position: I call myself disabled. But this cannot be the end of the story, because what counts as a disability is already overdetermined by 'white fragility' on one side and the racialization of bodies that are expected to endure pain, suffering, and injury on the other. As such, the latter is an understanding of biopolitical risk: to extrapolate a bit from Claudia Rankine's prose: 'I am in death's position.' And to expand: I am in debility's position.

'Disability rights' given to citizens of western countries coexist with genocide against disabled people, including those bombed in hospitals in Gaza, those forced to flee their homes under duress in the 1948 Nakba (Catastrophe) that killed and displaced so many, and the 2023–25 Nakba that shows no signs of stopping as I write these words, as we rage against the dehumanisation of Palestinians, of Arabs, of Muslims by the western world. What we need is not 'rights' given to us by nation-states that stratify our perceived levels of humanity by citizenship, race, religion, class, sexuality and gender, but disability justice.

Muslim women in western societies are more likely to be disbelieved. It was likely that Annah/s were Muslim – Indonesia has the largest Muslim population in the world – and we Muslims in the west are subject to the same dehumanisation, the same lack of belief, as Annah/s. As there does not seem to be an end to the atrocities committed in the Israeli genocide of Palestinians, a genocide condemned by Holocaust scholars, by the many Jewish anti-Zionist activists around the world, as well as Muslims, Arabs and allies, the force field of disbelief, of disregard for Palestinian pain, is the same barrage of unfeeling weaponry that Annah/s faced. The imprisonment of hundreds of children in Israeli prisons, subjected to all manner of violations, over decades, is part of the same imperialist machine. They took from Annah/s' lands as they continue to take from others' lands. The roots of trees are flooded with chemicals, as are the limbs and lungs of humans under military occupation – this is true of Indonesian-occupied Papua as much as of Palestine.

★

The concept of cure, as the writer Eli Clare argues, is also a weapon used to justify oppression of D/deaf and/or disabled bodies – in a world in which so many of us do not want to be 'cured' or justifiably are against a narrow, ableist and eugenicist notion of 'cure'. I know that with medication, pained bodies may deem life pleasant *whilst still* in a manageable level of chronic fatigue and pain. I know this with my body.

All this is to say that when I illustrate Annah/s as in pain, I'd like to illustrate them as one or some of so many pained bodies whose lives can be made worth living with proper infrastructure and support, that being pained should not define one's life as consisting of suffering alone.

In discussing pain, it is of paramount importance that we do not paint pained lives with broad strokes as uniform, particularly as: unliveable, unworthy of living, or the experience of all chronic pain itself as wholly 'bad'. Our perspectives on pain, as pained people, may have changed over time, and may change in the future, crucially in light of the fact that our healthcare is dependent on socioeconomic structures that are marked by geography, class, gender, sexuality, race, caste and other stratifications beyond our control.

I want my pain to go away when it is truly unbearable, but as a manageable thing, in times of ease, I do not want to be abled, ever. I love my body as is, my pained body, which is also fortunate enough to be loved. Even when pain is at toxic levels, I understand implicitly that I do not want to be abled – I want to be a disabled body that does not experience suffering, that can manage pain like others manage diabetes. The primary barrier to such managing is colonial ableism, which leads to lack of access, lack of resources, lack of being understood as human.

Annah could have been in pain. They also would have had their agency and the possibility of joy within being a pained life. At the same time, we must recognise the immense structural odds against this joy. Annah/s belong to the majority world, a world that has been debilitated by white supremacist, capitalist, ableist colonialism, including ubiquitous and persistent forms of it in the contemporary world.

The societal forces regulating a body coded young, woman and brown, in close proximity to Paul Gauguin, a man with a documented history of violence in many forms, would have caused Annah/s unnecessary suffering. Annah/s' experience of being a pained body – in a world where the architecture of buildings was harsh, the distances unforgiving, and with no access to proper healthcare, in a world in which they were most likely one of millions of Indonesians enslaved by European colonialism – would have been very difficult.

Through all these years when the torture I have been undergoing in plain sight has persistently been disbelieved, tracing the lack of belief for Annah/s has helped me cope, helped me understand how deeply and historically nailed into the ground this disbelief is for brown, female-presenting people. Annah/s have shown me I am not alone, and I need to honour their image/s in return.

By queer-cripping (that is, to both queer and crip as interrelated processes) stories of Annah/s, we open up understandings of debilitation, and widen the possibilities for historical interpretations of visual objects, as well as the lives they portray. Part of this queer-cripping is an understanding of pain as both broad and deep. I wish to avoid painting Annah only as victim, and want to create understandings of them as multidimensional – at the same time, I want to emphasise the terror that was likely to have been a part of their life in proximity to Gauguin and his coterie.

In *The Wretched of the Earth*, Frantz Fanon writes: 'Europe is literally the creation of the Third World. The wealth which smothers her is that which was stolen from the underdeveloped peoples.' The western world is the creation of a physical and social infrastructure, enabled by the plundering of other lands, that caters (by large, around the world) only to the abled, to supremacist understandings of who should be recognised as human. It has also been the creation of more and trenchant disabling, and of various ways 'disability' is understood in local contexts.

Vulnerability to painedness comes as a result of debilitation, created by western and other colonial forces historically, as well as vulnerability to lack of treatment and management. The physical-socioeconomic infrastructure of western countries has perpetuated selective disablement as more prevalent amongst majority world populations, women and LGBTIQ+ people. Structural disablement is always intertwined with global sociopolitics, racial imaginaries and fictions of supremacy. To begin to pay respects to pained Annah/s, we need to acknowledge the complex, gendered and racialised history of what we know today, within a colonial framing of world geography, as Southeast Asia. A place where literal enslavement and terrorisation of millions of bodyminds occurred over hundreds of years in unacknowledged pain.

Remember Annah/s and origin stories splayed across a vastly complex network of disablement and enablement, of perceptions of bodyminds, and the ways this determines the life courses of such bodyminds. Remember ocularcentrism, part of this primacy of visual perception, particularly with regards to the history of Western painting. Including the work entitled *Annah la Javanaise*. Remember that visual methods have been used to 'capture' and classify the colonised for subjugation, continue to do so through all the data being collected by governments and corporations daily.

Remember the painting, and that whether or not someone is regarded as being in pain is a fascinating and key indicator of how 'disability' and 'disabled' populations are labelled visually. Often, people who are disabled appear 'abled', and are more subject to the scrutiny of nation-states that portray disabled people as 'fakers', 'scroungers', lying about our own bodies to receive funds that are our rights. If we see the sitter for the painting *Annah la Javanaise* as a potentially pained body, we open up a poem that I have accessed through what I know in my body. The image refracts through possibility. Painedness is multiple possibilities, as there is a multitude of possibilities within painedness.

*

I wrote the poem 'Sliding Scale', which appears earlier in this chapter, in late 2011, early 2012, grappling with the many ways pain resists being described, how difficult it is to transmit pain's reality to another person. Years later, I read Elaine Scarry's seminal 1985 book, *The Body in Pain*, in which pain is portrayed as indescribable.

> Scarry claims that 'whatever pain achieves, it achieves in part through its unsharability', and that this trappedness of pain in the body is all the more overwhelming as extreme pain 'destroys the world' for the pained person, who is unable to communicate this destruction, for whom pain becomes the only reality. Scarry

links this to the use of torture as a way to inflict pain as an overwhelming fact that both takes over reality and denies the body of its ability to communicate it. Further, in war, a person's bodily pain becomes imbued with the side the body is on, its pains conceived as comprising part of victory or defeat. In order to move away from torture and war, and their attendant infliction of pain, Scarry postulates that democratic principles are necessary, and that acts of creation (such as art-making) are generative and are also movements away from the indescribability of pain.

Scarry has been criticised by the scholars Judith Shklar and Geoffrey Galt Harpham, who say Scarry's condemnation of torture ahistorically omits Western countries' use of torture in colonisation. Western 'democratic principles' have absolutely inflicted and condoned torture, continue to do so. This is crucial to note when discussing a pained Annah, and pained brown women, non-binary people and girls, in an era that is still colonial, whether past, present or (we hope not for much longer) future.

It is telling that one of the most influential works on pain in the Western canon erases the reality of tortured bodies from colonised lands. In visualising a human body, I contend, whether one's own body, another body in one's presence, or the image of a human body such as Annah's, there is always a hauntology of pain – there is the uncertainty of whether or not pain is present in a body (one might say also a hauntology of torture, in cases of prolonged extreme pain such as my own, inflicted through lack of medication and access). Even when there is pain perceived in one or more parts of the human body, there is the trace of painlessness or less pain in other parts. So if we see all human bodies in the context of a world's past, riddled with colonisation's abuses of the human body for political gain, pain and painlessness exist as *marks* of these acts in all of us affected historically. These acts are largely ignored, Scarry's detractors argue, as torture became a human rights issue for countries outside the West to be condemned by Western countries, without introspection into continued usage of torture by the West's own hands.

Pain research is still very nascent in medical history, and our neural networks are vastly complex. On a purely biological level, there are still so many neural universes that western medical science has yet to discover – and in the meantime, as ever, we pained people live with what our bodies know, beyond any doubt. And that is before we even consider social structures that create greater vulnerability towards chronic pain – the debilitation written of by Jasbir Puar – such as being poor, and/or living in a country without access to pain management services and information; systemic racism inherent in healthcare systems; being working class and in jobs without health and safety provisions that prevent injuries; or having the world discriminate against being a girl or non-binary, young, poor, migrant, non-white and disabled, Muslim or Sikh in the UK (or a villainised religious group in other contexts), Dalit, all categories that, in Annah's time as well as today, make one increasingly susceptible to chronic pain. Inciting 'injuries' such as these, however, would scarcely go into a medical report.

So now, let us think of Annah as a brown child in France in the 1890s, without any social support, a child who was captured in painting by and perceived as the possession of a known physical abuser of women; a child for whom the insinuations of their sexual association with Paul Gauguin were very much part of this possession. Though the causes of chronic pain are uncertain and widely varied, stress, lack of access to healthcare and increased vulnerability to hurt of both physical and mental nature (again, a vulnerability that Gauguin's record greatly increases the likelihood of) would have made Annah more vulnerable to pain. And yet, the young person in the painting is never described as anything but a kind of complacent, a kind of inviting, a kind of daring intertwined with sexuality.

Scarry claims art-making is the antidote to torture and pain, yet, as other critics of her have said, this is dangerously naive. *Annah la Javanaise* is classified as art, yet it very likely involved and *incurred* pain – abuse of physical, sexual, emotional, financial nature – at the hands of Gauguin.

Scarry states that acute pain resists language, yet we are constantly *in language with pain*, whether it is ours or others', whether it is acknowledged or not, through bodily movements, sayings and attempts at articulating a sensation we at times *need* to communicate with great urgency. Alyson Patsavas points out that there *have* been accounts of pain written by pained people with acute awareness and sensitivity, 'that there is a rich history of narrative representations of pain. […] Despite these interventions, for many people, pain *feels* inexpressible.'

All pain language is asymptotic, meaning it can only *approximate* an interpretation of pained feelings, as is all language.

There is the trace of both pain and painlessness in each piece of visual input we receive of a human body – terms that are not binary, but are often perceived as such – and this has vital political implications. *Annah la Javanaise* is a picture of a potentially pained body, where the existence of pain is liminal in nature (neither explicitly there or not there), but the likelihood of pain is astronomical.

This is all, of course, highly supportive of Sara Ahmed's groundbreaking work on 'the contingency of pain' – that pain can be and has been used for political purposes, to draw people towards or away from certain bodies, to support or decry policies. The pain of Palestinians under Israeli occupation is deemed negligible and necessary under the unbearable violences of genocide. Even the deaths of thousands of children are deemed collateral damage, even hospitals are openly bombed and shot at, disabled and pained people further disabled, disabilities created, no pain medication even for surgeries.

Notice how chronic pain prevention is intertwined deeply with violence prevention, yet the connection between them is rarely made, in the mainstream. Domestic violence, and other forms of violence against women, is a global epidemic and yet rarely framed as such because of the way women's pain is framed. Ahmed's work is also vital here in terms of what she writes about the 'stickiness' of emotions: how certain emotions do or do not attach to particular people or objects, through political, architectural, economic, social frameworks. The emotions related to concern, care, empathy, worry over, with regards to Annah as a young person, are made to seem extraneous and unnecessary by virtue of the literal framing of their body. Concern is an emotion that is not made to 'stick' to Annah/s.

In the 1996 study 'Beautiful faces in pain: Biases and accuracy in the perception of pain', it was found that 'physically attractive patients and male patients were judged to be functioning better than physically unattractive and female patients'. Clearly there is a contradiction in the interaction between stereotypes of a body interpreted as cis-male being 'more functional' or 'stronger' – and a body interpreted as cis-female as therefore being in more pain – against stereotypes of a cis-female body as being 'hysterical' and 'emotional', our pain as therefore not being 'real'. Empathy and belief adhere to some and not others, and, though in contradictory ways at times, enforce a hierarchy in which white people – always assumed to be within the colonial gender binary – are deserving of the most belief, most entitled to be regarded as fully human in colonial societies past and present.

For Gauguin, the entire function of Annah/s in the painting rested on them being perceived as beautiful, and the painter linked to them, therefore, as possessing this beauty. By framing them as a sexual object, whose purpose is to pleasure himself and other white people, he did away with the possibility of them being regarded as a person in pain – someone to whom we owe help and love, rather than someone whose sole purpose is to cater to the whims of the viewer.

Nor did it end with Gauguin. Long after his death, the context in which Annah's image exists continues to contribute to the illusion that they could not have been a pained body. Museums, galleries, libraries, lecture halls and the internet are places where Annah's image is displayed, and, I argue, the possibility of their pain completely denied or elided, in spite of circumstances that made pain very likely.

Hauntologies of pain persist. European colonisation of what is now known as the archipelago is nominally over, yet persists, in innumerable ways. The choke of debt to international financial institutions, the continued violent clawing of enormous swathes of the country for 'natural resources' to feed the machine, including the ongoing genocide of Papuans by the Indonesian government – a genocide fuelled from the start by US interests in Papuan gold deposits, now a militarised zone guarding the largest gold mine in the world, atop the blood of scores of families, of bodyminds. Structures repressing hauntologies of pain persist.

Think of *Annah la Javanaise* – perceived as a .GIF, .JPEG, in print in a catalogue, or, for those with access to the 'Private Collection' that owns the original, perceived as a material painting. We are at a remove from their possibilities of pain, even though they were a child being painted by someone who would be deemed an offender today. This remove is a deliberate one that upholds Gauguin's 'mastery'.

There are any number of ways in which we can scrutinise the direct flow of violence, from the Tate records labelling Annah a 'Polynesian female nude', to the biopics of Gauguin's life, such as *Oviri* or *A Wolf at the Door*, which aim to condone sex with Annah yet unwittingly frame it as assault, to the New York Times review of *Oviri* which, taking its cue from the film, described Annah as 'the gift of a Javanese gamine'.

This fantasy breeds sycophancy towards the actors playing Gauguin, whether Donald or Kiefer Sutherland or Anthony Quinn, at the cost of one's soul.

These flows of violence are something we must be aware of and rally against. By extrapolation, of course, this is something we must be aware of and rally against when thinking of pain in children and young people's bodies, especially in racialised and/or gender-nonconforming bodies, bodies who are often disbelieved.

Sociologist and poet Yasmin Gunaratnam writes in *Death and the Migrant* of 'total pain', a state of painful situations creating such conditions of vulnerability, particularly among the most disenfranchised populations in a society, that they are overwhelming. If Annah was not in physical pain, I warrant that due to being a very young, brown person of little independence in 1890s France, in the company of abusive people, there is certainly the possibility that they could have experienced, throughout their life in France, a sense of total pain. By 'total pain', however, I do not mean a one-dimensional suffering, and in characterising possibilities for Annah, we must keep in mind that possibilities for joy, for relief, for escape, were always present.

I wager that the lack of healthcare available to Annah would have made them potentially totally pained in a true sense of suffering, with few ways to alleviate the pain to a level where they could be pained and sustainably happy (an experience we who live with chronic pain may have). I think of opium or alcohol addiction, I think of orgasm with those who did not have their best interests in mind – avenues for pain alleviation that were dangerous and which compounded their vulnerability.

Pain exists in such variety, is challenging to describe. (I continue to ask how non-pain should be described: does pain always occur against the backdrop of non-pain, or is it the other way around? Why is the question of what non-pain feels like, in detail, never asked?) The fact that pain is difficult to describe, and that the daily descriptions of lived pain from those of us who experience it are so often misunderstood – at times fatally – is added grounds for the possibility of pain in every picture, that *every expression of a body could theoretically be an approximation of pain.*

It is wholly plausible, based on even extreme levels of pain in ourselves that may go unnoticed by another human being looking at us, and considering the situations Annah/s found themselves in, that they could have been pained body/ies.

Annah as a pained body presents a rupture in past narratives of them. The possibility of pain in every picture creates a fissure through which bone-deep histories may present themselves. How does this dismantle accepted notions of sex, consent, race, etc. in Annah's very specific context? Here is where we may first open the floodgates of such enquiry into a visual object, behind which are multiple possible lives.

*

The minotaur from my vision during reiki comes back in memory. She is too tired to move, in her pulpy, bloody flesh, shocked into stillness. Though she is unblinking, I sense her aliveness, electric. It occurs to me that the coliseum stands are blurred in this vision, out of mind's eye, while she is in such stark focus; that this may be because who is or is not in those stands does not matter, if they do not exist in her reality. Stripped to the bone. The charge of her animus only palpable to those who are quiet, observant, who detect it through an affinity with her. If people do not perceive her survival in a body of gore, if people do not perceive the gore, they do not deserve to be in focus. They live in a reality that is, in fact, unreal, one that occludes even the possibility that the bare, exposed sinews of the minotaur's scalped head and shoulders and torso exist. Even if they did, they may well not even acknowledge that she could still be alive. So very alive.

In the vision, the minotaur shapeshifted. She became another kind of creature, in another element: watery, away from the harsh coliseum light. She developed on her body a means of protection from the world, a gargantuan cloak made of stone-like scales, stretching further than the eye could see into the far reaches of ocean. This form existed, in my vision, at the same time as the minotaur. The minotaur did not disappear; in her new form, she was remembered.

Annah Clusterfuck

I. The Name

Mulatto Eurasian Dutch-Javanese and Indian
Malaysian pure Javanese the Javanese is
Annah la Javanaise am I the girl the paint
a chair the blue of the chair the shade of a
skin and the monkey the monkey is tame
and my feet are beside it my nipples somehow
a reflection of smile so hair up in bun and thirteen
indentured supposedly here in a Private Collection
the name is redacted and so I am worth I am bank

I am millions in the nude and mucho dinero when
clothed in olden-time photographs only because I am
constantly posed amidst men ah the men they are
pillars of art and Gauguin and Mucha and all the rest
never Paul never Alphonse but oh I am Annah I am
she though maybe 'like many Javanese, Annah goes
by only one name' these broadsheets say in English

so I am financial backings and I am art conservationists
signing NDAs I am the catalogue girl the .GIF the .JPEG
the crux of a Google search here is my name and begin
to read Nobel Prize-winning sir Vargas Llosa in paperback,
oh his impersonation of Paul perceives me savage
and lips so thick writes Vargas Llosa as character,
(or, as himself) that my plump, ready mouth could only be African.

Half-Indian half-Malay. Half-screengrab half-take care
of the brown girls of today in developing countries unless
museum-bound in frames where flesh will never pucker
from cold unless you cannot afford the few pounds
to send them for postal adoption instead of acknowledging
many-yeared days of weight in the form of carrying
the stripping away of land and food from our mouths
in order to gild your streets and now the world is alive
and changing but there have always been #rebels. They say
that I was one then and in Brittany sun they called me a witch.
Perhaps it requires magic to bloom in drought-filled earth,
in chilly-winded lands where you sit for long hours in order
to be claimed, as just the child opening expected of you.

II. The Pain

He made me sit for eleven hours on a broken nerve.
He bled me too hard. On the boat from Java,
when Madame Nina brought me over to be owned,
it had already happened. I ate a piece of glass

he'd cooked with the stew while drunk and he shouted
Sit. I sucked myself into the most imperceptible part
of a photograph, twisted myself into horsehair
brush, became the palette whose wood could no
longer feel sap dripping from it against its will.

I shut my mouth on Fridays, shut my eyes and
said to God on the Holy Day *kill.kill.kill.kill.kill.* I did not
specify a target nor did I understand who it should
be at that moment I thought I loved him. I think
I may have, there were no other little girls who did
not want him as well and Judith did, who he'd said batted her
eyelashes at him and in an accident of crime my parents
and siblings were separated from me, and they did not
know that all of Europe was here to fete their child,
that all of the world would be here to flatten their child
into two-dimensional form as his and theirs, not Java's.
I am the daughter of a domestic servant from Solo
whose eyes rolled back unalive childbirthing sister,
and a Dutch official whose eyes would nod at me
from the few times a week I would glimpse him in our
quarters, and then my mother passed. His white
children not shipped off with the next stranger; cradled.

I tried to cook rice in the house and Paul stung
my hand with the hot ladle *NO*. The sting in my hand
spread to arm and both legs my chest and all upwards
have felt as though they were gasping for air for the lack
of pain. He'd ▇▇▇ my ankles to ▇▇▇▇, sprain.
He'd love me the way he'd loved his wife in front of
his son, with a bloodying of cheek and bone. When
my arms began to shake and I felt a wound inside me
I could not venture to explain I did not dare to tell him.
The reason my death was not recorded despite my
prolific sitting was simply because such illness was
commonplace and misunderstood and almost-almost
made for the likes of us. Maybe. The debt of my life
was paid for leaving my baby sibling behind. There is
so much to be learned from the weights that make us
feel searingness agony tingling discomfort inside of
our migrained heads and the whole of my heart giving
way to a body that finally reflected: how it had felt to have
to hold breath, in bed, in front of the photographer
with my hands spread across my chest and all of this
carrying me into firelakes of body into pain that
was sparked by a hurt of bodymind distance away from
green forests and sambel terasi and heat and mother.

Once a dukun woman came to my bedroom,
sheets mine in Dream, with no one else there.
She said in the rainforests of Gunung Halimun
were eighteen plants very sacred to our people,
with leaves could cut through any kind of pain, make even
my firelakes bearable. That I would feel them simmer,
and stay a slower pace to calm them, lay body to the sky
to keep them at bay, paint and sing and dance in my way,
my way enough to escape. If I took my jamu medicine just so,
that she knew how to make a glowsun, oh that with a little
prayer to Gusti Allah and a Javanese rite, drunk with this
old medicine, I'd still be in the Hurt, but not firelakes-forever.
Just heat and tiredness and simmers, which to me now
sounds like a heaven. And I woke, in Brittany sunshine,
with Paul's dirty boots on the edge of my bed, caught smiling.

WE BURN DISBELIEF

This is a getaway story.

    Escape hatches sprouting from roofs and tunnels

    a window enlarging in a stray blanket,

    beige walls turning edible.

It begins with the distinct, danger-flooding-the-mouth possibility of being in a strange room, forced to contend with the question of how you want to be remembered by others. How do you condense a life into pithy, bite-sized obituaria? And if another person wants to consume you – yes, consume – in this way, and this way alone, does that not make them inherently unworthy of your story? For are they not universes apart from the people who love you, and who will think of you in shades and splatters of flaws and luminosity, who will see the remarkable architectural design of your being as singular and unrepeatable, and for whom brief labels are laughable insult?

Would you want to be defined by the worst thing that ever happened to you? There's a reason why many will never reveal that moment publicly, for we are prismatically more gorgeous than our crudest, most horrific memories.

What is shared in this book is not a definition of Annah/s – it argues that any such definitions so far are tattered shreds of half-truths. It is not a definition of myself. It is, rather, an illustration of persistent and very real adversaries that continue to cause violence in my life, and continue to cause violence against the memory of the child/ren called Annah/s.

Despite being told by a colleague 'Annah is you', she is most certainly not. The statement is frankly demeaning in the same way that every brown woman writing fiction or poetry in English is assumed by some to be drawing from her own life, especially if the narrator is (gasp) also a brown-skinned woman. However, around the same time that the sensation of hot axes began ripping my nerves apart from the inside, I learned of Annah/s, and I immediately understood the nature of their enemy.

The thought was complete and banal, 'the foe of my foe is—'

I clung to this one morsel of understanding, this possibility of friendship across dimensions, in a world of suffering that no longer made any sense to me. The potential of solidarity from Annah/s has kept me alive. We are not the same, but we are facing the same purveyors of narrative and physical violence. I hope we are escaping through the same routes, at root.

The bodyminds of Annah/s and I turn into letters:

WE BURN DISBELIEF.

Disbelief is an infrastructure. It moves at the speed of fibre optic cables, and permeates the ones and zeroes through which the world finds curiosity in disabled people, often under the guise of supporting and caring for us. What if we burned it all? We who are survivors of longstanding medical torture, neglect and/or malpractice from lack of belief. What if we burned disbelief?

This text will not be yet another space in which the physical and psychic violence the world perpetrates against chronically ill and disabled people is detailed at length; many of us have written, and spoken, and performed, and painted, and otherwise created any number of works testifying to this. These pieces – the talks and panels and artworks – are often asked to hinge upon the spectacle that is a marginalised bodymind's trauma, the perceived authenticity of the violence being disclosed. And this explicit or implicit invitation to reveal trauma, under the pretence of safety, a cajoling into doing so when it is not an inherent impetus of the artist, is in itself a bloodthirst.

It is a banal truth that people of the majority world are often told the pathway to 'visibility' and 'success' is to mine our own worst experiences, regardless of where we may be in terms of healing from them, regardless if they are still very much ongoing, regardless if the goal of doing so is to satisfy the twin evil urges of others to file disabled narratives into what can be called 'trauma consumption' and/or 'inspiration consumption'. In the name of 'care' or 'visibility', we are given narrative constraints.

Coercion into disclosure is a deeply destructive tenet, and it has much to do with the psycho-physical infrastructure of disbelief. By this, I mean the ways disbelief results in us being denied medication, care, access and safety from all forms of violence. We are still regarded as explicitly unworthy of care by virtue of colonial laws' persistent eugenicist tendencies. Those eugenicist colonial laws are not, in fact, of the past. They are the very present, and near future, manifesting in multiple livestreamed and intertwined genocides for colonial imperial resources, from Palestine to Papua, to killing disabled people through lack of care and public funds in the UK and elsewhere in the imperial core. Colonial infrastructures of disbelief endure in the structuring of welfare systems or lack thereof, the austerity measures, the capitalistic organisation of care that presupposes people are disposable, including the 'structural adjustment programmes' that wealthy 'global' financial institutions impose upon poorer countries in order to cut and privatise their public services, the lack of care for healthcare professionals themselves, and on it goes. Palestinian parents and doctors hold a camera up to dead and dying infants, and what is disbelieved is the humanity of all these people, wholesale.

That long tail of being disbelieved with regards to our personhood persists in brick-and-mortar buildings' and digital infrastructures' lack of access. It persists in the contemporary dictates of getting our needs met, in terms of having to disclose private accounts of our lives and conditions, simply to increase the odds of surviving and receiving access and safety. We trade a repeated nicking of the psyche – that is, such disclosure to sociomedical service providers who are trained or forced to disregard our humanity by virtue of brutally privatised systems of 'care' – for the possibility of salvation in a fundamentally violent colonial capitalist political economy.

It is a game of belief in which disbelief has the upper hand. We are perceived as non-disabled until otherwise 'proven', while the burden of 'proof' overwhelmingly relies on us to entrust deeply sensitive information to others who have already proven themselves to be uncaring, or will do so in good time, unaware of their own biases regarding what constitutes a 'proof'. You see this constantly reflected, for instance, in widespread ignorance as to the existence of ambulatory wheelchair users, leading to claims that we are 'faking it'. If someone has to hear the absolute worst things you have experienced, or parts of your bodymind you are proud of but do not wish to convey, in order to validate your truth, to see your story as worthy, they do not deserve this story. Yet often, to survive, we must cater to the undeserving.

So many of us are traumatised and have complex PTSD or PTSD, and identify as 'mad'. This also means that how we communicate with each other is marred by PTSD flare-ups, particularly because of constant stress. Thus, we may, as I believe many have experienced, bear the brunt of disbelief and cruelty from other disabled people who do not see our behaviour as cripnormative – i.e. how they think a disabled person 'should' behave – and who use interpretations of our words and actions to presuppose we are not in pain, or that our pain is 'not that bad' or the 'same as everyone else's'.

People presume, once they have heard your story over and again, that it is not still ongoing, and that crises are not acute. This is entwined with the violence of the assumption that brutal violence cannot stop and start and be ongoing in someone's life, and just as violent each time. There is a violence in the fatigue this brings. This presumption of lack of suffering is part and parcel of an infrastructure of disbelief and of systems of relating to one another based upon cripnormative assumptions, which are in turn endorsed in the ever growing popularity of 'crip' and 'care' as words that generate cultural capital in the creative industries. This creates forms of lateral violence within disabled communities, as well as violence from those outside disability circles, which people from the majority world are far more likely to bear the brunt of.

Disbelief as infrastructural violence, as a material infrastructure of violence and neglect, has overwhelmingly, within the past decades, come to be about personae online and offline. It has come to be about how our modes of self-expression and behaviour exist within intersecting forms of panoptic forces, which often require very different expressions of self. For instance, anyone using social media recognises that what we display there is rarely an accurate portrayal of the fluid and multivarious ways of describing how we are, or how our day has been, or the private joys and struggles we choose to keep to ourselves.

Disabled people, the largest minority group in the world, include the hundreds of millions who do not disclose disabled identity, or other personal bodymind information, for safety and survival. Disabled people are far more likely to be unemployed, by virtue of the fact that many of us cannot and should not be asked to perform according to colonial, capitalist markers of 'gainful employment', in addition to matters of stigma from employers and society at large, and the inaccessibility of most workspaces in the world. Performances of 'ability' and 'productivity' are necessary for survival in capitalist societies, especially in their current late stage. This is particularly the case in countries with vastly inadequate social safety nets for disabled people, such as Indonesia, and for migrants in countries like the UK, where many of us are cruelly denied access to public funds due to citizenship status.

Thus, we as disabled and chronically ill people are often caught in a double bind. In order to survive, many of us do not disclose aspects of disability or even anything about our bodymind conditions, in public or semi-public forums – in our demeanour at meetings, virtual and in-person, for example, we may perform so as to avoid violence and discrimination from those around us. Yet this very non-disclosure can be at odds with us trying to get our requisite needs for survival met in other contexts – we are accused of malingering (at times even by other disabled people) because we may 'seem fine', or because we meet colonial capitalist requirements of productivity. Furthermore, performing (in more ways than one) ablenormative work can certainly be disabling in itself. When, trying to survive economically, we do more than our bodyminds can take, our bodyminds often suffer grievously, continually, repeatedly. Yet our supposed abilities to conduct bootstrapping employable behaviour are praised as success stories, even though we should not have to work when we cannot, and even though the brutal socio-political, capitalist context for our 'success' means that overwork for disabled people – whether that means a month or a few crucial minutes more than we should – is likely.

Only when our demeanour cracks, and we disclose, are people likely to have more empathy for our condition, if they believe us at all. As our behaviour online and offline may vary, our behaviour with trusted loved ones and those we do not fully trust may vary as well. We will be judged based upon a juxtaposition of our traumas with how we 'appear in daily life'. And yet, our appearances are evaluated against laughable notions of how we should 'behave while disabled' on social media and in our places of employment, or around any people at all. Which face is considered 'authentic', 'our real condition', by the panoptic structures of late capitalism? Which facet?

These impossible double binds are deliberately caused by panopticons that are part of the same overarching ableist structures of colonial capitalism. Such impossible circumstances, which create deep suffering and violence for so many, are a product of: a) colonial destruction of communal systems and sources of welfare, including through austerity and privatisation measures that lead to scarcity-based systems of aid – and all the physical and digital infrastructures of these so-called care systems, all the taxonomisation and medicalisation – that rely on accusations of malingering until proven disabled; b) 'grindset' mentalities with regards to employment under capitalism, which necessitate obedient public personae reflecting 'ability' and 'employability'. This surveillance machine is built on all the data we provide every day to websites, apps, electronics manufacturers and governments. Metrics for what cripnormativity looks like – that is, the 'right' way to 'appear' as though our bodyminds are really going through what we know we are going through – are shaped by innumerable pixels and terabytes. These metrics, shaped by colonial capitalist ableism, are inherently racist and sexist, as Safiya Umoja Noble writes in *Algorithms of Oppression*; this nature is part of western technology infrastructure's imperial dictates. The exponential growth of surveillance systems is inextricable from welfare and so-called care systems, whether public, private, or both. India continues to build the largest biometrics system in the world, known as 'Aadhaar', which relies on the capture of biometric and demographic data that will determine the wellbeing of hundreds of millions of people. A system that will provide data to an inherently discriminatory medical field, which, as a result of the aforementioned double bind, has already caused trauma for disabled people the world over.

We are forced to contort our faces, our bodies, our lives, in order to secure things that are our right: livelihood, family, friendship, creative expression. Particularly as women of colour, regularly regarded as aggressive in Western societies, we must often 'hide' signs of pain, such as screaming, lest they are interpreted as aggression, to even gain access to clinics and hospitals. And that is just about literally getting in through the door, not to mention the hurdles that lie within such institutions. We are regularly gaslit by corporations and institutions about our access needs, based upon whether we appear to truly 'need' them, regardless of which of the various facets of appearance we must juggle are in play at any one time.

★

The infrastructure of disbelief consists of societal prompts and non-human materials. It is the fibre optic cables, lithium and cobalt mining for our phones, the abuse of employees in electronics factories, as well as the carcinogenic 'Erin Brockovich compound' that sickens people around Indonesian nickel mines quarried for supposedly green cars. It is every single electronic device used for surveillance being part of a chain of immiseration and exploitation. Disbelief is inherently tied to colonial, capitalist environmental extractivism, which has been coalescing for hundreds of years – with ecological crisis upon ecological crisis caused by the clearing of forests, open-pit mining and tailings, oil refineries, eviction of and violence against indigenous people for colonial gain – to create the current climate crisis.

'Mankind has caused this climate crisis,' claim western campaigners, trading on colonial notions of universalism. 'Humanity has been at odds with the earth,' claim media pieces. All of this discounts the very urgent and important work of indigenous communities around the world who are the best stewards of biomes, and are continuing to be killed and assaulted for opposing corporate and state destruction of lands. This is in tandem, of course, with the dehumanisation of people from the global majority, who have been environmental defenders throughout the ravages of colonial capitalism over hundreds of years. Environmental crises, including the climate crisis, are not caused by 'humanity'; we are very clearly living with the consequences of colonial capitalist policies, which have been resisted by generation upon generation of many peoples, and continue to be resisted by us.

Colonial capitalism is built upon disbelief: disbelief that Black, brown and indigenous peoples are human and deserve to be free of suffering; that there are thousands upon thousands of non-Western cosmologies and complex indigenous sciences. What it builds then – the aforementioned citadels of disbelief infrastructure that affect billions of disabled people – should not come as a surprise. When my mother was a child, remedies were found in her yard. Everyone in the village took from what was around them in natural form, freely yet respectfully, without an impetus for accumulation. In her early life she witnessed a profound and rapid shift towards the commodification of medicine, of healing as something to be bought and sold. Imagine going to a store and purchasing a product created by people one had never met as the only way to help one's body. Today, every single community where indigenous remedies are used is under threat.

In the film *Jungle Cruise*, Dwayne Johnson (aka the Rock) searches for a magical rainforest cure that will 'benefit humanity'. The film elides and Disneyfies the very urgent violences of pharmaceutical multinational corporations today, which extract materials from any rainforests spared by pulp and paper companies, mining companies and so-called 'carbon offsets' (which are essentially just ways for corporations to force indigenous peoples off lands, while continuing to pollute). The necessary condition for these extractive methods is profound disbelief in justice for indigenous peoples.

When a rainforest burns, cosmologies are consumed and turn to ash, as are cures, as is belief by those who perpetrate environmental genocides that indigenous peoples are human. When multinational pharmaceutical and cosmetic corporations take from plants that have remedied indigenous peoples for centuries, and make them available in Western markets for a profit, while destroying native communities, this is a profound system of mass disbelief. The world is covered with the aftermaths of profound disbelief. Buried in soils are the bones of those who were not given medicine, who were disbelieved about pain by medical institutions, who were misdiagnosed through systemic failures, who were beaten, killed and violated by corporations' long shadow.

And if you are in the books of a nation-state, if you are codified as a citizen by colonially created bureaucracies and systems that seek to mould name-giving and self-identification to their will, your bodymind is increasingly under digital surveillance. If your bodymind is non-normative, gaining any needed succour and aid will be through medical systems entwined with this surveillance, under governments that actually seek to minimise the amount of help given, and deny humanity of the most vulnerable – pandemic policies worldwide attest to this. And this denial of care relies on disbelief as the norm, not the exception. Disbelief is the entire machinery.

Indigenous ecologies are salvation ecologies, for disabled and chronically ill people especially. Under the radar as much as possible, there are pluralities of localised environmental justice movements fighting gargantuan, difficult, lifelong battles against corporate entities that disbelieve the right of all bodies to be free of violence and suffering. In an age where global 'environmental NGOs' participate in some of the worst offences against indigenous peoples on the ground (such as documented violation and assault against indigenous peoples under WWF's watch), there is the full impetus for these collectives to keep themselves hidden from surveillance and disbelief infrastructure.

The technologies we use, Zoom and social media and Gmail and Apple devices, are all part of an overarching structure of disbelief. How disabled people behave under these surveillance mechanisms can always be made fodder for disbelief under various panoptic gazes. The path forward is to fully recognise this. The path forward also lies with people who escape these surveillances the most. Salvation ecologies, distinct from any white-centric understandings of 'rewilding' that involve a 'terra nullius' – a colonial concept of nature as 'separate' from humans, and 'pristine' – are our way forward.

I am rooting for the salvation of thousands of cosmologies I do not know the names of. I am rooting for salvation through disability justices, in localised ecologies that brim with survival and resilience. And for all those in all nation-states who are actively resisting the increasing threats of surveillance infrastructures, who are organising against lithium mining for our meme-sharing at the cost of lives elsewhere, who are organising against child labour fuelling mining in the Democratic Republic of Congo to unearth cobalt destined for disabled technology devices as well as e-cigarettes, who are organising against government surveillance through our medical systems, who are organising against the collection of citizenship data in places of medical care, who are organising so that disabled migrants, including refugees, not given access to public funds can survive, who are organising so that we no longer must 'prove' our bodyminds to be what they are, according to abled and cripnormative ideas of how bodyminds should behave.

We remain firm in the truth of who we are, and our secretive bodyminds keep intimate knowledges to ourselves. We should share when we are truly protected.

*

I am under no illusions that bodyminds like ours are protected. Living in a world in which we are subjected to physical violence on a regular basis, to the point of numbness – the abuse and mistreatment of strangers against a disabled body – leaves me stunned time and again. Often just when I am regaining hope in the benevolence of the universe. When I share in this book the worst parts of my life, I know it is not safe for me to do so. I write these words and then baulk at having done so. You likely have done nothing to earn my trust, nor that of other pained bodyminds. Most likely, I will never even meet you. However, I now have a support system that tries, through trial and error, to protect me as a torture survivor. And I will put my faith in this system, this coalition of loved ones, to try to protect me, as I will try to protect them.

I am a survivor of torture, and a live-er of complex PTSD. I use the word 'torture' more and more these days, in addition to 'pain' or 'chronic pain' when trying to describe what I'm feeling to trusted people. In the past I have used the latter two terms, when it should have been the former – because when 'pain' is repeatedly used to describe what you feel, it is too easy to dismiss. Because 'pain' is variable, another person can, and will, reduce your 'pain' to the lowest part of the scale if their empathy for you is minimised. Some of them will never experience level ten pain in their lives. Fewer will experience it for long durations, at times for months over many years.

Being subjected to level ten pain, not only repeatedly but for long periods of time, over many years, is being tortured; it is torture whether delivered at the hands of an individual 'healthcare' professional who tells you nothing is wrong simply because they do not understand, or via a cruel globalised healthcare system, in which stolen-from countries are starved of healthcare through colonial extraction, and in the imperial core, in cities like London and New York, you are still excluded from eligibility for relief.

How long?

How much pain?

I am in an arena where people are gawking at the torture. I close the curtains around me. I disappear.

A tingling in your right pinkie becomes a firebolt up your entire right side, and your chest. Everything is burning. You have never imagined this level of hurt before. You feel it in the back of your ear, the right nostril, the right side of your lips. Knives, axes, exploding suns of pain. It is all-encompassing.

What happens to a bodymind when it is burned?
What happens to a burning bodymind when it is disbelieved, even as it continues to burn? This, I can very well tell you.

As a reader, you must be aware that yes, there is the danger of giving into some of the public bloodthirst for violence in writing from the positions of marginalised identities. And I am dismayed by the threat of having to do so in any measure. However, I would not be facing such threat if this book were not also about the escape hatch, the secret tunnel, the catapult into universes in which the gawking public does not exist, in which we are not reliving torture for others to look at askance, disbelieved and thus the recipients of stunning violence.

Those of us who partially disclose anything about our bodyminds from within infrastructures of disbelief, when doing so in the arts, we come up against the bloodthirst for violent 'true life' stories, and also against the laughable hypocrisy of institutions, groups, individuals, when they declare that your 'true life' story is not to be believed, does not still apply, is beyond the narrow scope of what they deem to be possible violence. Participating in colonial, so-called liberal arts industries as a disabled and/or ill person is to be in a state of captivity, wherein possible violence is the status quo and undergirds all structures, looms constantly, threatens you actively, harms you continually.

In this book is an escape route. I am writing this as a way of holding out limbs to also-survivors, keeping in front of us a map of hope in which we make our way to relief.

This is an escape story.

If you are not one of us, you will not follow us past this exit. We will, finally, be free of your gaze.

★★★

I am burning.

A nurse, tired from her shift, calmly tells you it's probably just electrolytes.

I am burning.

Hospitals cannot figure you out. Doctors say they have tried everything. They tell your family there is nothing to be done. They eject you from the emergency ward, half-paralysed, at two in the morning.

You are ejected from multiple hospitals who tell you your screeching supernovas of sword-stabbing pain have nothing to do with your nerves. Haven't you experienced psychological issues in the past of depression and anxiety?

Aren't you a brown woman's body?

I am burning.
Please help me.

If you were burning at level ten out of ten, 90 per cent of your waking hours, how long would you be able to maintain a hope in your situation easing?

If every full stop were a minute:

. . . .
. . ..
....

And if the Morse code of knifing pain lasted not only for minutes, nor hours, nor weeks, nor months. If every full stop were a month. Years, with occasional reprieve, from day to day, but always a return to the fire.

It is a chisel. A pulse. The human learns to regard the stabbing as punctuation, meditate into the knifing as though it is Morse code. One pulse at a time.

If you had asked dozens of doctors and was told there was no way out.

Imagine this repeating, at times for no discernible reason, your own neurology's unknown vulnerabilities. Imagine it is twelve years before the gaps get wide enough to make you feel like you have a chance of truly overpowering the force that fog of knifing has in your mind.

....
....
....
....
....
      . . . .
....
....
....
....
....
....
....
....
....
....

If you decide that you might as well approximate a 'normal' person, if this isn't going to end. You smile and post overly much on social media, through level ten torture, because at least positive responses to posts bring you joy, if, in the long run, they will diminish your 'believability'. You find your way into courage, put your art out there, travel with it. In multiple countries with a more robust healthcare system than your own, not a single moment in which you were told, 'There actually is medicine for you. Please go to the GP this moment.' If you behave 'normally' through screaming torture, because of that time you were shouted at to be quiet before you were allowed to stay in the ER.

If you go to an 'international' writing festival in Bali, and you request an accessible-for-you, no-step room. When you arrive late at night, if you find your room is up a steep flight of stairs. 'It's not that many,' says the hotel attendant. In the morning, if you are literally paralysed, and the knifing is surreal. If you realise you have been put in a room without a landline, and you cannot contact the outside world immediately. If you scream for help, and no one comes. When you finally get a signal with your own phone, the Australian woman yells at you that they don't have any other accommodation. You tell her you are paralysed. She goes quiet. Soon, someone from the hotel brings you food. No one apologises to you.

If four years after you begin to burn, you gain a scholarship to the other side of the world in the hopes of being afforded the time and resources to commune with more Annah/s. You go to a GP on a whim, and tell them you're in near constant pain. You are given painkillers that dull the edge slightly. You return to the GP and confess how little a dent the meds have had on your actual levels. She is stunned. She looks at you for a long time. She says, 'Why weren't you in a rehab centre for the past four years?'

If you forget what you say in response. Your cerebellum has forcibly protected you from much of the past years, salvation in the form of brain fog. The wall of knives that has hit you for thousands of days, shapeshifting, level-shifting, is a cacophony that overwhelms memory.

If for the rest of one's life, this threat.

If you request all of your access needs, double-triple-check, and then—
The wheelchair is left in a terminal with you in it. If a phone dies. If you scream.
then—
if you sit on your suitcase in the rain, while they bring the wheelchair you'd requested online but they had forgotten
then—
your accommodation dates are mixed up, and you must be driven to another town, you are out of painless energy units, you burst into flames
then—
if you are burning at a writing festival, you mention disability and a male writer literally rolls his eyes at you
if you imagine if his whole body were to burn (how could you not? if you were put in the same scenario?) just for fifteen minutes, and not for the endless…

if you want him to understand you have learned to contort your body like 'the normals' and 'appear normal' though you are in ten out of ten pain, because to do so otherwise is to be disruptive and to risk the nurse hovering screaming at you and denying you the possibility of help, and to risk not having creative fulfilment on top of burning all the time.

These are not in order, time is post-traumatically jumbled, which of course means trauma survivors are not believed.

Are you satiated? Does the violence make you want more?

If we are spent, at having to explain ourselves in the hopes that we will be helped and understood. The possibility of help as a tool is extractive as fuck. We are mirroring it right now, in this exercise, of you reading me. Let me describe to you just how much pain I may have been in, live in threat of. You will very likely not understand, or paradoxically, because of the fluency and frequency with which I describe my pain, you will recoil and roll your eyes and lose patience. 'You talk too much about your pain'. Eventually, no matter how helpful you are, unless you are part of my circle of protection, you will do this. You will work with me and publish me and still be incredibly surprised somehow when I tell you the level is ten out of ten. You will misunderstand every interaction, because you do not think that level is a possibility. You don't realise that a woman can 'behave unpained' through pain, in order to prevent violence against them due to misunderstandings, to maintain friendships, work, familial ties, and that this facade will inevitably break sometimes. *I told you I told you I told you I told you I told you*

When I stop burning, I'll be sure not to let you know.

★★★

If:
there is nothing you can do to fully protect yourself from ableist violence
anything you do while burning will not protect you
get a phd, through squeezing your bodymind into the imperial ignorance box
put on a show
make books of words where, having read them, those who witness you in violence they cause by neglect say 'i didn't know it was that bad' *ITOLDYOU*
find the correct life partner, sans mutual heartache, not another partner who echoes the disbelief you'll hear throughout, which is a form of both emotional and physical abuse for disabled people
then you are left to burn due to another case of access neglect from people who've experienced your work (what was it for?)
the burn lasts weeks

oh it keeps coming

a chest
a pulse
knifing

THE PAINED ARCHIVE

Here is what can also be read in the painting, and in photographic archives said to be those of Annah la Javanaise: a negotiation of imperial violence with refusal and defiance. I have looked through the archives, digital and in physical object form, dragging a pained body through libraries, seeking out ways to counteract the colonial insistence on 'rationality' with regards to belief in pain that is based on violent parameters.

In *The Promise of Happiness* (2010), Sara Ahmed refers to the 'unhappy archive' as a project derived from anti-racist and feminist-queer movements, and thus as a collective endeavour, which makes dissent and suffering palpable within archives:

> It is not simply a question of finding unhappiness in such archives. Rather, these archives take shape through the circulation of cultural objects that articulate unhappiness with the history of happiness. An unhappy archive is one assembled around the struggle against happiness… My aim is to follow the weave of unhappiness, as a kind of unraveling of happiness, and the threads of its appeal.

Thanks to you, Annah/s, I've been pursuing threads that unravel ablenormativity and cis-heteronormativity as part of this unravelling of happiness – pursuing the threads that reveal possible pain in every picture. Cripping pain is fundamental to this unravelling; after all, pained bodies are often immediately associated with unhappiness, despite the huge variety of experiences, including joy, that we as pained bodies may have.

Ahmed writes that 'emotions are both about objects, which they hence shape, and are also shaped by contact with objects'. Asking why a child is afraid of a bear, Ahmed suggests:

> fear is not in the child, let alone in the bear, but is a matter of how child and bear come into contact. This contact is shaped by past histories of contact, unavailable in the present, which allow the bear to be apprehended as fearsome. The story does not, despite this, inevitably lead to the same ending. Another child, another bear, and we might even have another story.
> […] Fear shapes the surfaces of bodies in relation to objects. Emotions are relational: they involve (re)actions or relations of 'towardness' or 'awayness' in relation to such objects.

If *Annah la Javanaise* is a painting that was created with the specific goal of inducing 'towardness' of people in its direction, in particular potential buyers of Gauguin's art, and in the present day is upheld as an artefact of his genius, we must deconstruct the ways in which this painting is not framed as an artefact of horror – a depiction of a child in dangerous circumstances, a child who likely was hurt and likely could not run away easily – but as an amenable, pleasing object.

Due to the profound and unbearable horror involved in what now constitute colonial archives, the theft of life and freedom and land and wellbeing from those who created artefacts, whose likeness now become artefacts, every colonial archive is for certain a pained archive. There is pain whether or not the archive administrators register it; it is a function of bureaucracy within cultural industries that they must not register its weight in the course of daily work.

Yet my point here is also that *all archives are potentially pained archives*, because *there is the possibility of pain and emergency in every image*. In every kind of artefact. This is something pained people know intuitively, though ableist conditions ask us to forget it, to forget the possibility of pain in others every time we see them, in the flesh or in oil on canvas.

Ahmed encourages us to think of emotions not as psychological states, but as sociocultural phenomena, and we can apply that to thinking about the sociality of emotion with regards to *Annah la Javanaise*. *Annah la Javanaise* is an object that is both physically proximate to Gauguin's paintings of Polynesian children interpreted as girls in arts institutions that sort prints, originals and the like by artist, to the point where the Tate Library could label the figure in the painting as a 'Polynesian nude'; the print of Annah was near prints of Polynesian children, and they are seen to resemble each other. Because depictions of Annah/s and their Tahitian counterparts are (a) marketed the same way, as objects whose significance is in their 'aesthetic' value, and their contribution to the myth of Gauguin; and (b) producing the same range of affect as each other (that is, the suggestion of pliancy and exoticism imposed on them by Gauguin), they are placed – literally – in the same boxes, and prone to interchangeability by workers at arts institutions, and by general audiences.

In other words, brown children interpreted as girls and painted by Gauguin are all marketed in such a way that the intended socialised emotions are not those of horror and fear at these artefacts of likely abuse, but aesthetic appreciation for the creator. The origins of the children depicted in a Gauguin collection are incidental – it is his (warped) vision that matters, that we the public are meant to consume. The 'affective economies' of Ahmed's essay shape the financial system that allows *Annah la Javanaise* to be highly priced, and preserved, and dissociated from images of living Javanese/Indonesian/brown children. There continues to be a 'towardness' socialised towards Gauguin despite knowledge of his relationships with young children. Arts institutions' uses of marketing to induce the public's appeal, 'towardness' with regards to Gauguin, condones behaviour which continues to make people vulnerable, particularly those bodies coded as brown girls and described by those who would use them as (colonial) commodities.

Annah la Javanaise, and the calm, appealing emotions socialised towards it, can be further understood as imperial in nature when one considers two contrasting ways in which the sociality of emotions are cultivated towards painted portraits: that of the National Portrait Gallery in London, and that of the exhibition *Black Models: From Géricault to Matisse* (2019) at Musée d'Orsay in Paris.

The National Portrait Gallery (NPG) aims to cultivate reverence and curiosity about the subjects of the portraits displayed, and about portraiture as a category of art; though they hold exhibits organised around portrait artists, the primary impetus of the NPG is to maintain a canon of notable Brits. According to its website, the NPG's mission for both its Primary Collection and Reference Collection is 'to display portraits of the men and women who have made and are making British history and culture' and 'to act as a national focus for the study and understanding of portraits and portraiture'.

In contrast, the galleries that display *Annah la Javanaise* (when on loan from its private owners), and all the related texts published so far, focus entirely on Gauguin; the subject of the painting is only seen as object, contributing to Gauguin's mythology. Even an Indonesian-American scholar writing feminist academic work on Annah once told me: 'I don't care about her, but what she represents.' The public is not taught that Gauguin was a menacing and abusive man by the arts institutions where *Annah la Javanaise* might be hung, nor is the public taught that Annah is a human child, nor is the public taught the power differential between a child coded 'Javanese' and an older man coded 'French', one that persists to this day. Let alone how Javanese people are colonisers within Indonesia, and other historical truths. Arts institutions that handle the valuable commodity of *Annah la Javanaise* are invested in maintaining the image of Gauguin as a master artist towards whom we are expected to be sympathetic, and so they notate Annah as willing participant in his journey – and, I argue, they notate the relationship between Java and France as benign.

The exhibition *Black Models: From Géricault to Matisse* at the Musée d'Orsay attempts to centre the Black sitters of paintings in a vaunted (and all-male) French canon of artists. In this exhibition, paintings by 'Théodore Géricault, Charles Cordier, Jean-Baptiste Carpeaux, Edouard Manet, Paul Cézanne and Henri Matisse, as well as the photographs of Nadar and Carjat' are renamed for their Black subjects. The exhibition is planned in a way that at least makes its intended audience aware of the fact that they had names, a step of 'towardness' in the direction of perceiving subjects as human. That said, *Annah la Javanaise* proves that one can be named in a painting's title and dehumanised by it simultaneously, and I posit that being named in the painting one sat for, to be displayed in a future public exhibition, might not in fact be the wish of the sittee. They might object to how they are portrayed, particularly considering racial power differentials.

All of the above is related to the *impression* that the painting gives when it is displayed, to use another of Ahmed's concepts – not only in a building owned by whichever private estate possesses *Annah la Javanaise* currently, but on our screens in Google Image searches, always as an object created by Gauguin, always bolstering the myth of the artist. There is also the myth of the muse as pliant and compliant.

The photo of Annah in fancy dress with Gauguin, Alfons Mucha and Marold is held in the archive of, and displayed by, the Mucha Trust. The Mucha Foundation website captions the image as follows:

> Mucha with his friends in the studio, Rue de la Grande Chaumière, Paris (c.1893–94). Mucha's snapshot captures a group of his friends in fancy dress gathering in his studio. Mucha, in his trademark attire, sits casually in the front. He turns his head, possibly to respond to Czech painter Luděk Marold, dressed in a dashing Renaissance costume, who looks towards Mucha as though trying to catch his attention. Behind Mucha on the left is Paul Gauguin, who sits tall in a Moravian folk hat, probably from Mucha's collection of hats. On the far right is Gauguin's teenage mistress and model, Annah la Javanaise, posing with an enormous Breton headdress.
> © Mucha Trust
> Media type: Photography
> Medium: Reproduced from original glass plate negative
> Date: c.1893–94

Here we see how possible pain is elided: despite no record of Annah's relationship to Gauguin as one of mistress, this is written in the copy as fact. The reader is thereby coaxed to look at this picture and think 'consensual relationship', the flamboyant costumery contributing to the sense that all four people are in congenial play together. The title says 'Mucha with his friends'; Annah is a friend of all three men. Everything is consensual, all of this argues. The fact that I easily duplicated this image by screenshotting it on my laptop is significant; these messages are so easily reproducible, embedded within the images that carry them.

A more incisive reading of this photograph is one open to possibilities of pain and abuse. My aforementioned artwork *Spectral Vision*, reproduced again below, is a manipulated version of the archival picture; though all three artists could have hurt Annah, I chose to make Mucha and Marold skewed and menacing in an abstract way, and focus attention on the dissonance and tension between Gauguin and Annah – and in particular how Annah here conjures for me a great fear of Gauguin, and of the men. Their hands are crossed over their costumed chest. They are not smiling. Only the person photographed might truly know what was transpiring in their interiority at that point. However, I would suggest there is the distinct possibility of pain and/or suffering and/or fear and/or anxiety in Annah in this photograph. And, as I repeat often and deliberately, in the presence of an abusive man this fear is absolutely justified – I repeat that Gauguin was recorded as being abusive in order to instil fear of him, fear and repulsion that is absent from most presentations of Gauguin in arts institutions. Can how emotions are normally socialised around the painter be disrupted?

132 Annah, Infinite

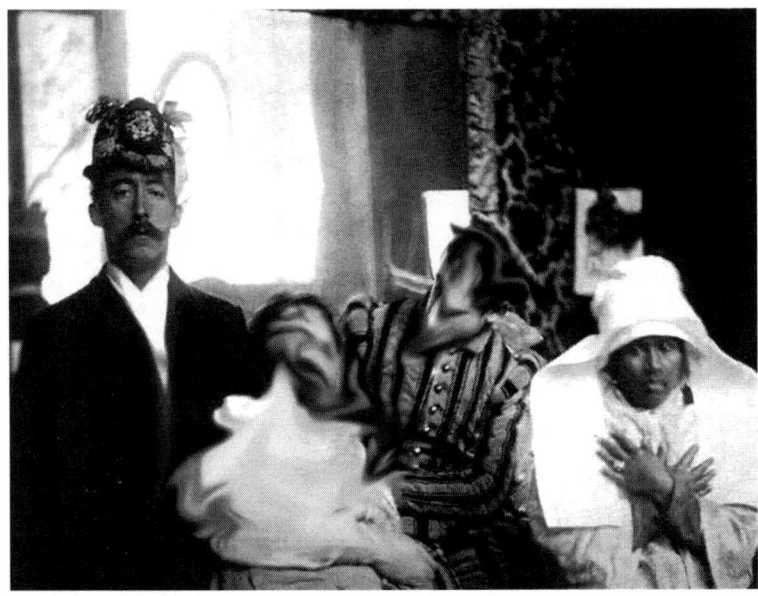

[Fig. 3.1. 'Annah with shadows: hands cross their body', also titled *Spectral Vision*]

Again, it is important here not to automatically equate all pain with suffering, suicidality and other associations abled perspectives may immediately tie to pain. However, excessive pain without relief may well cause these things – everyone's pain feels different, and induces different reactions – and particularly in situations where one is vulnerable, one is prone to the inability to manage one's pain, and prone to being around people for whom your pain is of no consequence.

Gauguin's painting and all prints of it should be recognised as a mode of tracking, cataloguing and constraining this heavily reproduced image of Javanese children's compliance to colonial France. However, the photographs and prints of Annah all contain registers of fugitivity beyond what colonial tracking mechanisms can control.

Though Annah/s may be labelled as 'mistress', 'faithless', 'model' (as if they posed happily, as if they chose to do so freely, and/or were paid), 'unmanageable', 'like a panther or a cannibal', the fact that all the words attributable to them are fictional (in Vargas Llosa's 2003 biographical fiction, for instance, as well as in *LIFE Magazine*, and in text written by the Mucha Foundation) means that all depictions marked as being Annah la Javanaise carry with them the great hum of possibility. Of possible different interpretations for who they were, for what a body marked 'Annah la Javanaise' felt like in 1893–94, in the presence of a dangerous Gauguin. There is the great possibility of refusal, of evasion, of defiance teased from accounts of their alleged robbery of Gauguin, of an unwillingness to submit. Indeed, I argue this hum of unwillingness, of refusal, whether in a pained body or not, and always with the possibility of pain, applies to every picture.

I draw possible Annah narratives from the hum of promise, of fugitivity. I do so in order to offer different 'impressions' of the image than arts institutions steeped in colonial values prescribe for us, by paying attention to how institutions stifle a *plurality* of registers for understanding human images, through ablenormative narratives.

Annah/s and other readers, I am offering you a template for how we may tease alternate, fugitive registers for visual archives of Annah/s – including ones in which you (they) are both pained and resistant, defiant, alive. Registers for how we may understand that this is not a contradiction – that there is not only the possibility of *a* pained archive, but the possibility of multiple, polycentric pained archives. Archives of escape, archives of safety.

NIGHTMARES OF 1965

The sun is shining on a brick school courtyard in the early 1990s. You are small and in uniform, your white, stiff shirt an imposition, your skirt regulation. You stand in the open and face your fellow pupils, little children all, clamouring to enter the school co-op. It's filled to bursting, many trying to push their way inside, exclaiming, in thrall. You do not try to enter that small building. You see the backs of their heads and are afraid to join in. You hear that day about the painting hung on the wall inside, the one whose eyes are live, the girl in a frame. You believe in ghosts, you all do.

Three decades later and half the world away, you lie awake at night and remember. Recall the violence of how false ghosts were placed inside your growing minds, ghosts that shouldn't have been there, because they did not exist as those stories told. At some point in your life, the words for 'scent of flowers' became tainted with these lies, that those words were used by forces of evil.

Decades later, you wear trails of bunga kacapiring and sedap malam and melati, because these scents are associated by your people with the general presence of spirits, and you refuse to give up their truths. You remember those fellow children and know they were trying to conduct an exorcism, for the ghostly, for the too much to contain at a tender age. You remember, and send them a fervent wish that the exorcism was successful, somehow. That they lived to be adults protecting children from untruths, from ghosts that once collectively burst out of their hearts and into a picture on a sunny Jakarta day, when they, and you, were small.

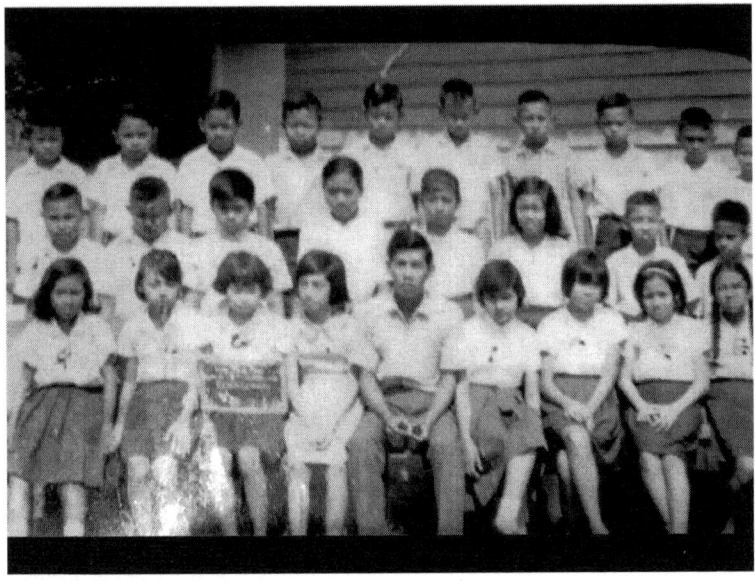

[Image description: in black and white, three rows of schoolchildren in uniform, facing the camera, with the teacher in the middle of the front row.]

This is a photograph of my mother as a schoolgirl in the fourth grade in Jakarta, circa 1965–66. She is one of the girls with a short bob and mildly petulant facial expression, indicative of a stubborn sulking called mabuduik in her native Minang language. I received her permission to use this photograph, an immediate yes, after revealing that I was writing a piece about 1965–66. It's all I had to say, those numbers in a row.

Simply mentioning '1965' for many Indonesians, of course, invokes a deep-rooted anxiety and distress, along with a deeper-rooted wish for catharsis and redemption. The years my mother was nine and ten, anywhere from 500,000 to over two million people – suspected and actual Indonesian Communist Party members, intellectuals, artists, ethnic Chinese, labour and women's rights organisers, non-normative sexual and gender minorities including indigenous identities, their families and friends – were killed. Many others were imprisoned, all caught in the choking swirl of local politics and the Cold War. The shape of their descendants' lives were forever altered, smothered by the thirty-three years of propaganda that ensued under Soeharto's New Order government, the effects of which have continued since the official fall of the regime. Our current president conducted war crimes for Soeharto as a general under the New Order. Though the CIA obscured their decisive role in it, this festooning of violence was backed by US, UK, and West German governments, with the intention of opening up our markets, in a manner it would not be untoward to call the slitting open of a wound.

Today we face a morass of forest fires and haze, mining and overfishing, tourism and deforestation decimating ecosystems from Kalimantan to Bali, where villages quietly harbour mass graves. We are over 17,000 islands in a warming sea. The wound was not only left untreated, but also unreported and spoken of surreptitiously, passed off as mere growing pains. 'Indonesia is an industrial giant now!' says a cab driver to me in England fifty years later. 'You should be proud.' I remind him of what had occurred to make it that way. 'I know,' he says, "That was terrible, terrible. I'm not excusing it. But tell me – when is history ever fair?'

The western-backed genocide installed a government that, having been borne of mass murder, made us citizens complicit in more genocides during its reign, and after. The genocidal violence of the New Order government across the archipelago, the violent occupations in East Timor and Papua, the violence in Aceh, and so on, and so on – in these days of Palestine-Congo-Sudan-Papua, we must flinch against the compulsion to make the word 'genocide' banal. We must continue to be nauseated by it. We must continue to feel viscerally how such violence makes our own bodies under colonial capitalism complicit. Our complicity is pooling in our throats.

On 30 September 1965, an alleged attempted coup occurred against then Indonesian President Soekarno. The exact circumstances of this attempted coup are much debated, but it resulted in six generals' bodies in a grave, and their deaths were blamed on Indonesian Communist Party (PKI) sympathisers.

As children, my peers and I were surrounded by rumours that the Indonesian Women's Movement (Gerwani) were behind an orgy of dancing women who allegedly ▮ the generals' ▮▮▮ during Tarian Harum Bunga, meaning the 'Scent of Flowers Dance' (even the scent of flowers was made identical to horrific rot). Lubang Buaya (literally 'Alligators' Hole') is the site of the generals' supposed graves, where the women were said to have thrown their bodies. When children were taken there on school field trips, the swirl of this rumour-as-fact was the perfume around small heads looking down.

In the 1960s, the Indonesian Gerwani movement (originally 'Gerakan Wanita Sadar', or the Movement of Conscious Women) was the largest feminist organisation in the world. Gerwani advocated against polygamous, forced and child marriage, and gender-based wage discrimination. They created schools and advocated literacy. They had campaigned against Dutch policies while officially under colonialism. As early as the 1950s, they were protesting the occupation of Papua and nuclear armament.

They were slaughtered in the genocide as a deliberate tactic against all that was perceived to be leftist. Dancer Jumilah was, in 1965, forced to confess to the supposed genital torture and murdering of generals, when she had done no such thing. Whether or not women were members of Gerwani, it was they – particularly labour organisers, artists, people of sexual and/or gender and/or cultural minorities – who were assaulted, tortured, murdered.

The extraordinary progressiveness of the Indonesian women's movement is still insufficiently acknowledged, yet it is profoundly important to our generation of feminists and activists. To learn the truth about their work, and how they were stigmatised and villainised, is to induce a shock of sadness I still feel viscerally.

Annah/s look on from above at surviving elderly women who, even in the 2020s, must live each day past the haze of millions of false scent trails. Women who were imprisoned as the scent cloud of slander hung around them, women who witnessed their peers' lives taken from them, and their legacy twisted into that of murderers. 'My kid is vicious, she's like Gerwani,' someone I know said to me recently. I felt the drop in my stomach keenly, as these older women have felt it in their guts their whole lives.

The Gerwani women were rumoured to have been singing 'Genjer-Genjer' in the lie of them killing the generals. This is a labourers' song about persistent plant life, a song that was banned by the New Order.

The overthrowing of Soekarno, and the instatement of President Soeharto as a dictatorial, capitalist Western ally, was key to the creation of the '65 – 66 genocide. Until he was forced to step down in 1998, when Indonesia is said to have become a democracy, the founding mythology of Soeharto's New Order regime was built on the alleged events of 30 September 1965: that the PKI tried to overthrow the government, and that Soeharto and his acolytes saved the day, justifying the violent dictatorship of the next thirty-three years. The massacre of hundreds of thousands, if not millions, of innocent supposed Communist sympathisers, Indonesia's own Holocaust, has been concealed, never mentioned by state-controlled media – nor school curricula – as anything other than the vanquishing of 'godless' adherents to Communism. The vanquishing of sadistic feminist psychopaths.

For many of us, the acts of 30 September 1965 as told by the state were our first real encounters with excessively violent tales. My own first real understanding of violence as an organising myth was inextricable from celluloid, sex, and ghosts. This was far from being my childhood experience alone. It is an imprint I share with millions of Indonesians who grew up in the Soeharto era, a psychological imposition I now understand as deliberate traumatisation on a mass scale.

In 2015, I have a night terror in London. It is extensive, elaborate. It begins with a drama of suspicion and menace between three people, which ends in a gory car accident in a dark wood, and discovery of the vehicle and its mangled victim in a tree by two quarrelling lovers on a motorcycle, corpse blood and bone in the headlights. The arbour's darkness grows wild, multiplies, and somehow the night reaches over into my room, personified as a dark cloud over my bed, beginning to take indistinct human form and bend over my body. Conscious in this dream, I watch powerlessly as the force proceeds to lick my collarbone. I feel warm saliva on my skin. My arms try to fight off the intrusion and are leaden. My tongue feels weighed and thick but attempts to scream, and finally, in the middle of the night, steeped in adrenaline and sweat, I struggle awake yelling, 'INI SIAPA?' 'Who is this?'

I continued to think about this night terror in the days that followed, as I thought about how violence first entered my subconscious. I think about how Indonesians of all socioeconomic classes and backgrounds were scarred by New Order propaganda. Scars many of us never speak of, that shape how my generation of Indonesians react to the blows of violence life deals us all in different ways. Scars we diminish and minimise as unimportant, that perhaps still haunt our dreams.

In 1993, I am a fourth-grade schoolgirl in Jakarta. Skinny in a uniform, sulkily mabuduik some of the time, a living version of my mother frozen in that photograph from twenty-eight years prior. School upsets me. I am informed of the truth of the dictatorship's structures by adults, and told never, never to repeat them as truths in school, to friends, to anyone in public.

It is funny growing up under a free market dictatorship masked as business as usual. A child cannot be too different, and the education system drills conformity like clockwork. Activist deaths and disappearances and suppression of freedom of speech are not on the news when we come home from school. Families affected by the long shadow of 1965 cannot speak of it, especially those with 'Communist sympathiser' lineage. Among people whose whole families are government-blacklisted for decades, some end up changing their names and/or going abroad to avoid persecution.

It is generally understood – despite political talk at home and leftist books filling our bookshelves, despite my friends and I knowing that there is a status quo – that it is dangerous to speak against the way things are. Most everyone toes the line in front of strangers, adults behaving as obedient schoolkids do: quick to ostracise. In Jakarta, life is supposed to be 'normal', but there is a tightness in the air.

In tentative ways I begin to try (with low to mixed results) to fit into resumed Jakarta life, returned to after five and a half years living outside Indonesia. I try to learn the slang of the era, to tighten up proficiency in my mother tongue, and to learn ghost stories. There is a painting of Ade Irma Suryani in the school commissary, and one day a throng of children at my school clamour loudly to see what is purportedly her image's ability to look around the room, eyeballs moving to and fro inside the portrait.

Ade Irma had been killed as a five-year-old girl. The daughter of a general who was supposedly shot by the Communists in the events of 30 September 1965, when they attempted to kidnap her father. This is common knowledge for us primary school students. I can't even fit into the school store to see the ghost; masses of small bodies are straining against each other to witness her spirit come back to life.

Perhaps it is no wonder that in adulthood I become obsessed with the portrait of another small being described as a girl, one for whom personhood and probable violence against them has overwhelmingly been obscured, in contrast to the 'stickiness' of empathy and recognition of victimhood for Ade Irma Suryani, that day in school when all my friends saw her ghost. I am still trying to catch a glimpse of feminine spirits, of the holy, in oil on canvas. When my schoolfriends erupted into hysteria, in the Jakarta sunlight, and I was standing there in the courtyard just outside the crowd, Annah/s was/were there.

The spirits of 30 September did come back to life, as it were, with regularity. From 1984 to 1998, the government enforced screenings of a film called *Pengkhianatan G30S/PKI* (*The G30S/PKI Betrayal*) on national television. *G30S/PKI* is an extraordinarily violent film, a work of New Order propaganda, screened in schools, as well as in homes. It extols the horrors of sadism at the hands of Communists. Communist men were godless traitors who had to be vanquished, and the film supported the rumours that Communist women – Gerwani – were evil villains. That they ███████████████ the six generals' ███, before killing them and tossing their bodies down a well. From before we could speak to our teenage years, this film was part of the national fabric, and part of the consciousness of my generation.

Back in the New Order decades, the film was shown on national television and in schools every 30 September: an act of mass historical disinformation made manifest as ritual horror show. If I was nine when I first saw images from the film, fingers over my eyes at fake blood that seemed to pop and ooze from the screen, realistic even in black and white, my classmates had seen it younger. One friend recently told me his parents had forbidden him from watching the film as a child, and this was the first time I'd even heard of such a pre-emptive policy. Whilst I remember the government censorship agency deeming other films too violent for children to see in the cinema, *G30S/PKI* was everywhere, inescapable. Not knowing its content of nightmares was simply impossible. Multiple someones would tell you before you saw it. And you would see it.

The nightmares deployed by the state to disparage anything associated with the left were both subtle, opaque, and everywhere. We who were born and came of age in those years inherited the traumas of generations before us that are not seen, but accumulate as a patina of anxiety on our lives, passed to us by birth, in schools, and through being raised by those similarly impacted. Though notable works of literature and visual art, from once-banned novels to plays and paintings, have more of a foothold nationally and, increasingly, internationally, and though activism has always existed, the government continues to refuse to apologise for '65, and there are still plenty of people in power with New Order ties. Apart from activists and artists, my young self knew of very few people who spoke publicly during the New Order era of the hundreds of thousands if not millions slaughtered or unlawfully imprisoned, both because many whose families were not directly affected were not informed of them at all, and because of the threat that adhered to speaking truths aloud.

Soeharto was ousted in 1998, when my peers and I were teenagers. As we grew into adulthood in fits and starts, so did our fledgling 'democracy' (undemocratic abuses are a persistent ailment). There would be political assassinations during and after 1998, including of human rights activists Marsinah and Munir, and the disappearance of those such as poet Wiji Thukul, and countless others besides. There is a great deal of discussion in leftist circles about the lack of policies to address crimes against humanity, freedom of speech and expression (evidenced by dozens of incidents of '65-linked intimidation reported to human rights groups and under-represented by the media), as well as the need for truth and reconciliation, and the fundamental need for the difficult separation of New Order elements from the current government.

What is rarely spoken of, and interlinked with all of the above violences, are the less explicit ripple effects of childhood traumatisation and conformity.

What happens to a very young brain that has barely understood violence, when they see images and hear tales of wildly, horrifically violent acts portrayed as a nation's founding mythology? What happened to our understandings of women when as children we were fed regular fables of violent sexual crimes – not against women, not thousands of unreported violent and sexual crimes against Gerwani and suspected Gerwani women – but in a terrifying reversal, lies of crimes perpetuated by them against generals? What did it do as small girls and boys to understand the term 'mutilated ▮▮▮'? How do these nightmares shift inside us throughout our life cycle? What nightmares literal and subdued have we carried with us and never shared with each other?

*

There is a direct correlation between the mark of knowing about sexual violence as something 'evil Communist women' do, women who were in fact social justice organisers, and the dismissal and outright perpetuation of violence against women in Indonesia, which – as it is everywhere – is sadly endemic. There is a direct correlation between the association of sex with horrible violence as one of our earliest understandings, and our struggles to include sexual and reproductive health education, including measures to prevent dating and marital violence, in school curricula. I see a deep-seated othering of minorities in destructive ways – with regards to ethnicity, religion, sexual orientation, disability and gender – which comes from our subconscious fear of the consequences of being marked as different, a tendency inculcated and exacerbated by the New Order in our formative years, and is also left over from European colonialism.

The genocide's rarely-spoken-of legacy also includes the violent disablement of millions of Indonesians. Not speaking of disability and disablement is another form of mind-conditioning: imperial violence exists by denying forms of disability, including and perhaps especially forms created by imperial violence itself.

There are acts of government censorship that gain widespread media coverage, but little conversation is given to even less publicised, subtler, often everyday forms of community-, peer- and self-censorship. Even knowing what I do, it has taken considerable inner work to overcome childhood fears of being attached to certain language and titles – 'Gerwani', 'PKI' – that we learned early on would lead to ostracisation and punishment.

We are marked by a form of trauma. So is our parents' generation. So is our grandparents' generation. This is suffering across generations on a biological level – what research scientist Rachel Yehuda calls intergenerational trauma. Such trauma is not only passed on from mother to child, but reinforced through the ways in which parenting effects psychology. We are all three generations survivors and strugglers, enablers and criminals by various definitions, ordinary people who didn't ask for harm, who have coped and are trying to cope the best we can. Our challenges, as a collective of many peoples in the archipelago, are enormous and interlinked, from environmental destruction to education to corruption to a colonial present with regards to occupation of Papua. Underlying all of these, however, are the psychic barriers we have to break through to enact change. Behind every policy-making act and gesture of activism are collectives of individual people who need to face up to the truth to move us all forward.

Children who grew up as internally displaced people, hiding for their lives, or those who witnessed their parents being abducted, with no way of helping them. Or those who saw and experienced any number of other violations against innocent people that the west deemed necessary in the 1965–66 genocide. These children were immediately thrust into a military dictatorship in which the only way to safety was to never mention their psychic wounds. The world became surreal – the official line was, and continues to be, that the genocide never happened. Your family's unbearable pain, your unbearable pain, is a fiction. These children, horrifically sentenced to silencing themselves, become our parents. These children, having been forced by society to never voice their pain, will not know how to encourage their own children to do so, nor how to react appropriately to, and aim to ease, their pain. The pain of the many disabled, ill children in our archipelago, beset with an intergenerational silencer whose shape we are not meant to recognise.

As my peers from elementary school have children, I wonder which of them will perpetuate the inculcation of violent myths that need to be dismantled, and which will educate in a different way entirely. I wonder if they, too, remember our furore around an animated ghost in the painting of Ade Irma Suryani, if they have heard of Annah/s. I wonder which of them have nightmares sometimes, and I want to tell them, if they're reading, so do I, and I am sorry.

ANNAH, THREE MONTHS BEFORE ESCAPE (ANNAH #835)

annah wakes on the bed in paris. rickety on the thin mattress, she feels a bruised and bruising hand on her shoulder, asleep, and heaving breath from behind her back. paul reeks of wine. the light is fluttery through curtains almost pirouetting with movement as the open window floods in the mistral wind, which reaches her bare chest, and she pulls a tan blanket tight to her neck, as softly as she can.

scratching her eyebrows, as softly as she can. it's difficult to breathe deeply in the very moment when he is not yet awake in the world, when she is the one alert, more alive, her own. a sense of freedom does not come naturally; the hand, her shoulder under it. this frustrates the child until she finally draws in one deep breath, trembling at its peak of intake, holding the power of it for two exhilarating seconds, observing the regular violence of somnolent breathing from behind her. she exhales. an unleashing of air, oceanic in scope from two small nostrils.

the sounds of street level below them are comforting; others exist. breeze continues to hit the front of her, small face right in its sights. annah doesn't want to be masuk angin, literally the wind enters, a phrase ubiquitous for us javanese. referring to a condition in which you are beset with flu-like symptoms – for being, for instance, out in the open chill, especially with wet hair – shivery, at worst vomiting, requiring warm drinks, heavy massages to coax a series of burps out. kerokan, which is to slather oil on a person's back when they are afflicted with masuk angin, to then take a coin and rub the edge of it against the back vigorously, not too quickly, in rows, until this back is striped with garish red marks, elongated, two columns of stripes resembling a palm leaf, or a tiger shin. these marks are the temporary cost of overexposure, a visual revealing of internal winds. they have been known to have the afflicted mistaken, by outsiders, for a victim of domestic abuse.

CHAPTER THREE: OF JAVA

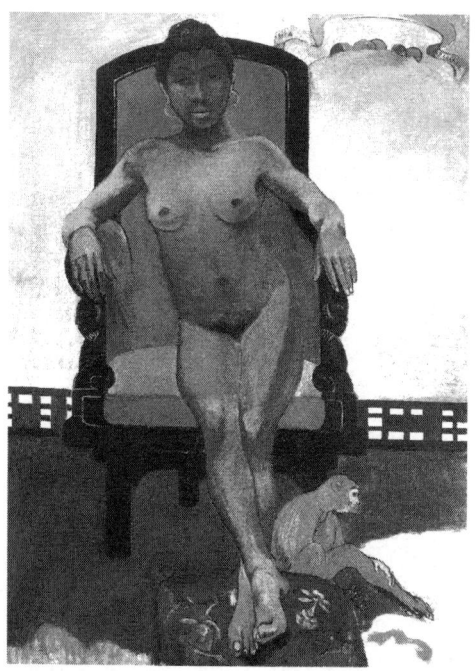

[Paul Gauguin, *Annah the Javanese*, or *Aita Tamari Vahine Judith te Parari* (The Child-Woman Judith Is Not Yet Breached), 1893–94. Oil on canvas, 45 1/4 x 31 1/2 in. (116 x 81 cm). Private Collection[4]. Painting of a naked child on a chair, their hair in a bun, their ankles crossed, arms on the chair. Monkey at their feet.]

---

4 Caption from Mathews, 2001: p.199.

152 Annah, Infinite

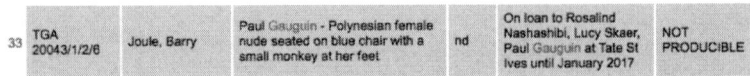

Figure 3.2. Tate Library Archive and Public Records Catalogue entry, accessed April 9, 2016.

[Image description: A screenshot of six grey columns to the right of the number '33', with black text, except where the word 'Gauguin' is in red. The first column states: TGA 20043/1/2/6; the second says 'Joule, Barry'; the third says: 'Paul Gauguin - Polynesian female nude seated on blue chair with a small monkey at her feet; the fourth says: 'nd'; the fifth says 'On loan to Rosalind Nashashibi, Lucy Skaer, Paul Gauguin at Tate St Ives until January 2017'; the sixth says 'NOT PRODUCIBLE' in capital letters.]

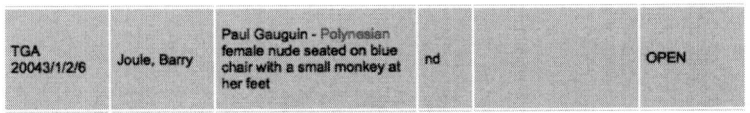

Figure 3.3. Tate Library Archive and Public Records Catalogue entry, accessed April 8, 2019.

[Image description: A screenshot of six grey columns, with black text, except for the word 'Polynesian' in red. The first column says 'TGA 20043/1/2/6'; the second says 'Joule, Barry'; the third says 'Paul Gauguin - Polynesian female nude seated on blue chair with a small monkey at her feet; the fourth says 'nd'; the fifth is blank; the sixth says 'OPEN' in capital letters.]

These, again, are the Tate Library Archive entries for a print I later confirmed is, in fact, *Annah la Javanaise*. This truth is NOT PRODUCIBLE until one regards it as OPEN, to interpretation, to claim by larger populations in Indonesia.

The effects of institutional disregard for the specificity of brown girls' origins, and of brown girls as distinct individuals, are not slight. That print was on loan, in April 2016, to Rosalind Nashashibi and Lucy Skaer for a project called *Why Are You So Angry?* (2017), which would contribute to Nashashibi's 2017 Turner Prize nomination. In this work, Nashashibi and Skaer recreated

Gauguin's portraits of Tahitian women on Tahiti, documenting them staring at the camera in an eighteen-minute video in poses echoing those Gauguin had placed his subjects in. In personal communication with Nashashibi in 2016, I alerted her to the fact that the print she had borrowed from the Tate was *Annah la Javanaise*. She had had no idea. Annah had been absorbed into 'Polynesian' heritage for the purposes of creating more art.

It is (ironically) a very crude, simplistic portrayal of Javaneseness as crude and simple that Gauguin employs, and one that deliberately relies on both presumed abledness and presumed lack of suffering. Gauguin's role in delimiting what 'Javanese' means, in a derogatory and simplifying understanding of 'Javanese', is to be expected if one looks at his role in the visual art movement of primitivism.

According to the Tate, primitivism

> is used to describe the fascination of early modern European artists with what was then called primitive art – including tribal art from Africa, the South Pacific and Indonesia, as well as prehistoric and very early European art, and European folk art.

It is important that this is what the Tate Gallery website gives as the public-facing definition for primitivism, the official, brand-approved definition of primitivism. One that frames how works such as *Annah la Javanaise* and Gauguin's other portraits of brown-skinned girls are presented – how the public is educated about them, and what colonial contexts are included or excluded. Colonial *presents* exist, and violences in the present towards populations made more vulnerable are the results of colonial formations. The interchangeability of Annah within art institutions is an example of this persistence, this endurance of colonial imaginaries and colonial violences.

If art exhibitions in a museum context are about 'how museums perform the knowledge they create', as Barbara Kirshenblatt-Gimlet says, what does it mean to title a portrait of someone who is very likely to have been a child under psychological duress 'of Java'? What does this mean for perceptions of Javanese women, young people (interpreted as girls), non-binary and indigenous gendered people today, both our perceptions of ourselves and others' perceptions of us?

It is so brutally apt that Gauguin's style of art is termed 'primitivism'. Primitivism heightened the colonial gaze that allows art from 'Africa, the South Pacific and Indonesia' to be deemed 'tribal', while European art is allowed to be 'folk' instead. It took elements of 'tribal' art and placed them out of context in an orientalist fashion – perversely using 'primitive' artworks that are actually deeply complex in order to perpetuate the myth of the simple native.

This involves erasing millennia of history. This involves drawing a crude image in its stead (the crudeness is important, the supposed simplicity of the original is important, the supposedly infantile nature of the original is important), 'inspired' by the most superficial understanding of what you erased, then improving on that crude image in comparison, and claiming you invented a thing. You do this over and over, until this becomes an enormous part of the western contemporary visual world, whether in 'tribal patterns' on necklaces sold to festival-goers, or the primitivist paintings sold for millions and kept in vaults.

When describing a photograph in his possession of the Javanese temple Borobudur, Gauguin said it was of Cambodian buildings. Java in particular has a specific role in Gauguin's career, life and ongoing mythos, not despite this ignorance but in line with it.

In 1894, Gauguin created a statue he titled *Oviri*, a Tahitian word for 'wolf'. The scholar Barbara Landy has noted that, in spite of its title, the influence of Javanese statuary – particularly Javanese statues representing women – on this piece is likely. *Oviri* was made around the same time as *Annah la Javanaise*, when notions of 'Javaneseness' were highly fashionable, so one might wonder why Gauguin omitted having been influenced by Javanese art. This may have been a tendency to deny Javanese influences in his art more generally, let alone admit to Javanese art's complexities. This may also have been a tendency to flatten 'la Javanaise', to render it primitive in European imaginations, as part of the European colonial project – including his own colonial project, in intertwined personal and professional realms.

By giving a Javanese-inspired statue a Tahitian name, Gauguin painted gross caricatures of Tahiti and Java simultaneously, *creating* a 'vague brownness' associated with vastly different Asian Pacific contexts. All this contributed to the fascination with and copying of Javanese culture among the French populace at the time, thanks in large part to the 1889 Paris Expo's Javanese Pavilion. Greta Garbo playing a Javanese woman on screen. Society women wearing Javanese clothing to parties in France.

Bringing four people (interpreted as girls) over to dance in the Javanese Pavilion of the Paris Expo – their names being Soekia, Taminah, Wakiem and Seriem – was part of Dutch colonial diplomacy, as was the construction of a fake 'Javanese village' there. Scholar M. Isaac Cohen argues that it was by colonial design that the Javanese artists' performances were framed in a way that reified, simplified and presented as static an incredibly complex island in constant upheaval and change. Just as the pulses of these four girls would experience the upheaval and change of travelling so far from home, to perform for strangers. (I think of them and feel grateful they had each other.)

The term 'la javanaise' has since become part of French vocabulary that exists to this day. A form of slang similar to Pig

Latin, in which vowels are rearranged as to render the original word *unintelligible* (related here to *uncertain or exotic origin*), as well as a dance called 'the java'. These meanings are all played upon in lyrics to the Serge Gainsbourg song 'La Javanaise'. As a Javanese person, 'dancing the Java' immediately conjures for me grinning Europeans equating an island of many millions with salaciousness, that 'the Java' is a form of dirty dancing from which actual Javanese people are absent. The point is to derive a sexual frisson from us, from the idea of us, from the land. Absurd.

The scholar Dick van der Meij pithily sums up this fascination with Java, as well as the interchangeability of cultures in Javanese performance for Western audiences:

> The 'artists' could call what they did as originating from Hawai'i, Bali, Burma, India, Hindu, Buddhist, it does not seemed [sic] to have mattered: everything was blended to the delight of one and the exasperation of another, depending on the amount of naked female flesh that was displayed, which alternated between visual belly buttons to complete nudity.

The 'newness' of these encounters is manufactured. The first person known to write of Java in Europe was Ptolemy, who was born in 100 AD; what is now known as the Indonesian archipelago is not the 'remote' (yes, shudder at that word) outpost to Europeans that colonial frames portray it as. There has for nearly two millennia been travel and trade of ideas in some form between supposedly 'unexplored' Southeast Asia and Europe. The notion of exploration, however, is key to conquest. A place cannot be colonised without the self-righteous adrenaline of the colonial 'explorer' to rename, to extract information from, to 'translate' without knowing a word of the language, to declare a map blank.

This manufactured vagueness, a blurry canvas on which to enact the observer's pleasures, is in line with the *non-person-*

hood attached to colonised or racialised brown bodies in Western countries, in the fin de siècle period and now. This includes the bodies of the child/ren named Annah la Javanaise. In order to abuse someone, you attach non-personhood to them. Someone deemed to be a non-person is more vulnerable to having their pain ignored, even to the point of having their lives eliminated.

Gauguin is widely accepted as having played a key role in primitivism as an art movement, and this is in line with the myth of the 'primitive' as simple and pliant, open to subservience with an enticing, orientalist spark. Anthropologist Paul van der Grijp calls Gauguin 'the first primitivist'. The more the artist associated himself with primitivist tropes, the higher the price of his paintings, the more the mystique of him as closer to 'savage' heightened his appeal:

> Gauguin called himself a person adept to an instinct and experience of 'the civilized savage', a description that biographers have eagerly taken up and used to make sense of his outright rejection of certain practices, prohibitions, and relations that characterized nineteenth-century bourgeois social life in France.

He'd 'gone native', like Leo in *The Revenant*, like *in Dances with Wolves*, like in all of the Gauguin biopics. A white man is able to attach 'primitiveness' to himself, sexual salaciousness to himself, through association with brown people, in a way that does not detract from his allure to other white people in late nineteenth-century France – but adds to it, hiking up his capital, his allure as well as that of his paintings, while those same connotations attached to 'natives' continue to suppress their personhood in society.

    These tactics to build up his own wealth, fame and ego are the building blocks of every single portrayal of Tahitian women

Gauguin has created, and also of *Annah la Javanaise* – crude caricatures of colonised peoples.

The late Banaban, I-Kiribati and African-American scholar Teresia Teaiwa has written incisively on how Gauguin's time in Tahiti was marked by his being wrong about all manner of things, including, at one point, knowledge of what island he was on. This was not merely bumbling ignorance, but a baseline of 'not knowing' on which he grafted supposed expertise, a tactic to exploit a notion of Tahiti, particularly of Tahitian women, through a colonial paintbrush. Tahitian people and Annah/s were branded by Gauguin with the same terrifying marks.

The potential sufferings of Annah/s are as intractable as stone, writ in oil on canvas – the painting *Annah la Javanaise* is not merely a parting gesture of colonialism, but a solid marker of colonialism's persistence, irrespective of changes in national borders. Irrespective of pronouncements that colonialism's systemic oppressions have long been put to an end – you can go into plenty a museum in the western world, observe how they caption the wealth that is kept, how they keep that wealth, and see these pronouncements' falsehood, as clear as a pane of exhibition glass. Just as the racist commentary underlying early European 'science' exhibits of so-called 'tribal' objects was presented as fact, so too do displays of primitivism in contemporary art institutions continue to fail to incisively critique the colonialist presumptions and politics of this art movement.

Cultures deemed 'other' by European art were, and continue to be, simultaneously stolen from and advertised as infantile. Simple, crude images. They may be stolen and stolen from because they are crude. Blurred masses. Drum beats sans specificity, at least a specificity beyond enticing the outsider to feel a 'primitive' emotion. The 'tribal' women playing music that studios record and turn into science fiction soundtracks, evoking a barren, diabolical desert, evoking aliens, evoking the non-human.

★

So what do we talk about when we say 'Javanese'? As you may well know, you are liable to be scoffed at by a confused westerner, in academia or the arts, if you point out that on the island of Java, there exist multiple forms of Javaneseness, as well as indigenous cultures that are not called 'Javanese' – Betawi people, for instance, and Sundanese people (around 40 million in population, including historically related groups the Bantenese, the Baduy, and the Kasepuhan), as well as other minor but culturally distinct group identities, such as the Tengger and Osing peoples in Eastern Java, and the Sedulur Sikep in Central Java. Javanese people from Central Java differ in language, dress, culture from those in East Java, and there are even more granular differences. The person who scoffs at you when you try to explain this tends to, at the same time, look down on those who don't know inherently that Great Britain consists of England, Wales, Scotland and Northern Ireland, that there are different peoples from each. #WhoseGranularityMatters

Classifications of 'Javanese' defy simplistic organisation. For instance, there are those on Java who were born there, lived there all their lives, and may identify as, for instance, Indian-Indonesian, Chinese-Indonesian, Arab-Indonesian and/or one of hundreds of Indonesian cultures not originating on Java Island as far back as its first inhabitants. And there are also people for whom their origins or cultural heritage are located on Java, but – in the case of Surinamese and South Africa's Cape Malay peoples – were transplanted from Java to other Dutch colonies through slavery, indentured servitude and/or other colonial routes.

These migrated populations have come to adopt varying forms and levels of affinity with 'original' Javanese cultures. For instance, Surinamese people of Javanese origins speak Javanese, but not Indonesian. For these people, their Surinamese culture predates so-named Indonesian nationalist movements, so the concept of 'Indonesia' as a unified republic of disparate provinces doesn't apply; Surinamese people of Javanese origin are, I would argue, very strongly Javanese in a way that has been shaped by their colonial iterations, by the specifically Surinamese/Latin American flows of cultural influence and people.

There were also, of course, many native Indonesians who had European parentage, whether forcibly (as is the overwhelming case under slavery and colonial military occupation) or not. In her 2005 book *Race and the Education of Desire*, Ann Laura Stoler writes extensively about the denigration of Indonesian people by European colonialism, and the endangerment of women and girls in particular, including in the fin de siècle period in which *Annah la Javanaise* the painting was produced. Among these vulnerable groups were children labelled 'métisse' or 'mixed'. Here is a key to who you might have been, Annah/s, another strain of possibilities. The 'nativeness' of mixed children, born to native women living under duress, meant they were undesirable. Meant they were to be abandoned. Meant they would be vulnerable to trafficking, vulnerable to Paris.

All these elements of what 'Javanese' could mean have mixed between cultures and interbred, and the dynamics between them are influenced not only by creeds (including different manifestations of Islam) and ethnicities, but along lines such as coastal/maritime communities and the cultures of those who live inland.

So what kind of 'Javanese woman' is the person whose words you're engaging with? I am a Jakarta-born woman who calls Jakarta home, who is both Javanese on my father's side and Minangkabau (otherwise known as Minang) on my mother's side. My paternal grandfather was a Bantenese man whose family settled in Ngawi, East Java; my paternal grandmother was from East

Java, specifically the coastal town of Tuban, and she was born in a hamlet in the Kendeng mountainous region; both paternal grandparents worked in (what was before 1945 deemed 'native') education, and lived in various locations before settling in Jakarta. My mother's family, too, migrated to the capital of Jakarta in the fifties, from their home village in West Sumatra. This is a common, age-old Indonesian story of mixing, journeying. Of various points coming together to form a human that is just one version of 'Javanese woman'. There are manifold variations, of course, of 'Javanese woman'.

I'm not indigenous to Jakarta, which is the indigenous home of Betawi people (hence, the Dutch word for the capital in colonial times, 'Batavia'); my indigeneity is related to my home village in West Sumatra, where my family has an ancestral home, and to my Javanese grandmother's land, near where farmers have for years been rejecting the threat of national cement plants that would ruin indigenous waterways. Indigeneity is, as always, relational, contextual.

As Fred Moten and Stefano Harney would say, I write in a space both 'for and against': as a practising artist and writer who identifies as Javanese, with the many complex possible meanings of this term, and one who is also Sumatran, who deplores the many violences Javanese people have committed as colonisers within our Southeast Asian archipelago, *and* as one who performs in colonial spaces that have historically whittled down so many complexities, spaces that have been built on the plunder of empire.

As Ambalavaner Sivanandan said, 'We are here because you were there' – I am here in the UK because, over centuries past, European countries including the United Kingdom stole resources, land and people from what is now Indonesia. My presence here is *of course* tied up with capital, and survival, especially as a chronically ill woman. But while I am here, I reserve the right to aim at the self-built mythos of Gauguin propped up by colonial states.

Being Javanese itself (in its many multiple variations) is a form of 'for and against'. Indonesia's government has been heavily Javanese-centric, and the capital city of Jakarta is situated on Java Island, the most densely populated island in the archipelago. The centre-periphery model of capitalist conquest applies on so many scales.

If this is an escape story, it is also a fleeing from all the ways Javanese peoples have been brutalised, whether in chains or in a gilded, mounted frame.

When I use the word 'Javanese' in this book and in my Annah performances, there is a liminality with regards to what the term means, for it is an umbrella term of many different kinds of Javaneseness. When I speak or write of Javanese as a culture and language that comes from my personal frame of reference, it's not meant as a blanket assertion of Javanese culture and language as monolithic. This blanketing of complexities is key to Gauguin's visual portrayal of Annah/s, his characterisation of the island and its inhabitants.

Rejecting the idea of a static, reified notion of Java, and of what 'Javanese girl' means, is crucial to our understandings of Annah as potentially plural, and thus potentially in pain and under threat. A very caricatural representation of 'La Javanaise' appears in Gainsbourg's lyrics, and this is in itself a violence. Similarly, in the painting, innumerable violences proliferate, as all the many multiple existing variations of 'Javanese' are cut out of Gauguin's use of Annah: a reified, simplified idea of 'Javanese girl' as one thing, easily digestible, as prop for his mythos of wildness and genius. McJavanese Annah. One could say that 'Java' is in this way opened up to speculative, virtually infinite violences, to historical, present and future realities. One could say that multiple Annahs exist in these spaces, forming multiple possibilities of resistance.

And yet, *Annah la Javanaise* continues to be (literally) framed by arts institutions, including museums, galleries and universities, in a way that acts as though the colonial context is not one of violence. This is in alignment with understandings of Gauguin's work as 'timeless' – and in attendance, the notion of the subjects of his portraits, bodies presenting as young, brown girls, as interchangeable.

Simple.

Existing for pleasure.

A crude image of 'the tropics'.

And of those who inhabit them.

If you exist solely for pleasure, you are, of course, seen as incapable of suffering. You are presumed abled. What do we write about when we write about 'Javanese'? What would it mean to seek a different understanding of 'la Javanaise' than Gauguin would have us possess?

Gauguin isn't solely responsible for how *Annah la Javanaise* is positioned today by institutions, nor for the vulnerability of Annah/s in relation to him, which allowed the painting to exist – all of this is a product of systemic inequalities, violences and oppressions that are inherent in coloniality, modernity and patriarchal white supremacy.

Much of western art 'history' relies on the assumption of a linear Eurocentric progression of art from realist to postmodernist, of this as the only timeline of art that exists, the only one that matters. Scholars Ella Shohat and Robert Stam write:

> Endowing a mythical 'West' with an almost providential sense of historical destiny, Eurocentric history sees Europe, alone and unaided, as the motor, the primum mobile, for progressive historical change, including

> progressive change in the arts. An arrogant monologism exalts only one legitimate culture, one narrative, one trajectory, one path to aesthetic creation.

As Shohat and Stam point out, this narrative has little basis other than in the myth of European superiority, and obscures the crucial understanding that European art history itself is 'limited and ultimately provincial'. In Indonesian, there is the unfortunate usage of the word 'kampungan' (my approximate translation: 'village-like') to mean 'provincial' in a pejorative sense, often employed by middle- and upper-class urban denizens, including in Java. However, Shohat and Stam use 'provincial' here to explode the centre-periphery model that privileges supposed 'centres' of power such as Europe and European capitals; they argue that this power also belongs to places marked 'periphery'.

Communities of, say, different sensorial modes of creating and consuming art, as well as communities of different cultural denominations, would in an ideal world be respected equally. Not only are Javanese aesthetic movements sophisticated, but as Shohat and Stam argue, there has not been a clearly demarcated division between these European and Asian arts in the first place. European arts have long been indebted to Africa, Asia and First Nations arts. European art movements have long appropriated aesthetics from elsewhere whilst deeming them inferior, 'primitive'. Fanon's observation that 'Europe is literally the creation of the third world' is profoundly true of the arts.

Even considered through the limited realism-modernism-postmodernism rubric that dominates the western narrative, art that comes from outside Europe is, by such measures, considerably more 'advanced' than most European art. Shohat and Stam point to the fact that much art from Africa, Latin America and Asia – and to this I would add threatened Indigenous and other cultures of North America and Europe – has not been invested in realism to begin with, noting in particular South and Southeast Asia (Southeast Asia being a region that includes, of course, Java) as examples. And it is precisely these art movements that 'liberated' European artists, who appropriated these cultures in ways that can be seen everywhere, from Picasso's cubism to Gauguin's primitivist work.

All of the above is in keeping with how Gauguin himself took from the art of Java, flattened its rich cultural contexts, and used it to add to his self-mythos of grandeur in a European context. A context that essentially rewarded cultural appropriation for being novel – whilst portraying a young child from Java as constantly sexually available and willing, causing harm to all of us who might be labelled 'la Javanaise'. I argue that Gauguin presented the young children of Tahiti and Annah la Javanaise as similar, in his flattening of their art histories, while simultaneously framing them as willingly vulnerable to harm, that it is not a coincidence that the Tate Library would confidently label *Annah la Javanaise* as 'Polynesian female nude'. Indeed, that is what Gauguin's entire oeuvre of brown girl portraits gestures towards – the interchangeability of populations both infantile in intellect and sexually mature, primarily to be consumed. And Western art institutions continue to present these children as consumable through this lens.

Because of the unequal power dynamics between France and Java, dynamics in favour of Europe that have persisted since the late nineteenth century, the beholder of a print of *Annah la Javanaise* in the Tate Library is nudged (through aforementioned website copy and general framing of primitivism) towards a view of Java as not only consumable in the form of young girls, but falsely static, falsely nudging the viewer towards essentialisation.

Let's turn these dynamics on their head. The possibility and indeed, as I argue, probability of violence contained in *Annah la Javanaise* is not a matter of Paul Gauguin as a lone abuser. It is structural, and this is confirmed by a dominant narrative surrounding it in which violence is ignored and thus condoned.

If we are speaking of moving away from Eurocentric analyses of art, and into opening up Annah la Javanaise to possibilities of pain, then it must be understood that 'Java' itself consists and has consisted of many centres, with interlocking, overlapping power structures. To understand the cultures of Java Island as polycentric and fluid, rather than monolithic and static, is a step towards multiplying even more the possibilities for bodyminds that Annah/s could have inhabited.

In my work, I focus on the possibility and, indeed, probability of disabled bodies in the presence of abusive figures and structures, particularly with regards to chronic pain. The numerous different iterations for what 'Javanese' could mean also encompass many different kinds of bodyminds that would fall under the term 'disability', that are interpreted differently in Javanese cultures than they would be in, say, white western British contexts.

As notions of 'disability' and 'ability' are inherently cultural, there are variances in what different bodyminds signify. Disabled Indonesian scholar Slamet Amex Thohari identifies at least four different competing frameworks for 'disability' that evolved in Java after the fall of the dictator Soeharto in 1998. These include the western 'social' model, as well as Dutch Christian missionary-introduced frameworks, and models that draw on interpretations of Islam. Thohari also, however, traces the presence of Javanese interpretations of disability that predate colonialism, persisting into the present. These frameworks include the presence of disabled gods, and honour those who are disabled as spiritually touched.

All of these are possible frameworks through which one might view a pained, disabled, Javanese child interpreted as a girl. However, it is the model of disability as being connected with the holy, with disabled gods, that I believe is most relevant to a framework for understanding a possibly pained Annah as not simply abject, but as a person who could have had agency in a pained bodymind. They could well have come from a pre-colonial Java in which disabled bodies were revered, protected, cared for, deemed spiritual.

Thohari argues that despite the marginalisation and stigmatisation of disability in Indonesia,

> many people in Indonesia, especially Java, see the disabled as exceptional and possessing invincibility [here is another reason, incidentally, why Annah could be Infinite], have incredible powers and must be respected. This view is related to the position of disabled people that is part of the cosmological system of Javanese society, a most important element that is inextricable from its people and daily life. [my translation]⁵

Thohari summarises several stories from Javanese cosmology that are relevant to our understandings of disability, and of indigenous Javanese concepts of 'pain'. Here are just two of them, by way of example (the text here and above is Thohari's, the translation is my own):

> in a wayang creation story, Durgandini or Dewi Lara Amis [...] was a disabled person with a bodily strangeness, her skin was peeling and smelled rancid, so she

---

5 Throughout the original Indonesian version of this article (2012), Thohari uses the term 'difabel' to refer to disabled people, a term which has become most prominent in Indonesian disability discourse. It is an Indonesian acronym for the English 'differently abled'; I argue that this term seems to erase society's role in disadvantaging non-normative bodies, and also does not question calling ourselves 'different' *in relation to* bodies deemed normative, thus othering ourselves. I therefore translate 'difabel' here as 'disabled'.

> was exiled to the Ganges. Until one day the Ascetic, Palara, came to help her, and made her invincible, beautiful, and made it so she would have a child who was also disabled. This child was incredibly invincible, and was able to solve complicated problems that normal people could not [...]

And:

> 1. Another element reflecting disability in Javanese society is the punakawan [...] Usually the punakawan are portrayed as 'little people', with patterned clothing and strange-looking bodies. Despite this, the punakawan are invincible, born of the gods. They are even manifestations of gods who are disguised as poor people, who become saviours, those who bring balance, and are present with all their wise ways.

What the above mythologies show is that categories of 'abled as empowered' and 'disabled as not empowered' do not apply easily to Javanese mythological characters. As Thohari writes, notions of 'disability' are multiform on Java, colliding with each other and jostling for prominence. In other words, Java has always had many different frameworks for pain and disability among Javanese bodyminds, which have existed for millennia.

Even Thohari's descriptions of these disabled deities' stories contain inherent tension and ambiguity with regards to maligning or celebrating the disabledness of these gods. Durgandini's 'strangeness' becoming 'beautiful' is quite an ablenormative ugly duckling story, and society seemingly takes for granted that her bodily 'strangeness' requires exile, while the 'invincibility' of her child echoes modern day forms of the idea of a 'supercrip', a disabled person whose abilities are deemed extraordinary (as, for example, Paralympians) and thus 'compensate' for their disabled nature and for the pain that may be involved in both the hurt of exclusion and in bodyminds more prone to varieties of pain.

For potential Annahs, these fluid, competing, notions of painedness, disability and what it is to be a deity – or a combination of these – would have been very immediate, real, part of the fabric of reality. Not 'magic realism' or 'fantasy', or 'myth', but tangible, touchable reality. This opens up myriad possibilities for how a pained Annah might have conceived of themselves.

There are many possible stories for many possible Javanese Annahs. In my fictionalising or extending of the universe of these disabled Javanese gods, these deities visit Annah, and some are pained. Some have the ability to heal in the aftermath of pain-induced traumas, and the ability to tolerate daily, consistent pain while bringing balance to the universe and even potential succour for Annah/s.

From possibly as early as the first century AD, Javanese cultures have twisted linear concepts of time. Disabled people traversing space and time is not a novel invention, but a truly ancient part of Javanese cultures. This fact is likely to be subconsciously part of my compulsion to create multiple disabled Annahs, across time-space continuums.

This space-time traversing in non-European storytelling is often called 'magical realism', when that term denies the fact that depicting reality the way European realist artists do has never been the main modus operandi of non-European cultures. What is called 'magical realism' or, I contend in addition, 'science fiction' and 'fantasy' are, in other words, realities unto themselves. As Javanese people, to imagine disabled people queering time and space is also to create possible scenarios that we can imagine Annah la Javanaise inhabiting.

I am Minangkabau as well as Javanese, and Minang people are the largest matrilineal society in the world. Though we are now overwhelmingly Muslim, there were waves of Hinduism and Buddhism that came after indigenous Minang spiritualities as well. In Minang indigenous spiritualities, there is the concept of 'semangat' (literally 'energy' or 'life force'), the notion that humans have something like two souls, one which is the true semangat, and another spirit within us that can be closer or further away from the semangat life force. When our semangat forces are aligned, we are in possession of our full powers; when they are separated, I personally interpret this as feeling far from one's own conscience, one's truth, one's path, one's fire.

A girl marked 'Annah' could well have been Minang if she was of what was then the Dutch East Indies, even if she was taken from Java; part of my interpretations is therefore that Annah's pain could be a manifestation of her semangat acting in the face of danger, a grave spiritual warning sign. My visual as well as written and performance work contain various versions of Annah that could be described as science fiction or fantasy – however, I would like the audience to entertain the possibility that spiritual worlds other than Western-prescribed rationality exist, and that goddesses, Minang and Javanese spiritualities interacting with their pained body might be, to Annah/s, fundamentally real.

In terms of engaging with indigenous histories, including histories of diaspora, it is not only the contents of artefacts and stories that must be deconstructed and moved away from ablenormative interpretations. Let's think through the marks *Annah la Javanaise* the painting and persons make, as mediated through different bodies and senses, including through non-ablenormative bodyminds.

That is, when the painting is described in histories, it is universally with the assumption that all who regard it are sighted (and with the insinuation that we are all universally neurotypical and sensory-typical more generally). To privilege different senses as absorbing and creating histories – oral, textual, and so on – is a step towards greater acknowledgement not only of diversity among bodyminds, but diversity among cultures, particularly with the denigration of many oral cultures, as written histories and laws were among tools of colonial subjugation (though of course there are many written indigenous languages as well). We urgently need to recognise these non-ablenormative modes for interpreting archives, modes which include a recognition of many different interpretations of painedness and disability.

For instance, as the blind scholar Georgina Kleege writes, it is important to understand that access to visual cultures and analyses thereof are not the province of sighted people alone, but also of blind/seeing-impaired people. The use of visual tools that are accessible only to seeing peoples in particular (that is, made inaccessible by design) are a mode of power. This includes museums, paintings, catalogues, websites and the like using visual material in a way that is inaccessible to blind/seeing-impaired populations, without descriptions in audio form or Braille for instance.

(Too often, 'blindness' is used as ableist metaphor in the arts for 'unknowing' or 'ignorance'. Such linguistic violence does not belong here. Annah/s could well have been blind or visually impaired.)

This is a main reason why the entire book you're reading is one caption. It is, in fact, my caption for the painting *Annah la Javanaise*. It is a translation of the visual into text, another kind of material.

When the complexities of Javanese and other cultures and histories are applied to understanding possibilities for who the person or people in *Annah la Javanaise* could be, this opens up so many possible interpretations, even within the assumption that Annah was Javanese at all – so many varieties of possibly pained soulbodies, so many possible stories, and Annahs, and escapes.

★

If Annah came from the island of Java, by birth and/or heritage, they would have come from cultures – plural – that contain myriad understandings of the human bodymind/soulbody, of pain and how to live with it, to heal and ameliorate it. Cultures with healing practices passed down through matrilines, and with legendary goddesses and heroines who did not simply sit in discomfort on a chair, nude and in waiting for a European man, with no other purpose than subservience. Gauguin's dependency on *Annah la Javanaise* as a static portrayal of a Javanese young person with no implied agency or wants beyond sexual servicing of Europeans means that signifiers of pain that abled, Western viewers would understand are not there.

I *do* see potential painedness in this painting. I perceive signs of it all over this painting, and all over how arts institutions continue to uphold it, and to uphold the myth of its maker.

However, just as we pained bodyminds are not automatically passive, all-suffering and otherwise flattened versions of the fully-fleshed human beings we are, Indonesian women, girls, non-binary and/or indigenous gendered people throughout history are not reducible to our suffering alone. Even the millions of Indonesians who have died as a result of colonial violence and violence caused by imperial duress stretching into the present day are not merely victims – they had families, friends, interests, lives, and they also resisted.

I would laugh at anyone who describes my family, friends and me simply as 'victims of the New Order regime' or even 'survivors of the New Order regime', without further depth of understanding. Surviving is the art of weaving – weaving in and out of danger, weaving artforms together, stitching communities back together where we're ripped. Survival is decades of embodied knowledge, communal knowledge.

Some art looks at our peoples as objects of despair and trauma alone. Some art focusses on the rips without studying the seams that pulled the fabric of families back together, as best as people could.

Western observers, if they have heard of the 1965–66 genocide, are likely to have encountered it through one of two documentaries directed by Joshua Oppenheimer and Anonymous (an unnamed Indonesian filmmaker): *The Act of Killing* (2012, also co-directed with Christine Cynn) and *The Look of Silence* (2014). Writer and media scholar Intan Paramaditha has written a powerful argument on how Western media-makers, even when purporting to spread the word about Western violence, tend to reinforce their own narratives in a way that is harmful to and erases the resistances of Indonesians. In Oppenheimer's documentaries, Intan argues, 'The entrance of the 1965 massacre into the global stage could be seen as a reproduction of a paternalistic scenario that begins with the Western discovery of a "dark secret" in the Third World.'

I have heard tell of who co-director Anonymous is, and want to honour the work that they and the Indonesian crew of these films did under an environment of persistent government repression, the legacy of the New Order in the post-New Order era. Yet the way the films are positioned and spoken of by Oppenheimer, the focus on suffering and brutality, does not resonate with what I know of how Indonesians interpret this violence. It does not resonate with how resistance is woven into the texture of lives and art, by the resilient activists, artists, ordinary people who were persecuted by the New Order, people who I have known, loved and looked up to all my life.

Women are mourners or brutalised in this film. A genocide perpetrator is filmed speaking of ▆▆▆▆▆▆▆▆ of women's ▆▆▆▆▆▆. The personhood of those women affected was separated from the hyperfocus on their horrific wounds, deaths.

The shock-doc portrayal of feminine-coded Indonesian people has parallels to the description of Annah/s in Mario Vargas Llosa's 2003 biographical novel of Gauguin's life, *The Way To Paradise*:

> [...] he would superimpose the image of his lover over the unfinished study of Judith. And so he did. The painting took him a long time because of the incorrigible Annah. She was the fidgetiest and most unmanageable model you would ever have, Paul. She was always moving, changing her pose, or, when she was bored, pulling faces to try to make you laugh – the favorite Thursday evening game, along with spiritism – or, tired of posing, she would simply get up, toss on some clothes, and run outside as Teha'amana would have done [...]
>
> Annah hadn't asked to be what she was; she didn't even realize the incandescent power she derived from her origins, her blood, the untamed forests where she was born, just like a panther or a cannibal. How superior you were to ossified Parisian women, Annah!

A panther. A cannibal.

Indonesian women were literally ▆▆▆▆▆▆▆▆ in the 1965–66 genocide. My body revulses when I read these lines by Vargas Llosa.

I watched Oppenheimer's films finding myself hungry for fuller stories of what happened to those who survived, and those who had to say goodbye to the potentially millions of women and people of other genders who were assassinated and/or violated in those times. I was hungry to see people with agency, with families who lived on, to see souls.

What is noteworthy in interpretations of Annah so far is not that they have no 'voice' (to adopt an audiocentric view of self-assertion) and no self-determination in them. Descriptions such as those in Mario Vargas Llosa's *The Way to Paradise* portray them as unknowable – the haziness of their background being part and parcel of their flightiness and unreliability – in a way that implies this unknowability absolves Gauguin from responsibility, as caretaker. Of and to 'that devil in skirts [...] that magnificent savage [...] A true savage to the marrow, in body and soul', wrote Vargas Llosa. Someone 'who not only was not French, European, or white,' he continues, 'but also had the gall to show her breasts, navel, mound of Venus, and tuft of pubic hair'.

Annah's role, in this novel, was to supply Gauguin with renewed vigour for life, and their own welfare was immaterial:

> In bed, it was hard to tell if she was enjoying herself or pretending. In any case, she gave you pleasure, and she entertained you at the same time. Annah gave you back what you were afraid you had lost since your return to France: your desire to paint, your sense of humor, your will to live.

In the aforementioned 11 September 1950 issue of *LIFE Magazine*, the feature entitled 'GREAT LOVES OF GREAT ARTISTS' includes writing on Annah as having betrayed and left Gauguin to suffer for the rest of his days. Entitled 'Gauguin's Faithless Javanese', the section is accompanied by the painting *Annah la Javanaise*, infusing the painting's impression with 'faithlessness', Gauguin's 'rightful' ownership of Annah, and so too an imagined biography of Annah.

In her work *The Dance That Makes You Vanish: Cultural Reconstruction in Post-Genocide Indonesia*, Rachmi Diyah Larasati 'trace[s] how the female dancing bodies obedient to the state's agenda are able to attain mobility while simultaneously erasing the unruly bodies that are not'. It is life or death for you in New Order Indonesia depending on which dance you dance – metaphorically as well as literally, meaning the difference between dancers who are suspected leftists, versus dancers affiliated with, for instance, docile, government-approved troupes. These are facts about the movement of our bodies as Indonesian women that are innately, physically understood, if you also grew up in the New Order. You are meant to keep your bodymind far away from anything that could be remotely tied to Tarian Harum Bunga – the orgy dance in which women ▮▮▮ generals' ▮▮▮ (a heinous accusation disproven by an army doctor's report, yet one that has persisted in the collective psyche). I realise my bodymind knew these warnings as a child, being taught certain dances in school, certain movements acceptable to girls, and so did my peers. It was the fragrance in the air.

Ibu Rachmi's mother was a dancer who was vanished in the 1965–66 genocide, as part of a group of dancers suspected to be Communist. The writing of a book by a genocide survivor on the very trauma that has shaped her is a form of weaving survival, of persistence, and layered persistence, that shock-docs cannot convey.

We have long used our bodies in the face of violence to protect ourselves with our own creation of art.

These are the narratives that need to come to the fore with regards to coded 'Javanese', coded 'Indonesian', coded 'brown women and girls', not as mere conduits for redemption or lust. Nor as mere victims of imperial duress, but as people, who have negotiated all of this throughout our lives, and must face futures containing such violence – with as much joy as our bodyminds can possibly contain.

INTERLUDE ONE:
QUEERING AND CRIPPING TIME

[Caption for *Annah la Javanaise*]

The three time zones for Interludes One, Two and Three are 300 AD, 1890s AD and 2020s AD – simultaneously.

[Annah is being continually called by the Annahs in the other interludes. It is the most constant of hums, it is a thrum in the very neck.]

Dimulainya begini: Your body is the truth. You should trust it. You should notice the ebbs and flows of sensation, the prickles, the irritations, the reliefs and kinetic workwomanship inside you. Dalam Bahasa Indonesia sebutannya jiwa raga. So you should remember that jiwa (soul) and raga (body) are linked, together, one phrase, one being. Your soul asks you to honour the truth of your body. If it hurts like hell, and keeps hurting, take it somewhere safe. Bring it all the wailing of emergency, hellfire begone, give it care, take it home. And if you can't take it home, make it home. Understand that even in the worst weather, that will not abate for years, what is underneath is the jiwa raga of yourself, indestructible shelter. Impermeable to others' assertions. You know who you are, your name is your own.

'Juminten.'

Madame Nina is laughing at my name. 'Ju-mean-done? Ju-mented?' Her tea is literally snorting out her nose. We are in her parlour, it is 1890s Paris. I suppose women can snort their tea out, it's fine. I suppose some women can ask for a slave girl just like another cup of tea.

...

I begin to see visions on the wall of her house. My body feels bending and then starts to break. First softly, in my hands, then throughout my frame. Down the middle, the chest. It feels as though a hole has been blown in it, short-circuit ventricles. But from the paint in Madame Nina's parlour, a vision hits me the wall is an ocean and Nina is gone, it's an ocean surrounding me I'm in it I'm wet, I realise it is the year 300 AD (as opposed to the time in Javanese years).

My body was made from thousands of women. God now I feel it. And they are all inside of me, and their laughter rings each cell and wrings a voice together that runs through my nerves that have gone awry in this parlour, they say: *Swim. We are here now, long before this building or this woman existed, swim in this sea and come home. Your body was not meant for this shithouse dressed in finery. This air that reeks with thievery and the slitting of thieves who had no choice.*

Srikandi appears before me with a bow, and she who is also he tells me that I am the arrow, I am the arrow. And I do not know what they mean. I don't need to be a symbol for warfare, I am too small to be feeling this blasted, this damned, this sinking. Madame Nina threatens to sell me to the brothel when I miss a spot, and I think perhaps there are other girls like me in that place and brighten, then I realise what it is that is threatened.

...

Madame Nina's suitor is another demon. She learned of his breaking into my closet-room, and promptly sent me away with what she called an 'arts man', who'd looked me up and down in Nina's parlour and snickered, 'Domestic dispute indeed.' And the arts man in turn sent me to Paul's house, alone, with a sign. *Oh no oh no oh no oh no oh no oh no—*

White out. My lungs want to escape through my mouth. I breathe shallow, each gasp a punctuation mark a full stop dot dot dot dot dot dot.

'Annah?' says Paul as he opens the door and his grin turns his lips, poisoning his face with intent.

I miss Ibu so much, I broke something. Something has cracked inside me. I think, it is the realisation that conditions are overwhelmingly in favour of me staying in this country where hateful and/or lustful are de rigueur. What is Paris now for a brown child. I am twelve and wise. I've escaped much by dexterity of thought. It was not Madame who first wanted to take me; back home it was the plantation owner near Jogja who wanted me for housekeeper. He did not smile but told me with his eyes that proximity to his house was a yawning maw. I begged Madame Sarah to take me instead, before he could. A month after cleaning at her house, she introduced me to Madame Marie, the wife of a banker who knew a certain opera singer. I'd enjoyed listening to her chatter when she visited Madame Sarah, but she looked at me as though

I was furniture, and when the two Madames got me in a room and told me I was to leave for Paris, it was not an ask. I hugged my friends goodbye with so many tears: Bejo, Siti, Zaenab, and my younger sisters: Bilqis, Dhitta, both bewildered. I don't understand the concept of crying as anything but relief. It is not a crack in the armour, but the armour speaking to the world.

And in Paris no one could pronounce Juminten (even Nina's original pronunciation was shite) so they called me Annah. I'm Minang and Bantenese, but was born on Java and lived there, so I became: Annah la Javanaise. They don't understand more than what they make up, do they.

I'm having what in the twenty-first century is known as a panic attack and I also have PTSD from so many near escapes already in Paris, I don't want more. I don't want to enter gaping holes when I should be with my mother. And I should be with my friends. And the next five days are a blur but already I feel it, the cracking, I am in such pain. How do I beg Madame Nina to take me to the doctor when she smirks at me in the salons of their coterie that Paul takes me to.

I cannot possibly be in pain when in a frivolous European dress. I cannot possibly be in pain when Paul, who I know wants to hurt me and is closing in, gives me such shelter and access to the finest young European painters. They photograph me in costumes at Mucha's studio, they have a game they all play when drunk that involves persuading me, wooing me, and I white out then as well I nausea my way through it and the version of reality in my mind is just that I hurt and I want to be home, and everything else is a dream, isn't it?

Day six, however, I begin to be summoned. At night, an ocean appears on the ceiling of my small room where I stay when I clean until late, and Paul is too drunk to stay awake painting, so I can breathe easy and be more alone. From this ocean comes Nyi Roro Kidul, and I ask her why she did not take Paul when she takes so many other sailors all the time. What is the purpose of a goddess of the sea if not to smite the right humans? He went to Tahiti and I see those paintings and speak to those girls and say god I am sorry, please tell me how you got him to leave. From the whirlpool on my ceiling, the goddess comes closer to my face and says *a light at the end and so many voices are calling 'Here, come here with us.'* She disappears; all I hear are the voices, and my body's thrashing pain, for it has been thrashing, through all the smiles, through everything it has been its own ocean of fire and I am supposed to keep clean his house and it's only because he has been too busy and drunk and I know how to disappear when he wants me that nothing has happened, but he tells the world we are lovers while I grit my teeth back into my gums and watch the doorknob at night I am screaming screaming screaming inside my nerves blazing so what are these voices I do not know but I am desperate for salvation, and I have just seen a form of God.

CHAPTER FOUR: LA FILLE FRANÇAISE: A CHILD OF THIRTEEN

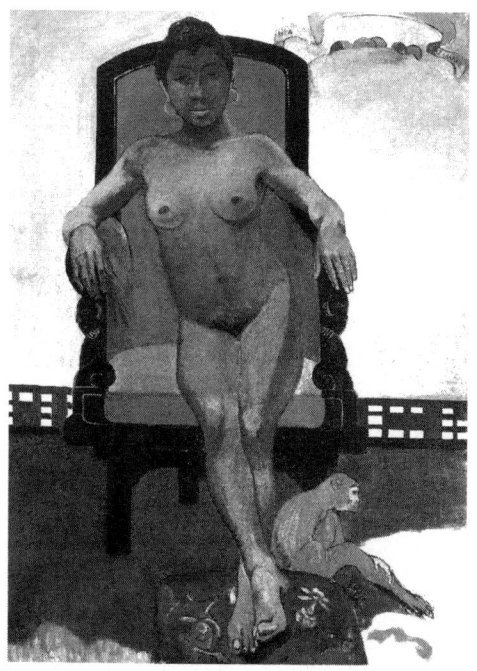

[Paul Gauguin, *Annah the Javanese*, or *Aita Tamari Vahine Judith te Parari* (The Child-Woman Judith Is Not Yet Breached), 1893–94. Oil on canvas, 45 1/4 31 1/2 in. (116 x 81 cm). Private Collection.[6] Painting of a naked child on a chair, their hair in a bun, their ankles crossed, arms on the chair. Monkey at their feet.]

---

6 Caption from Mathews, 2001: p.199.

A few moments to sit with, if you would oblige. When each panel of text and/or imagery appears, kindly take a beat and notice what thoughts, what imagery, each page brings up in you.

This is a space for further impressions of sex and age of consent, of whether or not it is possible that Annah/s could have been pained bodies. Within this chapter are strains of art practice as research. I would like to gesture at these as elements which have been present in the making of the work. I want to hold space for our emotions, and to recognise that reading about and grappling with these histories requires emotional energy, emotional labour. Only you can decide what stories you are able to, want to, acknowledge.

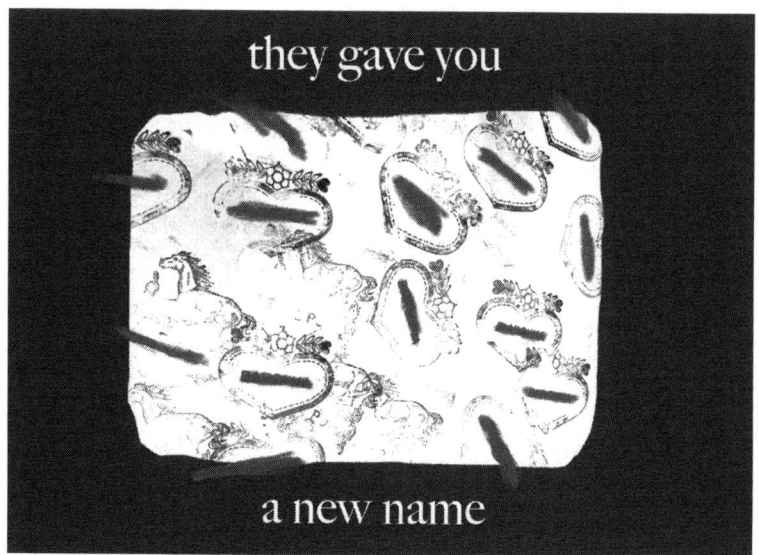

[Panel 1 caption: Black and white version of the image described as follows. In light brown text, 'They gave you [rectangle of a child's multicoloured name-in-a-heart stamp, used many times over on a tan sheet of paper, with the space where the name should be scribbled over in purple] a new name'.]

There are versions of Annah's story which claim they were half-Dutch, half-Javanese, elsewhere they were described as 'mulatto'. When Indonesia was the Dutch East Indies, there were populations of abandoned, part-white, part-Indonesian children sparking contradictory colonial policies.

Speaking of both Dutch and French colonial regimes, Ann Stoler writes:

> Colonial officials wrestled with the belief that the Europeanness of métis children could never be assured, despite a rhetoric affirming that education and upbringing were transformative processes. Authorities spoke of abandoned métisse daughters as *les filles françaises* when arguing for their redemption, but when supporting segregated education, these same authorities recast these youths as physically marked and morally marred with 'the faults and mediocre qualities of their [native] mothers' as 'the fruits of a regrettable weakness'. Thus, abandoned métis children not only represented the sexual excesses and indiscretions of European men but the dangers of a subaltern class, degenerate (*verwilderen*) and lacking paternal discipline (*gemis aan vader lijketucht*), a world in which mothers took charge.

verwilderen

La Fille Française

gemis aan vader lijketucht

[Panel 2 caption: Black and white version of the image described as follows. In purple text over tan background,
verwilderen
La Fille Française
gemis aan vader lijketucht]

In 1977–78, Michel Foucault made clear his view that all age of consent laws serve the purposes of regulating norms of decency and criminalizing certain forms of sexuality. He took part in public conversations in France in 1977 and signed a petition, along with Jean Danet and Guy Hocquenghem, to abolish all age of consent laws. He maintained, [sic] that '[a]ll the legislation on sexuality introduced since the 19th century in France, is a set of laws on decency [la pudeur]', but now, '[w]hat is emerging is a new penal system, a new legislative system whose function is not so much to punish offenses against these general laws concerning decency, as to protect populations and parts of populations regarded as particularly vulnerable'.

—Judith Butler, 'Sexual Consent: Some Thoughts on Psychoanalysis and Law'

Why, for Foucault, [do] colonial bodies never figure as a possible site of the articulation of nineteenth-century European sexuality? And given this omission, what are the consequences for his treatment of racism in the making of the European bourgeois self? More troubling still are the implications for those of us who have sought to extend Foucault's approach to sexuality and power into imperial settings. Do we run the risk of reproducing precisely the terms of colonial discourse itself where any and everything could be attributed to and/ or reduced to the dangers[,] contaminations, and enticements of sex?

—Ann Laura Stoler, *Race and the Education of Desire: Foucault's History of Sexuality and the Colonial Order of Things*

I am trying to get through this manuscript without entering the search term 'Southeast Asian girls'.

Last year (at the time of writing this), I flew Thai Air from Jakarta to London, with a stopover in Bangkok. On the plane, we were all made to watch the most bizarre commercial I'd ever seen. The advertisement, made by the Thai government, interspersed horror-style red- and black-tinged frames, reminding us that human trafficking is illegal, with tourist-friendly frames following a genial older white man as he greeted Thai person upon Thai person, ate their food, smiled with them on the beach. From the tourist-friendly advert to the admonishment of and the illegality of human trafficking again. The final scene was of the smiling white man with each arm around a Thai adult, also smiling.

Splintered frames of reference colliding. Asking white men *nicely* not to engage in human trafficking. Are any of these ads targeted at asking thieves to *kindly* not steal from Thai stores? In whatever country you come from, would you ever see an advertisement asking thieves not to steal items, let alone people, trying to persuade them to treat humans as humans?

Come to our shores, give us your Euros and dollars. And here's a small reminder: do not forsake your hosts. Back to the beach!

I imagine us Southeast Asian women, girls, non-binary people as levitating, each of us witnessing a rope attached to the opening of a door that allows people into our lives, our bodies. We wish to repel them, send them away should we not wish them there, but the rope is tethered tightly to some and not others. I imagine Papuan and Acehnese and Minangkabau people who have been assaulted by Javanese and other Indonesians holding their ropes, above the ground. Asked to be calmly tethered to constant threat.

Age of consent laws, and how governments police consent – including through the media and adverts such as the Thai one – rest on international geopolitical and socioeconomic relations.

possible prayer #467 from annah's mother

calm the waves
reverse their flow
bring her brine to my door

possible prayer #786 from annah's father

because more might befall her
the further she's made to walk from us

196 Annah, Infinite

how far would Annah/s be from a paediatrician

would they treat brown, slave children

how far are they from traditional healers, whose aeons of wisdom continue to be decimated into the present by dint of palm oil plantations, mining, factories, 'development'

how far would Annah/s be from a rainforest

I was working in my flat in South London on this book, when I came to a realisation — eight years into thinking about this project, and four years into a programme of focussing on it deeply.

At the Q and A for my performance *Annah: Nomenclature* (ICA, 2018, Aditi Jaganathan as moderator), an audience member who was half Indonesian, an art curator, said that 'Annah' sounds like 'anak', the word in Indonesian for 'child'. I agreed, and noted that in Tagalog, it also means 'child'. However, it took about another year for me to realise that the child who was given the name 'Annah' might have been called this because, when asked who they were by their slavers, they had replied with 'anak'. They may have said, in an Indonesian no one understood, in defiance of a nonsensical world:

> 'I am a child'.

CHAPTER FIVE:
IN A WORLD WHERE NO ONE IS VOICELESS, THE SOULBODY YELLS THROUGH THE NERVES

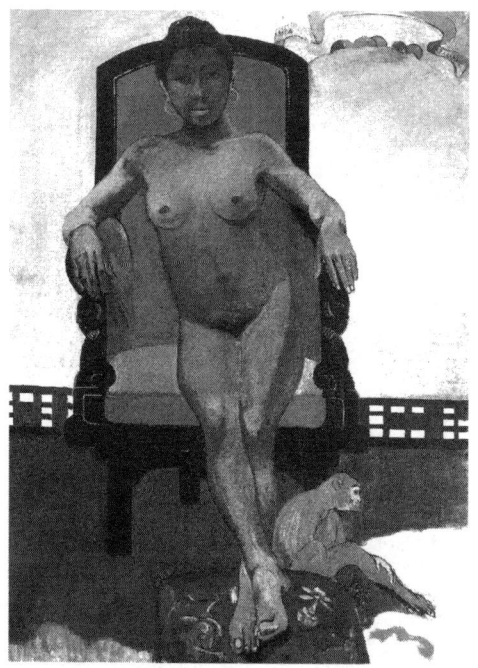

[Paul Gauguin, *Annah the Javanese*, or *Aita Tamari Vahine Judith te Parari* (The Child-Woman Judith Is Not Yet Breached), 1893–94. Oil on canvas, 45 1/4 x 31 1/2 in. (116 x 81 cm). Private Collection.[7] Painting of a naked child on a chair, their hair in a bun, their ankles crossed, arms on the chair. Monkey at their feet.]

---

7 Caption from Mathews, 2001: p.199.

In a 2010 article called 'Is It Wrong to Admire Paul Gauguin's Art?', in response to the Tate's so-called blockbuster Gauguin exhibit of that year, the *Daily Telegraph*'s art critic Alastair Smart wrote:

> Life's not easy as a Paul Gauguin fan. You are on the defensive too much to be effusive. Gauguin was both a syphilitic paedophile and an artist more important than Van Gogh. See the problem? Foul man, fine artist. Some say our knowledge of the former should change our opinion on the latter. Others, myself among them, think otherwise.

It is not, in fact, hard out here for a Gauguin fan, in a world where the artworks of your idol are casually mentioned even in the TV series *Succession* as being stored in a vault by a billionaire.

For Gauguin fans to feel hard-pressed, there needs to be a distortion of the past of the kind that allows Jane Austen and *Little House on the Prairie* heroines to be deemed 'relatable', but which renders colonised people – who were living through exploitation and sadism at the same time as when those stories are set – 'ancient history'.

In her article 'Affective Economies', Sara Ahmed challenges 'any assumption that emotions are a private matter, that they simply belong to individuals, or even that they come from within and then move outward toward others'. Rather than being internal or external, she contends, emotions shape the effects of boundaries or surfaces between self and world. Ahmed analyses the language of Aryan Nations material in which 'love' is tethered to 'hate' – their love of white people and hatred of the other. She writes, '*It is the emotional reading of hate that works to bind the imagined white subject and nation togethe*r' (her italics).

Thinking of the story that Gauguin had 'Here there is love' written in the studio where Annah supposedly sat, and of the many sources alleging the two were lovers, I extend this reading to assert: *in continuously reinforcing the narrative that Annah and Gauguin were in an equal, loving relationship, what binds imagined white subject and nation together is, in this case, also the emotional reading of 'love'* – specifically of love towards Annah and other Black, brown, Asian and indigenous children as automatically worthy of reciprocation, and of 'love' being used to characterise master-slave relationships and abuse.

If Ahmed writes, '*Together we hate, and this hate is what makes us together*' (her italics), with regards to racists, it seems to me that part of this hatred of the other is the compulsion to hurt and capture vulnerable members of 'other' groups under the guise of 'love'. *Together we claim people, claim 'love' between them and us, and subdue.* Perversely, Annah framed as both beloved and exotic contributes to the idea that Gauguin was not only not racist, but 'closer to natives', serving as a beacon of acceptance so different from other French people with their bourgeois values. We should be extremely suspicious of the trope of the happy native who is willing to fall in love readily, to offer their body readily, and to nullify arenas of abuse by making them arenas of pleasure. 'Love' as abuse is another way in which white supremacy operates.

It took me a long time in my own life to recognise that denial of one's illness in a romantic relationship is abuse, both emotional and physical. It took me nearly a decade to recognise that my fury for Annah/s comes in part from personal experience of having the word 'love' given when also being mistreated in the most intimate of contexts. It feels glorious to be on the other side of a certain escape, but there are legions still seeking the exit hatch.

Here are the statistics in the UK alone, from a 2018 BBC article:

Disabled women are more likely to experience domestic abuse than 'abled' women – 16.8 per cent of us as opposed to 6.3 per cent of 'abled' women. Yet only one in ten refuges for domestic violence survivors are accessible to physically disabled women. 'Domestic abuse can include physical, sexual or emotional abuse – as well as withdrawing care from people with long-term illnesses or disabilities.' Or not ever giving proper care in the first place.

What these statistics do not show is that abuse can, and too often does, create disability. I know deeply that such incidents of disablement as a result of abusive relationships are underreported and widespread. Such is our chests feeling, sensing the truth in ways scientific verification cannot capture.

Disability and sexuality are intrinsic in readings of Annah as a possibly pained body: they are presented – as part of Gauguin's creation of self-mythology, and by those who perpetuate it – as a sexual creature. Sexuality becomes a mark of violence when one regards Annah as a developing young person or child – and this intertwines with painedness in myriad, complex ways.

The colonial project is predicated on capture. It is thus no surprise to learn of the vulnerability of young, brown children, especially 'native' and mixed children, in what was in the 1890s the Dutch East Indies and is now Indonesia. Dismissing the vulnerability of Javanese children as a direct result of colonial, capitalist expansion in the Dutch East Indies is part and parcel of that violent, plundering process. It is the covering up of harm done to these children by virtue of denial of rights, less access to resources, psychological damage and increased vulnerability to every form of pain without recourse to managing it on their terms.

If *Annah la Javanaise* is a colonial depiction of a supposedly Javanese child, it is a typical denial of their right to be perceived as a fully human child in need of care. It is in the colonial interest for them to be denied the possibility of being a pained body – not only because Gauguin was a citizen of France as colonial power, as well as being coded white, male and abled (all attributes that increase the likelihood of power in European colonial governance), but because Annah was turned into a commodity. Images of Annah/s are still regarded as a literal commodity, worth millions of pounds; the project of capture remains firmly in place.

Annah was commodified through the mythos surrounding their supposed consensual sexual relationship with Gauguin, which again cannot be proved, yet was what Gauguin intended to portray. A sexual commodity enshrined as such by being depicted in the nude, with a soft smile, with body language coded as inviting, with jewellery befitting an adult woman, coding them specifically as grown. As you have read, the more sexualised and seemingly consenting, seemingly adult, unruly and independent Annah was, the higher the monetary value of Gauguin's paintings, as boosted by his 'wild' reputation.

Once again, I emphasise that many of the varied retellings of Annah in media, art and research mentions them as teenaged: thirteen, or 'around thirteen', the age of consent in France at the time the painting was created. Such prevalent determination of a very specific age marker for Annah – when their photographs might be interpreted as depicting a much younger child, and when so many other details about, say, their ethnicity are written of so variedly – is part of the legitimation of Annah's position as potential sexual paramour for Gauguin and his ilk. Paul Gauguin's Tahitian bride Teha'amana was also written of as being thirteen years old, which is not to my thinking a coincidence of framed consent. Determination of age for brown children in Gauguin's life is part of the racialised determination of brown people's social status for the western gaze. *Annah la Javanaise* is a prime example of how racialised negotiation involved the tacit approval of framing brown children's ages as more 'adult', in order to justify making them vulnerable to pain.

How are we prompted to interpret Annah/s' demeanour by the painting *Annah la Javanaise*? And what effect does this have on our understanding of the relationship between Annah/s and Paul, predicated on understandings of what a certain demeanour supposedly *permits*, and with what degree of enthusiasm?

In the painting itself, Annah is portrayed as being – according to simplistic abled understandings of outward demeanour – calm and smiling, open arms on the chair, legs crossed in comfort. There is the suggestion that they are at ease with their naked body being in such close proximity to the monkey, an animal symbolising neutered Indonesian men; the film *King Kong* (1933) was, after all, set on the island of Nias off Sumatra, in what is now Indonesia, and similarity to apes has long been an insulting descriptor of enslaved and colonised peoples. The juxtaposition of this wildness in monkey form and Annah's nude body within a Parisian domestic setting all go towards the suggestion of consent, and a legitimisation of the interaction between observer and objectified Annah.

Thus Gauguin depicts Annah as willing participant before various histories chronicle them as being so – people have taken the painting as cue. Annah's characterisation as passive person who thus, it is assumed, is in a willing sexual relationship draws on aforementioned colonial tropes of colonised and enslaved peoples as happy to be so. But so do histories of Annah as a spitfire, such as Vargas Llosa's depiction, which play into the idea of the unruly, sexually exuberant and exotic native girl. Both characterisations deny the notion of Annah as a child in peril.

Gauguin's efforts to push Annah/s' status as a child, and their vulnerability, out of frame take on additional significance when considered in light of changes to French laws on the rights of children at the time the painting was made.

Historian Rachel G. Fuchs writes of 'the increase in and types of state intervention for the care of abused children' after the 1880s:

> Modern concepts of child abuse date only from the 1880's [sic] in France [...] Prior to the 1880's [sic], only 2 acts, abortion and infanticide, constituted crimes against children. Child abandonment, rather than a crime, was the state supported, societally acceptable alternative to abortion and infanticide. After abandonment, malnourishment and neglect of these children, even to the point of death, likewise were not crimes. With changes in attitudes of the 1880's [sic], parental neglect, assault, and starvation of children became defined as child abuse, as did perceived immoral behavior of the parents such as habitual drunkenness and debauchery. Under these new definitions of abuse, state officials could deprive parents of their legal rights and make the children wards of the state for their own protection. The state became *in loco parentis*.

The fact that *Annah la Javanaise* is not regarded as a portrait of an abandoned child, I contend, is because that interpretation would be a clear sign of the French government's failure to care for a child vulnerable to pain, at a time when protection of children's rights was coalescing at the national level. Western concepts of 'childhood' were invented in the nineteenth century, yet French laws designed to protect children applied, practically and in spirit, only to white children, both in France and its colonies. In contrast, the French state's pillage of colonies meant brown children were seen as resources to be exploited, just as they were for the Dutch, the British, the Portuguese and other European colonisers of now-Indonesia, rather than citizens to use resources on protecting.

Another aspect of the racialised negotiation of age for Annah/s and others like them is the usage of notions of non-Western 'cultures' as being more promiscuous and amenable to younger ages of consent to justify the harm of majority world children. Time and again, brown children's supposed openness to sexuality at a younger age is given as a reason for why Annah and visual subjects like them could not have been hurt by a recorded abuser, even when there is as blatant a power imbalance as there was between Gauguin and Teha'amana or Gauguin and Annah/s. (After all, if someone literally owns your land, and to refuse them could injure your life, what is the possibility for meaningful consent?) This is blatantly apparent in exhibit literature, in art reviews, in how Gauguin's relationship with his Polynesian 'partners' and Annah are written and spoken of. In the Gauguin exhibit at the National Gallery where I was wheeled around by a colleague one winter, a short film showed a Polynesian woman praising Gauguin for his more 'authentic' depiction of Tahitian women, as he painted them bare and without western dress. Another instance of papering over the violent gaze of a recorded abuser, and weaponising 'brown cultural authenticity' against the memory of these women. I desperately wanted the late Teresia Teaiwa to have intruded on this film, bursting onto the frame with her life's work of denouncing Gauguin's violence against communities she belonged to and loved.

Such myths of imperial duress shape the production of art as well as the interpretation of it. In an interview with an artist working supposedly directly in counter to Gauguin, which I conducted for my PhD research, she said that Tahitians were sexually promiscuous, and married earlier, at the time of Gauguin's sojourn to Tahiti, that Gauguin's behaviour was in line with native practices and expectations. Even in creating work supposedly attacking Gauguin's patriarchy, the artist perpetuated the omission of Gauguin's role as recorded abuser who married Teha'amana and associated himself with young Annah to imply they were sexually involved. The rights of the vulnerable child are moot if the child is seen as adult in French contexts as well as in 'native' colony contexts, a double condemnation for a brown child like Annah in 1890s Paris.

After 1897, fever for 'the Festival for the Crowning of the People's Muse' swept France. Historian Aro Velmet writes, 'In *fin-de-siècle* France, communities around the country were obsessed with [...] a musical procession of varying length and complexity, centred around the crowning of the Muse, a working-class girl, symbol of virtue and youth, elected from within the local municipality. The festival drew from similar ceremonies that often dated back to prerevolutionary times, but substituted their monarchical and religious trappings for a discourse of fervent nationalism.'

The pageant, historian David Pomfret argues, was part of French society's negotiation of the social ascendancy of women and girls. An example, he writes, of how 'age situates individuals within implicit or explicit hierarchies of power, further complicating gender, class, and race'. Much like contemporary beauty pageants like Miss Universe, which also codify women's bodies as 'national', older political figures selected girls for this festival on the criteria that they were 'young' and 'beautiful'.

Here's how Annah's position in 1890s France was as a body who could not represent France – but as a subjugated body *owned* by France, whose very likely pain was made negligible. 'The People's Muse' was an attractive, confident young woman, as Annah was positioned to be, but Annah's strength is portrayed as a threat, alluding to wickedness and potential duplicity, and they are not a symbol of what France could be – a 'natural', if subdued and sexualised, component of the ideal nation-state – but of what potent, 'exotic' mysteries France could conquer. At that time, writes Pomfret,

> Contemporary commentators made frequent reference to biological models in explaining evidence of 'degeneration'. Pathologies (*neurasthenia*, suicide, *prostitution*, and a worryingly low birth rate [my italics]) were believed to be upsetting the balance of the social organism and undermining the 'virility' of the French nation. The concomitant efforts of women to move beyond bourgeois models of domestic femininity and to claim social and political rights thus became a major source of conflict.

One version of Annah histories is, if you recall, that they were found in the brothels of Montmartre, with the implication that they were a sex worker. I argue that the bringing in of Annah into a male artistic coterie – taking them out of sex work, which was seen as pathology – was precisely to boost this sense of French 'virility' in the form of Gauguin's power over them. The nation of France as virile compared to colonised nations. The body of Gauguin compared to the body/ies of Annah/s. To Judith's body, which was protected by her mother, who lived in the body of a white woman.

Neurasthenia is broadly defined as bodily disturbance stemming from emotional disturbance. It is associated with Chronic Fatigue Syndrome (CFS), a catch-all phrase used by medical institutions when they cannot identify more specifically the causes of pain, especially in women, especially in women of the majority world. How CFS manifests in some of us belies the almost gentle nature of the word 'fatigue' – a word that does not conjure the knives and knifing of reality for many of us. Annah/s would very probably have been under great emotional disturbance, conditions conducive to total pain. The heart is of the body, wholly – our hearts may rip all our nerves apart. And yet, any possibility of pain whatsoever, physical and emotional, is taken from Annah/s' images. If one is unascribed a full emotional life, unbestowed the full potential of a soul to react to life's violences and joys naturally, one is not regarded as human.

Annah/s were taken in from supposed degeneracy and made palatable as an *owned* sexual object, boosting France's sense of virility through visual artefacts of them. That the perceived pathology of sex work was also regarded as being in opposition to virility is part and parcel of eugenicist thinking, which aims to wipe out bodies that pose a threat to nationhood. It is never in France's colonial interest to allow Annah to be a pained or ill person: sex work as pathology, as a form of illness within the nation-state, is regarded as something to be wiped out by a virile, eugenicist, colonial nationalism. Chronic pain, on the other hand – persistent pain of the sort that is often incurable, that the person may not wish to be cured of, though they still deserve protection from suffering within it – is never allowed to be a possibility. Because of Annah's supposed overt sexuality, they must be immune to any kind of incurable, permanent harm or damage. The only possible bodies depicted must be those that the state can cure of the 'illness' of promiscuity.

In fact, if Annah/s were perceived to be a sex worker, the stigma around sex work that persists to this day, and makes sex workers vulnerable to this day, would have contributed to Annah/s being seen as sexually voracious, indiscriminate, always consenting to sexual activity, and immune to harm, pain and danger.

The assumption that Annah is attracted to men, specifically Gauguin, is a form of heteronormativity also acting in service of probable abuse: though there was certainly the chance that Annah was not only unattracted to Gauguin and his friends, but to men in general, or to anyone sexually, this is never mentioned. It is important to emphasise that I do not conflate heterosexuality with consent here.

To think of Annah as possibly being anything other than strictly attracted to Gauguin is to oppose Gauguin's self-mythos, perpetuated in imperial duress, and also to make obvious the prevailing likelihood of abuse. We should bear in mind that if Annah/s were around thirteen, or even younger, they may not yet have begun to explore their own sexuality and self-agency, were in a process – possibly still very nascent – of becoming. We must remember this, in spite of persistent myths of brown children being more sexually advanced, as well as capable of threat, at a younger age.

Also of importance in addressing disability and sexuality from an anti-colonial perspective, in this case when it comes to potential painedness, is the understanding of how, when and why a person discloses that they are in pain – or that the actions occurring will cause them pain later – in a potentially or explicitly sexual situation. Comfort with disclosure requires safety and consent that may be negotiated and manifest differently from case to case (including, for instance, pained people into BDSM/kink, as scholar Emma Sheppard has written of). However, if the relationship is in fact not perceived as being between two people, but between a person and a commodity – between Paul and Annah, Annah who is sub-human by virtue of being brown and a child in colonial times, and potentially further dehumanised by being disabled – I argue that safety and consent are made impossible for the commodified person in sexual situations.

Throughout my years of research, Annah/s have revealed crack after crack in official 'histories', possibility after possibility for their potential agency, ingenuity and capacity to survive, even in close proximity to an abuser. The preponderance of stories about Annah's spirited demeanour and their thieving, while in the presence of culturally powerful men, may point to clear possibilities of incredible resilience and initiative on their part/s. Particularly in sexual situations that may be forced, and in great risk of such situations, I sense a quicksilver thread of intuition for survival from what is still a developing mind: a child's pluck and nerve.

Another possible jiwa raga framing for a pained Annah, another kind of possibly pained Annah, is that of a child for whom pain is managed and lived with. However, it must be emphasised that considering the availability of healthcare, the possibility of pain management would have been incredibly slim for a brown child alone in 1890s France. Affording Annah/s agency over their pain to a level where it could be lived with is also unlikely.

Intense dis-ease, unsafety and harm manifested in the jiwa raga of a brown child in the 1890s would likely, in my view, not be trackable or traceable to child welfare authorities.

I believe that if visual archives of Annah's body/ies conformed more to ablenormative, sighted-normative notions of what disability looks like – if they were 'visibly disabled' in a way that ableds understand – the already incredibly high risk Annah/s had of living with violence would have been impacted by a fear of the 'other'. Very likely in a very different way than how 'la Javanaise' exoticises the 'abled other' as consumable exotic commodity. If a child is brown and thus regarded as adult, when they were actually likely robbed of their childhood in the presence of Gauguin and his friends in 1890s France, how would their life be different if they 'appeared to be disabled' according to sighted, abled understandings of disability?

The ways in which disgust and erotic appeal might interact with each other upon the same body would of course be variable, depending on how Annah's disability would be visible, who the beholder of their body was and their relationship to Annah/s in terms of sociocultural power hierarchies. Both disgust and erotic appeal would make Annah/s extremely vulnerable to harm and painedness, including sexual harm, as it does for millions of children today.

What are the ways in which ocularcentrism, as determined by abled cultural workers, refracts different bodies being depicted visually, across history – especially if disabilities are seen as something to be 'clocked', registered, documented, so that undesirables can be subject to the violence of patriarchies and patriarchal states?

Anti-colonial, cripped perspectives on ocularcentrism, coming from feminisms outside mainstream white feminism, reach towards Annah/s and are, simultaneously, overwhelmingly crowded out. As the circulation of art objects such as *Annah la Javanaise* shows, colonised bodies continue to loom in contemporary life in the sphere of white intellectual histories, yet are still rarely allowed to be interpreted according to non-white, D/deaf and/or disabled frameworks. There is such neglect of a cripped, pained perspective on artefacts such as *Annah la Javanaise* and the histories it is bound up in, bound by (a rope).

The further I went into my PhD in visual cultures, the tighter this rope wound around my writing on art and on Annah/s, the tighter the grasp of normative interpretations – approved by colonial, white feminism – on the work I had ostensibly been recruited to perform as a researcher.

Margrit Shildrick's *Dangerous Discourses of Disability, Subjectivity and Sexuality* is a touchstone text in the field of disability and sexuality studies for western academia, and delves into how disabled people are perceived as non-sexual beings or objects of disgust in Western societies. Shildrick's work has gained notoriety in the field of disability studies in the Anglophone world, and is a strong example of how racist configurations of neoliberal globalisation permeate the field.

In my doctoral dissertation, I offered a critique of Shildrick's work, pointing out how she writes of twenty-first century economic globalisation as a positive force with regards to disability, sexuality and subjectivities – without any writing on colonialism, mass violence or disablement, particularly *by* colonial capitalism. Writing, as Shildrick says she does, from the 'Anglo-American' perspective, she pays no attention to the ways in which the United States was built upon white supremacist ableism as a violence imposed upon slaves and the colonised, certainly including large swathes of disabled people, and certainly including large masses of people made disabled by such violence. Including the genocidal murder of what could well have been two million people in the Indonesian archipelago in the name of ableist colonial capitalism. Ignoring these realities allows her to maintain the fiction, in her work, that West is best and will free all disabled people.

Academic critique is the job of a PhD researcher, ostensibly. Yet my argument above nearly cost me my doctoral degree, as my scholarship was for a limited time, whilst racist abuse as a result of this simple critique of Shildrick – which I refused to tone down – stalled my dissertation. My offering of an alternative viewpoint, one which exposed the lacunae in hers, was characterised as a threat to Shildrick, to an established, disabled white woman academic. In positioning my defence of brown children in Shildrick's hole-filled theses as a threat, my own status as a disabled woman was denied. (Content warning for the next sentence: self-harm.) By telling me that my intellectual, emotional truths as a brown woman, my elucidation of colonial infrastructures, were the kinds of critiques that could actually cause (white) people to commit suicide – and yes, this was said to me explicitly – my own psychic pain, and that of billions of people, was elided.

Annah/s' voices whipped around me stronger than ever. The denial of *our* pained perspectives, as 'brown island women', hadn't let up an inch over more than a century. Their hands remained at our throats. How we regarded the truths of our jiwa raga – our histories, our lived understanding when it came to torture, and pain, and disability – is deemed violent. Even within disabled communities we are othered, and our understandings of how the world truly works are deemed inferior; their rights come at the expense of our bodies through capital flows, and always have; when we dare to say this, our whole selves may be slapped down.

Throughout the years of persevering at this book, Annah/s' foes presented themselves as gaping traps, again and again, the institutions and lackeys of liberal whiteness revealing themselves in supposed benefactors. They loved Annah/s in theory, until Annah/s' potential truths, our ocean of stories, truly came for them – for their sense of superiority, of needing to be centred, their denial of colonialism as fascism, their need to be 'good', their Main Character Syndrome. The dying throes of an impossible system. For if there is anything impossible in this world, it is to regard the minority of the world (so ignorant of the wisdoms of billions) as human, and all other worldviews, all other people, as inferior, moot, painted shut.

My episodes of torture were signals to my jiwa raga that situations were untenable, that I was under holistic violence, both from colonial medical neglect and colonial intellectual institutions, at once; the shockwaves of pain were screams from all the parts of me that heard Annah/s, which is to say, everywhere. That torture continued as, without fail, I faced the arrogant dismissal of my views, of my peoples, was not surprising. To carry on with my work on the *Annah, Infinite* project, with the slowness and deliberation of crip time, allowing for my post-traumatic mind to recoil again and again from the writing, and heal bit by bit to be able to continue it, was all I could do for them, for ourselves.

Annah/s' possibilities surviving, our knowledge of these possibilities, are themselves evidence of the banal absurdity of colonialism – for they cannot be stamped out. Annah/s' continuance belies their simple, violent lies. And so does ours.

Recalling that Annah may have been called 'a little negro girl' by Mme Nina Pack, who asked for them to be brought to Paris in one version of Annah's origins, the intersection of Blackness and brownness in racist colonial logic needs to be a cornerstone of understanding with regards to Annah stories. The Dutch East Indies Company was in power when Nina made this specific request; of course the banker would know what she meant – their infrastructure had created the possibility of this transaction happening in the first place, multiplied, then buried.

Scholar Therí Pickens writes of her book *Black Madness :: Mad Blackness*:

> *Black Madness :: Mad Blackness* rests on the idea that ability and race are intertwined ... Suturing madness and Blackness together, I debunk the perception that the title is redundant, oxymoronic, or excessive. In [...] white supremacy, Blackness is considered synonymous with madness or the prerequisite for creating madness. [...] Mad studies perspectives mobilize activist and scholastic impulses in their refusal of the historical definitions of madness as 'irrationality, a condition involving decline or even disappearance of the role of rational factor in the organization of human conduct and experience' and the equation of madness with lack or inability.

This resonated with me in terms of how, in white supremacy, natural emotions in Asian cultures have also been literally categorised as madness. Witness how the Indo-Malay word 'amuk' (with linguistic ties to Maori and Filipino as well) means 'rage' or 'to rage', but was translated by colonists into English, Dutch, Danish and Portuguese to mean 'indiscriminate, pathological, homicidal killing'. Most likely, colonists witnessed slave uprisings in what is now Malaysia and Indonesia and categorised these as killings, with no reason other than 'native bloodthirst', thus turning the word, eventually, into the English term 'running amok'. 'Amuk' now carries the colonial definition even in the official Indonesian government dictionary. Our very rage, and our language for rage, continues to be in the process of having its meaning twisted, stripped and stolen. This reminds me, always, that 'mad' to some means insanity, while to others it has been about being angry, being mad in the sense of reacting naturally to injustice.

Thinking such as Pickens', combined with my understanding of my own histories, as well as of disability and ability in Indonesian spiritual structures and stories of deities, opens up space for understanding Annah/s as potentially disabled child/ren, including disabled in the sense of 'madness', a form of sociopolitical, and deeply intimate, resistance. An uprising within a child's body. My speculative works and performances of reaching out to potentially pained Annah/s are a recognition that racialised, gendered, colonial, anti-child trauma could well have manifested in chronic pain within the body.

The possibility of Annah as a pained bodymind, or jiwa raga, serves as the starting point for understanding their body/ies as being potentially non-ablenormative in any number of ways. Possibly concurrent ways, ways possibly interacting within one person. Acute psychic pain could have damaged their nerves, and this would not only be possible, I argue, but a *natural* outcome of living in a society from which there was likely no escape into safer, more nurturing situations, in a body marked as brown girl, brown child. One's jiwa raga could well, should well, tell us we are in danger, that we are in harm, and manifest that in pain.

Pain, in other words, could be read as a form of resistance and generative possibility, as a state of soulbody alertness/recognition, rather than the ableist understanding of pain as a monolithic marker of suffering. Pain is a shrieking alarm. Pain is a jiwa raga's intelligence, saying *stop*, saying pain does not want to exist but does.

Annah la Javanaise as potentially pained is a marker of disability as a manifestation of white supremacist ablebodiedness, both in terms of an 'othering' by such a society of those deemed abnormal, and in terms of such a supremacist society creating the conditions through which the soulbody manifests what is *deemed* disability.

This call to imagine disability as vaster, more open to refractions and permutations of what 'disability', 'madness' and 'ability' really mean in racialised contexts deeply echoes with and in my own work of speculative Annahs. What happens to the jiwa raga of a child in danger in different understandings of the world as we know it, in different cosmologies – including, for example, in Javanese or other spiritualities indigenous to what is now known as Indonesia, for which the interactions of nerve endings and cosmologies reach far beyond what is recorded in Western art histories – means that the equation of Annah's potential pain as suffering pure and simple must be questioned.

Much like Pickens' assertion, the refusal of jiwa raga to submit to ableist colonial norms – for instance, by recognising the real, physical, psychic impact of unsafety and harm by internalising it and manifesting that harm in the body, a process which is in fact natural – is a sign of resistance.

By being the truth, pain is resistance. Denial of pain's truth in our bodies is a denial of natural reactions to danger and injury; a denial of that danger and injury itself.

I do not want to glorify anyone's pain when it is at an intolerable level (including mine); any pain that is suffering should not be romanticised. This is in no way incongruous with recognising it as the soulbody's reaction to a state of emergency, a completely plausible reaction when one looks outside Western rational frameworks for the body. Looking outside Western rational frameworks for the body, and for painedness, also opens up possibilities for pain narratives that are beyond the scope of my knowing, even as a pained person myself. These possibilities include different pain narratives in a (brown) child's jiwa raga than in an adult's.

It is not my goal to map out all possible pain narratives, as that is impossible; indeed, the project of all-knowingness and supposed 'universality' is one inherent to colonialism and white supremacy. Thus admission of how much we do not and can never know, as individuals, is a refusal of such imperialism. What I'm trying to do here is to open up a starting point for understanding that pain narratives in Annah archives *exist*, and for understanding that in many frameworks, including contemporary rights-based discourses, Annah was a child or children and thus a member of a very vulnerable group, in addition to recognising the vulnerability of being brown in Paris and being interpreted as a girl or woman, and the vulnerability of being the only one of their kind in all known archives in which they exist.

This point is even more trenchant when one considers the vulnerability of disabled majority world children today, as well as the vulnerability of millions of migrant workers, refugees and human trafficking victims, including hundreds of thousands of domestic workers from Indonesia who work abroad each year, virtually all of whom are women. (Annah too was potentially a foreign domestic worker, though more likely a slave.) These include millions who have been working with scant protections from both their home government and the places where they reside, and are vulnerable to exploitation and abuse, including sexual, including human trafficking. This vulnerability extends not only to the women themselves, but to the families they leave behind in their home countries, for whom '[p]recarity chains effectively *remit persistent dependence and future precarity*', as Rachel Silvey and Rhacel Parreñas write of Southeast Asian migrant workers in the Middle East.

The possibility of pain in every picture is a layer of potential vulnerability that is often omitted from art historical narratives. But of course. The narratives by which marginalised groups are made precarious – especially groups of the majority world, including Black, brown, Indigenous and Asian women, girls, non-binary and/or indigenous gendered people, trans people – and thus more vulnerable to pain, are precisely those that imperialist ablenormative narratives seek to erase.

Going back to Talila Lewis' definition of 'ableism', our whole world is shaped by what constitutes 'able'. Able to perform within colonial capitalism.

How pain narratives or lack-of-pain narratives exist in histories of Annah/s is inextricable from how Annah/s were and are expected to perform sexually under colonialism. To perform sexually in a specific way, that is: sexual ablenormativity, what abled people think sex should be like, which also points to sexual functioning in these certain ways as part of being regarded 'abled'.

What stories are told about Annah repeatedly, always in relation to Gauguin, and with Annah as a minor character, show a limited, ableist understanding of sexuality as being diametrically opposed to pain, in a way that studies like Emma Sheppard's of

BDSM and kink as part of the lives of some chronically pained people, undo. Because of an ableist, limited framework, sexual pleasure, or sexual pain as at least consensual, in the narratives of Annah's relationship to Gauguin, is embedded in the violence of Annah's colonial archival portrayals.

Saidiya Hartman says the aftermath of slavery is an aesthetic problem, with regards to how Black bodies carry the past, present and future. Sexual ablenormativity is also an aesthetic problem, in terms of how we impose sexual ablenormativity on depicted humans across many eras. I'm attempting to highlight that understanding for us, as brown bodies capable of pain, whose bodies show us how much pain we are capable of, how much pleasure we can derive from life.

Jasbir Puar's book *The Right to Maim* calls attention to how rights-based discourses in Western countries coincide with discourses in which human populations within and outside those countries – but indelibly marked by the West's foreign policy – are deliberately made more vulnerable to disablement and debility in the name of profit. Puar argues that the focus on the disabled person as a neoliberal subject, a subject deserving of rights, obscures how countries in which these neoliberal subjects live continually oppress marginalised populations with economic and other forms of violence, reserving the right to maim and disable some while upholding the rights to safety and welfare of others. This maiming and disabling, Puar argues, also includes the dismantling of material and social infrastructures that would prevent such maiming, whether public healthcare or child protection services.

Her examples of those that are maimed by neoliberalism include Palestinians in the Occupied Territories as well as Black Americans in places such as Flint, Michigan, who are the recipients of life-altering environmental racism. Both the Black children of Flint and the Palestinian children of the Occupied

Territories have been and continue to be maimed due to their classification as populations which others have the right to maim. The brown child/ren named 'Annah' in *Annah la Javanaise* and Annah archives, I argue, fall inside this category as well, which explains why young schoolgirls in the West may increasingly be made aware of their right to sexual self-determination, agency and protection, yet are told to revere work in which brown girls are hypersexualised and laid bare to deeply searing forms of harm.

There is a lack of empathy for these children's narratives in the most-circulated media of the western world. Indeed, considering disabled women and gender nonconforming people, girls, children in general are multiple times more likely to be abused in myriad ways than abled counterparts, and thus at much greater likelihood of being chronically pained, disabled women and gender nonconforming people and children are not always included in the conversation around consent and safety. This is also tied to the lack of sexual education for D/deaf and/or disabled children.

In visual perceptions of pained people as non-sexual, and of all people with agency over their sexuality as non-pained, lack of empathy is (re)produced. Also note the difference between empathy and sympathy for pained girls, and the difficulties of expressing the lived-inness of pain to 'abled' bodies as related to this difference. The pain of us pained people can exist on lower registers than it does for abled people, or only occur days after an injury is incurred, or exist in any number of ways in the bodymind that are difficult for others to understand. Pain and its possible manifestations are thus deemed counterintuitive to 'abled' bodies, and so the possibilities of its entanglements with sexuality and age of consent are also deemed counterintuitive – which they never are for us as pained adults. Queered, cripped temporalities also underscore how many different kinds of pain may exist simultaneously.

Subini Annamma, a scholar working within a US context, has written about disabled brown children's characterisation in a way that illuminates why the (lack of) conversation around age and the age of consent for Annah/s contributes to the possibility of them being a pained person. Annamma draws on dis/ability critical race theory, or what she calls DisCrit, which provides a framework for understanding the confluence of racism and ableism in Black and brown children's lives in the US as multiply marginalising. She writes:

> I utilized the work of an intellectual ancestor of Critical Race Theory, W. E. B. Du Bois (1903) who [...] found that Black people had unique knowledge and gifts to share with the world, specifically due to the oppression they faced. Therefore, this Gift Theory, as Reiland Rabaka (2010) later identified it, required me to refuse the notion that the girls were inherently dangerous or deviant. Instead, I conducted this work with the central assumption that multiply-marginalized disabled girls of color had Gifts I did not possess.

I find resonance with Annamma's ethos in my approach for addressing Annah archives. For over a decade, as I experienced persistent and regular torture from systemic medical malpractice and systems designed to injure and neglect, I have tried to listen to these Gifts I do not possess, that potential pained Annah/s possess.

It is important, however, to note that what constitutes 'pain' is extremely variable and fluid, ranging from extremely acute pain from which a person is desperate to be relieved, to low-level chronic pain that someone has learned to live with, from occurring instantaneously to much later on – because of this, we must examine the following quote from Annamma while gesturing towards the multifaceted nature of being pained:

> Situating this work in DisCrit means that I approached this work understanding that there is *nothing wrong with our students, their families, and their communities* [my italics]. That means I did not approach this work seeking to understand how to fix the girls in this study. I did not assume they were lying or seek to inform them how to live better lives.

I wholeheartedly agree with this approach, but as someone who has had innumerable experiences of acute pain from which I should have been and wanted to be relieved, I would want possible Annahs not to suffer such pain – this does not, however, mean that I want to 'fix' them, but rather, I want to fix the *unnecessary* conditions of suffering, the social mechanisms they were caught in. Potential Annahs who are pained at a level they can live with, however, or in a manageable way, may not want their condition to be 'fixed' (I myself am a pained woman who does not want to be abled if the pain is manageable and escalation is avoidable). It depends on jiwa raga experiences of pain across time, and within specific cultural frameworks of pain. Considering the existence of anti-colonial frameworks for time here, it is also possible to have multiple kinds of pain exist simultaneously.

In thinking of Annah/s as possibly pained brown child/ren, I too intend to open up the possibility of their Gifts, rather than paint them as one-dimensional, lacking anything to offer the world.

Annah is written of, whether in *LIFE Magazine* or by novelist Vargas Llosa, as criminal, deviant – they steal from Gauguin and break his heart after reinvigorating him artistically and sexually. As mentioned, this deviance is connected to racialised stereotypes applied to women and girls who might be labelled 'Javanaise', 'mulatto', or any of the other labels applied to Annah/s. The effects of these racialised stereotypes of deviance, dangerousness and criminality are also, I argue, to make the children who were Annah/s even more at risk of being harmed by being characterised as adult. This imposed adulthood is fundamentally important for increased risk of sexual, physical and emotional abuse, including by, as Annamma writes, institutions. Institutions here include art institutions, and governments who determine realms and modes of punishment and care.

Annamma writes that Black and brown children in the US are more susceptible to being labelled as 'dis/abled' in the classroom setting, and that this increases their likelihood of being shunted into the school-to-prison pipeline. This resonates in how the criminal acts of theft and sex work in 1890s France were attributed to Annah in some accounts of them, accounts that did not describe them as a child. In other words, Annah/s are/were criminalised in a way parallel to how disabled children of colour, including pained children, are in the US today. US schools are ostensibly tasked with protecting the wellbeing of their pupils, and labelling a child 'dis/abled' in a way that makes such children more susceptible to the US school-to-prison pipeline allows such institutions to easily relinquish this mandate of care.

How France has historically mistreated young people racialised as brown, including in arts institutions, involves perpetuating myths related to these disastrous US systems: that only adults can commit what the state deems a crime (i.e. stealing from Gauguin), that only adults can be in proximity to a sexually active man, that Annah/s are abled, that young people who are disabled are universally cared for by western countries. And that disabled young people are abject objects of charity or pathologically toxic for society, by virtue of their criminalised nature.

All of the above is important, because *Annah la Javanaise* the painting and the Annah archives circulate, and are preserved, in countries where the rights of the child are a professed tenet of contemporary law – yet Annahs are never treated as children under these contemporary rights.

The possibility of Annah as a pained child seems 'counterintuitive' to those ascribing to abled colonial white supremacist narratives, because the possibility of Annah as pained and Annah as a child both expose fallacies in the notion of rights-based discourses being applied consistently to both children and disabled populations by Western countries. All the while this image continues to be part of the mythos of not only Gauguin's artistic genius, but the supreme importance of white male artists and arts institutions that uphold them as central to colonial white supremacism's ablenormative hold on nationhood.

And so, the real person or people portrayed in Annah la Javanaise was, or were, not only possibly pained, but more likely than not to have been pained or abused due to being in a dangerous childhood, made vulnerable by virtue of being racialised, and sexualised as commodity. Because Annah/s' bod/ies were brown, art historical archives and contemporary art institution texts and fiction writers conspire to eliminate their childhood by making them consenting adults at the age of around thirteen, by making them a sex worker, by making them 'panther or cannibal', by making them a thief whose takings were unjustified.

Against these falsehoods and fallacies, against arts workers complicit with colonial keeping, stands the ultimate authority of what our own bodies experience, what we know with our bodyminds. No one can tell us we are not being tortured when we are, though innumerable people have told me so, in words and gestures that ate at my mind over the years, as I desperately sought help. The truth of our jiwa raga is final and indisputable and ours.

In university settings, I baulked at having to cite academic references for the Soeharto dictatorship, when I was born into it and lived under it, live with political legacies of it. This is embodied knowledge, generational knowledge, and a firsthand survivor's account; my jiwa raga feels a twinge of concern at having somatic knowledge forms seen as less 'accurate' or 'truthful' than the work of white, Western academics. Over and over, I saw people in academia who did not know how to treat brown, disabled people as human claiming to have spawned a 'universal' theory for all humankind. Their idea of humanity is cauterised by white supremacy, occluding all of our universes, our mitochondrial truths, our subatomic pulsings, our pains and our pleasures as records, as archives, our bodies as archives of truth, constantly asking us to trust in our own histories.

To deny our bodyminds the truth of extreme pain in the aftermath of trauma is to assault our own spirits.

The world will consistently attempt to suffocate the truths of our souls. It is nonsensical, it is outrageous, it is true horror that throughout the years of writing this book, I and so many others have been disbelieved – I know so many others because I have met them, and acknowledged them, because I see the systems that perpetrated this suffocating of my own truths as vast in their grasp – yet nothing can take away our wholeness, our pain as shrieking truth, our pain as resistance to 'being alright' when met with extreme violence. It is not we who are extreme; it is what we have had to endure. Our pain is an anger. Our torture-level pains are meaningful because they are bodily truths, and by being so they resist the twisting of what is true by ablenormative gazes, by colonial supremacies.

Working with archives, as an archives consultant, I have seen visual artefacts and read accounts of all manner of torture being unleashed upon peoples I come from, by colonialism. This past year, I was confronted with a page in a book describing in detail the various methods that European colonists used on prominent peoples from the islands I come from, and it hit me like a forcefield, sunk me into perceiving what I've survived as part of a seemingly endless lineage of colonial torture tactics. I thought of my grandparents and how devastated they would be, having survived all they have, to know their granddaughter was a torture survivor, and lives under continued threat of further torture if at any time surrounded by disbelief.

Some time after, my perspective shifted. My body asked me to be kind, kinder. The key is not the word 'torture' that threatens to waylay me, take me down into depressive depths, stun me with the shock of memory after memory. The key word is 'survival', for all of us who need it most. The key is a coming to terms with pain as a warning siren, that wants us to find safety.

If my grandfather were here today, he who was a political prisoner once, and clawed his way back to a good life for his family, I would tell him that his granddaughter has been continually met with violence, and remained indestructible. That she was taught by a ghost or ghosts from a painting, a ghost or ghosts who defied suppression, to understand the body as truth and the truth of our bodies. I would tell him how I crawled through the years in secret sanctuaries, moment by moment, until I found as much respite as I could. That I understand how for us, jiwa raga, the soulbody, screams through the nerves. That I am always imagining, and laughing into, all of our escapes – all my ancestors as children, we are escaping the frame together, towards tenderness, as we always have been.

INTERLUDE TWO: QUEERING AND CRIPPING TIME

[Caption for *Annah la Javanaise*]

300 AD. A Minangkabau woman foresees her offspring moving to Java, and one of them moving to Paris, France. She is also met with women in India, in Guyana, in South Africa (Cape Malay), in Sri Lanka, in Malaysia, in Polynesia, in Nepal. You know, in any case, they made up some of our names and so many borders.

'But I feel that they are in pain and no one believes them,' says the woman in what is today Bukittinggi, West Sumatra.

So do I, says the woman in what is today Ahmedabad.
So do I, says the woman in what is today Máncora.
So do I, says the woman in what is today As Sarriyah.
So do I, says each woman in each shapeshifting village, township, city and shore.

They are visited by Nyi Roro Kidul, Javanese goddess of the Indian Ocean, in the incarnation of when her skin was deemed ugly, and she had to swim into the waves. And the women pray with their bodies across time and space, for their children who are their children's children's children's children's – on and on and on – children.

OUR LANGUAGE OPENS UP

Indonesian, or Bahasa Indonesia (*never* 'Bahasa', which just means 'language'), contains such sophisticated understandings of humanity in some cases, an unboxing of empathy, an ethics of true care. Our pronoun, 'dia', is gender-neutral. A word can be either plural or singular, depending on context. And then, there is the matter of time.

There is the time that we use to determine the order of our days and nights – twenty-four-hour days, three-hundred-sixty-five-day years, sixty-second minutes, sixty-minute hours. Weekends and weekdays. Names for each day of the week, and the division of time for labour and time for rest. The presentation of time is cultural; I once met a PhD student, in Germany, studying the creation of the weekend as a construct. The existence of Western, universalising, psychological notions of time-space are so ubiquitous as to go so often unremarked upon.

In my home language, Indonesian, lies what I find to be a fundamental loophole in these systems – consisting, if you will, of time portals; galactic alternatives to what we know of time, baked into the grammar of our language. That is, Indonesian, or Bahasa Indonesia (literally, 'Indonesian language') lacks time-based tenses for verbs – there is no 'present', 'past' or 'future' tense; instead, everything is happening at a time that other words may make apparent, may contextualise. For instance, 'Saya makan' could mean 'I ate', 'I eat' or 'I will eat'. 'Saya makan kemarin' means 'I ate yesterday'; 'Saya sedang makan' means 'I'm eating'; 'Saya akan makan' means 'I will eat'.

The absence of time tenses contains profound presences. It makes me feel comforted when I write, for instance, 'Keluarga saya di sini' ('My family is/was/will be here'), because there is not only the possibility of the meaning 'My family was here' or 'My family will be here' – both important in maintaining that tie between eras and familial connection – but also the possibility of the presence in the now of both past and future; the presence of the past in the now and future; the presence of futurity in what is past and what is now. This means that *people* and other spirits in the past and future potentially exist in the now. And that we who are in the now are part of a river, a thread, a flow of time that defies easy distinctions; a gorgeous plurality of contexts.

There is, of course, a peace in this understanding of time: those we love who have gone onto another plane of existence are always potentially *here*, with us, and will continue to be in the world. Our existence is tied to the expanse of pasts, is a part of many possible futures.

★

Annah/s may well have belonged to these differing time tenses, or lack thereof, corresponding to hundreds of Indonesian spiritualities, belief systems from before contemporary nation-state configurations existed. Codified in language. I personally only understand what I know and live – an Islam understood with a bit of Kejawen (a Javanese manifestation of Islam, syncretic with so-called animism and other spiritual elements), Minangkabau spiritualities and the occasional foray into other spiritual worldviews that I find resonance in, that don't necessarily contradict my interpretation of Islam. Having loved ones of other religions than my own has only strengthened the need to understand all of our energies as not disparate, however you choose to understand that.

That distinct tenses hold no tensile strength in Indonesian, so to speak – or, one could say, that the possibility of all forms of time are contained within every Indonesian verb – is powerful. It is both a rejection and an expansion of time. What is expansive is the possibility in a single word of far more worldviews than the Western-imposed, masculinist, positivist thinking handed down from European Enlightenment about what is 'rational'; an understanding of rationality still used to tamp down indigenous cultures, to justify violence and theft. Words like 'supernatural', 'fantasy', 'science fiction', 'witchcraft' and 'the occult' have often been used to describe things that are generally thought to be fictional, non-existent – including concepts of transcending space and time, and spiritual presences that defy time distinctions. 'Magical realism' is used to describe some fiction, as though these 'magical realist' events are not very real for people with certain understandings of the world. This goes along with the denigration of many forms of spirituality, which persist despite genocidal attempts. As Lou Cornum wrote in a piece in *The New Inquiry* entitled 'White Magic', accusations of witchcraft were part of settler colonialism's tactics to decimate Indigenous and Black bodies in the Americas, as well as settler bodies deemed unruly. 'Actual witch hunts of the past such as the Salem witch trials followed from a fear of Indian women and their role in forms of governance alternative to those of the foundling country,' Cornum writes.

Yet Western, European-influenced science is now confirming what Indigenous communities around the world have known for hundreds of years: that plants have sentience for example, or that climate change could well revive long-dormant viruses. That intergenerational trauma can be passed down from body to body. However, there are those of us who eschew the need for Western science to prove something true and deeply significant to our communities – Indigenous, Black, brown, and Asian knowledges that have resisted decimation. Here there is an important distinction between the proliferation of fake news that is anti-science, which is a very real issue (for instance, climate change denial), and the instant denigration of Indigenous, Black, brown and Asian beliefs and worldviews about the natural world as fanciful, 'of the past', rather than timeless concepts of fundamental communal importance that have survived the continuing marks of genocide and colonialism. That have allowed us to survive, and are the keys to our continued survival.

Science has always been political. What counts as 'the truth' always is. So what the many planes that verbs without temporal tenses means to me is an acknowledgement of plurality of truths, of ways to feel at home in the world, of ways in which our relationships to plants, animals and each other exist not only in the here and now. And that people before us and after us knew, will know, of these relationships. There is a comfort in believing that all our ancestors' understandings of time and space, however met with destruction, live on in our soulbodies somehow – just as our flight or fight reactions today come from the ancient need for survival, chemical reactions as present now as they were when we first discovered how to make fire.

★

The late performance studies scholar José Esteban Muñoz writes about 'queering' time, envisioning queer futurities and notions of time beyond the usual strictures. I'd like to think he would love the Indonesian language's understanding of time as expansive and filled, potentially, with possibilities for different understandings of it, understandings beyond capitalist ones: non-linear notions of time.

In the performance installation I did at London's Institute of Contemporary Arts, entitled *Annah: Nomenclature*, I speak to various potential Annahs as various possible spirits who existed and persist. It felt real to me; it *was* real. Throughout the past fourteen years, these possible Annahs have felt so present. When an audience member told me afterwards that they, too, had felt Annah's presence in the room, it was all I could ask for.

So when we say that those who are departed are still with us, that we can feel them, this is a truth also found in and reinforced by our language. All the energy our ancestors created on this plane of existence lives on in how they changed us, in more publicly palpable material things they created or altered, but also according to understandings from myriad spiritualities and languages. Reclaiming this embodied knowledge may be as simple as understanding that our language – in my case, Indonesian – does not automatically nor easily translate into the supposedly distinct notions of past, present and future in English. That it contains larger truths: the speculative, the spiritual, the sacred, the bodily acknowledged. That it holds what is plainly felt and simultaneously hidden from a world that so often seeks to co-opt, to explain with harmful forms of rationality.

What is being acknowledged here is simultaneously subtle and ubiquitous, all-encompassing – a glowing, untranslatable patina of possibility. In language, and in the emotion it evokes, it is possible to be grounded in a comforting understanding of existence beyond oppressive notions of time and space. Here we know the peace and the comfort of justification for the spirits so many of us feel among, and for how we feel about existing as spirits in others' futures, in others' pasts. What frequently gets lost in English translation regarding the understanding of time can instead be saved, clung to, and understood as a gift – albeit one so vast as to be, fittingly, uncapturable. In this we can find a reminder of ancestral strength, as well as a warning: not to bend others' timelines and universes to fit the shape of our own.

★

We aren't numbers. We aren't Arabic numerals. We're colours, sounds, your pulse. And more. We've seen universes you haven't. And we live there. Why would we be simplified mathematical integer? We are moral philosophies you have no business bottling up to 'help others on their journey', people who couldn't name the communal biomes we come from, with free worldwide shipping.

I wrote and researched this book in scraps of time, jagged runs of compulsion, non-linear, non-continual. For writing about Annah is a fundamental revisitation of such gargantuan scales of trauma, and by gargantuan, I mean so all-pervasive that it invades your very mitochondria; by overwhelmingly large, I also mean minute, subatomic.

The fact that I often write about trauma, others' and my own, means that whether or not I write in English, I experience the words subconsciously as closer to Indonesian in the sense of time expanding. Trauma is remembered non-linearly, straddles time constraints, operates on an underworld agenda in which all clocks working with oppressive linearity go awry – to protect us, to get us to trust our innate, often denigrated as 'nonsensical', understanding of time first.

And this is part of how you saved yourselves, Annah/s. Their very language cannot wrap itself around you. When a single word in Bahasa Indonesia cannot be translated just one way in Dutch or French or English, whether it's in terms of time tenses, or in describing you as singular or plural, or in terms of gender – for our verbs are not gendered, our pronoun gender-neutral, and any singular noun in Indonesian can also be read as plural – they will never be able to definitively say that they are telling a universal truth. Such a truth, after all, does not exist. The imperialist project is doomed to forever fail. And whilst we are looking at the rubble underneath such grandiose pronouncements of 'truth', you exist an escapee from all the nonsensical manoeuvrings of your captors. Whether or not you were hurt by Gauguin physically – as however likely such hurt was, there is always the possibility you were not hurt – the unequivocal insistence that you were an unhurt (or unharmable) being, in love with him, would hurt deeply. Hurt accumulated over each year of the century.

Their concepts of space-time are rubble to the ground that the earth would not respect. In marronage, you gathered all your possible selves together and cloaked your truths in the vastness of other truths – the truths of how narrow and laughable colonial 'facts' ultimately are. Their records are nonsense. And you know that any writing about you, including my own, any portrayal of you in the future, will never be your life or lives. You own your own truths. You always have. The lie in your enslavement is exposed by this fundamental, unassailable truth: you owned your selves. You always will. And so, as formerly or currently enslaved, will we own our selves.

*

we'll let you guys prophesize
we gon see the future first

—Frank Ocean, 'Nikes', *Blond(e)*

The singer Frank Ocean's second studio album, released 2016, is spelled *Blond* or *Blond(e)* – and thus is both. At the same time. An ambiguity that has been called culture-jamming, a mocking of uniform corporate labelling.

I have always thought of *Blond(e)* as akin to Annah/s. Or, I should perhaps say, Anna/h/s.

'Annah' is the name given to a girl in France, so Vollard said: given to her by French people. In French, the 'h' on the end of such a name is silent.

However, in Bahasa Indonesia and Boso Jowo and many other Indonesian languages (there are over seven hundred in the archipelago), the 'h' is pronounced. Hard. Like 'ach' for Anglophones. If I shift into my Bahasa Indonesia personhood from ever-enveloping English, I pronounce the 'h' in Annah. In Indonesian and Boso Jowo, the 'h' is hard, so for it to be a silent one in French for that name means Frenchfolk's Annah is spelled Anna in many Indonesian languages (using the Latin alphabet, of course, which is all-encroaching).

Finally, I realise what has been right there in front of me, known in my bones, perhaps realised at some point and forgotten, as painful things sometimes make themselves helpful by being forgotten.

Even when we pronounce 'Annah' as 'Anna' instead of as 'Annach', we are part of the linguistic system binding Annah histories – one that marked them as colonial property. I myself have to remind myself to say Annach, but then also, when I do say Anna, I console myself by thinking that perhaps the spelling the child/ren would have wanted *was* Anna. After all, the infinite possibilities of them, and so on, et cetera.

The ambiguity of spelling and pronouncing Anna/h/s is sui generis culture-jamming. We cannot be claimed. You can never be claimed. And the more they claim to have you, to define you, the freer you are, just by knowing yourself to be other than their property. Knowing yourself to be whole universes of otherwise.

This very particular consistency and the attendant inconsistency of every other 'fact' in various accounts of Anna/h/s are a mirror of how the French colonial state self-polices its norms, even after the supposed end date of colonialism, a violent force we know continues into the present. Yet it is unable to police the language of Anna/h/s – the pronunciation, the number/s of, the time-space location.

Anna/h/s, in these ways, in the possibilities for spiritual protection in afterlife or afterlives, you have always been free. It is you who have taught me this.

how do you write history
in a language that has
no past tense?

—Ko Ko Thett

The answer is: in so many ways. The answer is: vastly beyond the scope of their imagination, an escape hatch for all of ours.

There is the possibility of pain in every picture, and therefore the possibility of escape. If they think you're not pained, and you were, it means that in a way you are not beholden to their stories, you have escaped their truths by being your own.

You have always already escaped.

You don't need to tell anyone where you are, who you are, when you are.

You exist as possibilities. You roam universes, including possible universes where the horrors of imperialism, in every form, truly do exist in the past and are not forgotten. And realms where they never existed in the first place.

There is a place for all of you, I promise. There is a space that none of us on earth have been made privy to, where your marronage spits fire in the face of likely hurts. Where you do not constantly have to explain your pains or hide them. Where existing is brisk and calm, both, easy, a resting, a flow, a movement, a loving of those you love who are near you and reciprocating in this possible universe. A universe where Javanese cultures do not in turn dominate others, where cycles deemed endless come to an end.

ANNAH #0.000000015 ATTENDS THE FIRST INDONESIAN WOMEN'S CONGRESS, IN 1928

I was never summoned into slavery by a brutal white woman 'creative' on the other side of the world. I was never given to a man known to take and take too much. Can you even imagine?

I was kept safe as anyone could keep a child under our weights, even as an orphan, by a coterie of aunties, by grandmothers. My Bu Des and Tantes, my Eyangs, sewed stories onto my back that I have taken with me.

I am here now, as an adult in this meeting place, where other women beam inside their sarungs and dresses. We pay no mind to the Dutch. We are against polygamy and forced marriage. We speak many different languages and dialects. We carry within us the sense-memory of having been many different genders, not the slight binary that colonies have beaten into us. Some of us love each other in more ways than one.

Our ideas will survive.

They can never undo our lives, and then give us charity and 'empowerment' in the form of aid money we are dependent on. They can never erase these many meetings. They can never claim, as slavers, that they invented what it feels like for a woman to feel free.

In 1965, I will be in my eighties, and live to see the flourishing of my sisters, my daughters.

They can never murder our faith in each other.

Can you even imagine.

Did you see the diagrams in that earlier session? Such attention to detail. And that one cerulean fan in the hands of the Mbak over there, the way the light hits from the window – a joy!

CHAPTER SIX:
THREATENING SYSTEMS OF DURESS

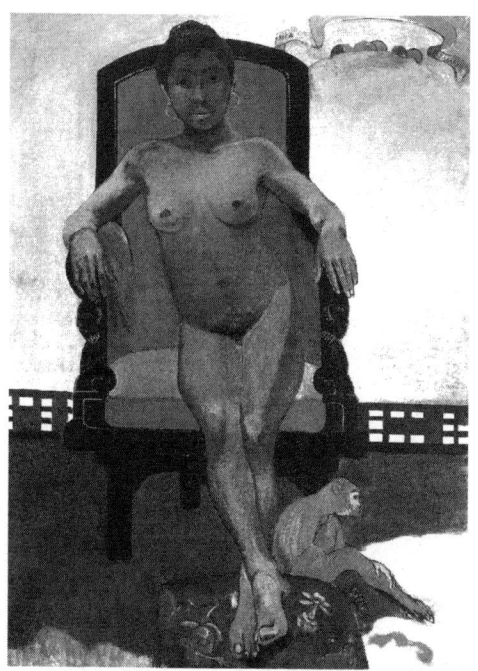

[Paul Gauguin, *Annah the Javanese*, or *Aita Tamari Vahine Judith te Parari* (The Child-Woman Judith Is Not Yet Breached), 1893–94. Oil on canvas, 45 1/4 x 31 1/2 in. (116 x 81 cm). Private Collection.[8] Painting of a naked child on a chair, their hair in a bun, their ankles crossed, arms on the chair. Monkey at their feet.]

---

8 Caption from Mathews, 2001: p.199.

Seorang pejuang harus bisa menahan resiko, apapun yang terjadi...
Seorang pejuang harus bisa melaluinya.
[A fighter has to be able to take risks, no matter what happens...
A fighter must be able to get through it all.]

> – Nurma, a West Sumatran woman whose family suffered during the Soeharto dictatorship, quoted and translated by Yenny Narny

The possibility of Annah being in pain, and of *Annah la Javanaise* being a painting of a child in pain, is an outcome of Annah/s being in situations where they were deeply vulnerable to harm, isolated and only in the company of older Parisians who did not see them as human. There are systems that collude to make this so. I present to you four.

They are all in the following quote from a text written by Ambroise Vollard, Gauguin's art dealer, published in 1936.

> An opera singer, Mme Nina Pack, was on friendly terms with a rich banker who had business relations with the traders of the Malayan Isles. The singer happened to say before the representative of one of these, 'I would like to have a little negro girl.' A few months later a policeman brought Mme Nina Pack a young, half-breed, half-Indian, half-Malayan, who had been found wandering about the Gare de Lyon. She had a label hung around her neck, with the inscription: *Mme Nina Pack, rue de la Rochefoucauld, á Paris. Envoi de Java.* She was given the name of Anna. Some time later, in consequence of a little domestic drama in which Anna was implicated, she was dismissed. She came to me, as I had known her at her employer's house, to ask me to find her a good situation. I judged her qualifications as a housemaid to be very middling, and thought she stood more chance of succeeding as a model. I told Gauguin about her.

'Send her to me. I'll try her,' he said.

Anna pleased him, and he kept her.

I repeat Vollard's words here in full, to highlight how shockingly immediate the connection is between the institutions mentioned above, then and now. How Annah became a likely indentured servant and likely abused child, and how there is a direct link between the structures that imperilled Annah/s and imperilment of majority world people today, who include disabled children. For these are all, ultimately, the same interlocking systems of white supremacist, ableist, capitalist oppression.

The institutions in question are:

(1) The international finance and banking system: the banker who worked in the 'Malayan Isles' who allegedly facilitated Annah's capture, transport to Paris and ultimate abandonment to further slavers;

(2) State and institutional violence: Annah was allegedly found and brought to Nina Pack by a policeman, and policemen allegedly watched on as Annah, a child, became a slave under Nina Pack, and was then sent to live with Gauguin, surrounded by European male painters;

(3) The arts: Pack, Vollard and their coterie, including Gauguin;

(4) The international 'development' industry: this was formed in the wake of decolonisation, and was not present in the 1890s. However, its existence is extremely important in conjunction with the other three interlinked structures, in the contemporary world of neoliberal globalisation within which *Annah la Javanaise* circulates.

Each of these structures relates to memories and materialities, of Annahs past and also Annahs present. Each creates debility and vulnerability to suffering for Black, brown, Asian and Indigenous adults and children, children who continue to be treated as Annahs were.

It feels like an overwhelming task to summarise the entirety of what Annah's potential painedness represents, the thread of duress into the present – from their pain to that of others now living. The point is that it is impossible to describe, that it is infinite how many ways one can describe this thread.

I think about all the forms of resistance to socioecological crisis that are currently and have been underway in Indonesia, all the people whom Annah/s's bodies represent: the vagueness, as I've written, of the term 'la Javanaise' encompassing all brown people with feminine characteristics. The majority of the world, with our infinite number of experiences, thousands of languages and cultures, many at risk, subsumed into one non-specific category. I think of all the ways we could be pained, for all kinds of reasons, many reasons imposed by other bodies, whether cancer epidemics from pollution that stems from industry lobbying, land grab for factories to destroy women farmers' lands – as is the threat currently in Kendeng, Java, Indonesia, and a vast number of other locales – carelessness and disrespect for human lives that are, like Annah, seen as objects, accessories, incapable of pain.

The task before us, to undo these structures, seems to stretch out to the very edges of our canvasses of existence. The first step, it feels to my small self, must be to recognise these monoliths in order to plan any attempts at dismantling. This recognition need not be in the form of writing out their names – this recognition, in homage to Annah/s, can be and is felt at the cellular level by those of us who have been, who are, who are most likely to be, entrapped. The recognition of these four structures and violence by them is a bodily kept series of emotions, enacted by the flesh, with flesh-felt impacts.

STATE VIOLENCE AND MONEYBANKS

As an Indonesian citizen raised by activist parents, I grew up understanding how enmeshed neoliberal capitalism is with genocide in Indonesia. I've known, since the age of at least eight or nine, that the state was capable of mass murder, and that the Western-backed genocide of 1965–66 led to the disappearance and murder of activists and to capitalist expansion.

What happens to Annah/s is also interlinked with the legacy of this genocide: the mass slaughter, abuse, imprisonment and suppression of artists, activists and other civilians that began then, but continued throughout the thirty-three years of Soeharto's dictatorship, a regime installed by the genocide (which itself was blamed on the Indonesian Communist Party); the ongoing genocide in Papua, as a direct result of US interests and backing.

I address the genocide again here because of the fundamental importance of 1965–66 in all the socioecological crises that have happened since, and to the four institutions I've listed above. Simply put, the genocide was an instrument of the Cold War, and wiped out alternatives to a capitalism that has continued to decimate the fourth most populous country in the world. Recall that the Indonesian Women's Movement – which, even under colonialism, had been working to imagine and bring about new socio-economic structures – was specifically targeted by post-genocide New Order propaganda in an attempt to terrify generations of women away from Indonesian feminisms. With the World Bank and International Monetary Fund imposing structural adjustment loans that create huge debt, and neoliberal economics that destroy public welfare, Indonesia is among the many countries that have been 'underdeveloped' due to policies enforced by Bretton Woods institutions: the World Bank, the International Monetary Fund (IMF) and the World Trade Organization (WTO).

This neoliberal encroachment ranges from the world's largest gold mine – the Freeport-McMoRan mine in the Indonesian-occupied province of West Papua, protected by the military, seeding violence and deathly pollution for locals – to Trump's resort-building in Bali, presumably in ignorance of how the island is the site of mass graves as much as rich culture (if any thought at all is given to Balinese culture), a place where farmers' paddy fields are being bought by foreign investors, where ties to the land, sea, rivers are spiritual, yet have been glossed over in favour of tourists flocking to re-enact Elizabeth Gilbert's *Eat, Pray, Love*.

'I want to go someplace where I can marvel at something,' says Julia Roberts in the cinematic adaptation of Gilbert's book. What is marvelled over, objectified, includes Indonesian, Balinese people and their lands and waters. There is a throughline of violence via visuality that reaches to European colonialism and even before, and the violent marks of Soeharto's dictatorship, which continue to this very day, are a part of this imperial continuation.

Among these forms of New Order-era duress are the politics of remembrance and forgetfulness, and here I focus particularly on the Indonesian women's movement. Violence against women did not stop with the 1965–66 genocide, far from it. The labour organiser Marsinah was ▇▇▇ and killed during the New Order era, alongside many other instances of sexual and physical violence against women instigated by the government. Leftists continued to be 'disappeared', including poet Wiji Thukul in 1998, the year Soeharto was ousted. Brutalities continued to occur everywhere since the genocide, including in Aceh, Papua, East Timor, and were enforced by a governing and societal culture in which a warped interpretation of Javaneseness was used to dominate others.

Banned art included songs such as 'Genjer-Genjer', a proletarian song composed by Muhammad Arief about the titular plant that Javanese people were forced to eat to survive under Japanese occupation. The tune was tied by the New Order to Communist women and banned for decades, a song that my musician friends still face opposition in performing in Indonesia. I've sung this song in a number of artistic works, including in performance installation *Annah: Nomenclature*, commissioned by and performed at London's Institute of Contemporary Arts in 2018.

In an otherwise positive review of *Annah: Nomenclature* published in *ArtAsiaPacific*, a white, male reviewer wrote that I needed to delve more deeply into the 1965–66 genocide, and that it was a shame I hadn't, as this was important. He was not, of course, aware of the multiple inflections of my visual and song choices. The songs in the performance were not merely children's songs or lullabies, as he had written: each contained political subtext. Indonesian viewers, who approached me after the show, understood and appreciated these, that they carry deep meaning if you know our histories. The reviewer was not aware of the very real fear I had to break through to even sing 'Genjer-Genjer', as a woman who had grown up in the New Order, who was at that time in the UK scholarship-funded by an Indonesian government still ruled by so many New Order shadows. The past is now, and is embodied. The review of *Annah: Nomenclature* reminded me that even my own embodied trauma and artistic catharsis may be distorted on a mass scale through the lens of white male 'experts'. I mention this because I want to emphasise the many, at times 'minute', forms of cultural violence linked to the politics of 1965–66 remembrance, in this case in the reception of work I have created about Annah/s. For Annah/s.

This is a form of what Havi Carel and Ian James Kidd call 'testimonial injustice', which I experience repeatedly as a disabled, racialised migrant woman. In the case of the review of *Annah: Nomenclature*, my testimony of pain's possibility in Annah/s as related to the genocide is denigrated as insufficient. This is because my womanhood, my race, my nationality and my disabled, chronically ill and chronically pained status, as well as the cripping and anti-colonial perspectives in my art, are all factors linked to what Carel and Kidd call 'the presumptive attribution of characteristics like cognitive unreliability and emotional instability that downgrade the credibility of [...] testimonies'.

All of this discrediting, you may imagine, contributes to why I was compelled to write this book, as a pained person who has been repeatedly disbelieved about my own body over more than a decade. Though other Indonesians understood my hermeneutics of Indonesian cultural cues – such as the choice of songs to sing, and the exact moments in which I chose to sing them, against specifically determined visual backdrops in my installation film – that these cues even existed is negated by a white male reviewer's perception of truth.

Though much academic work has been written on Indonesia's legacies and ongoing violence, this remains a 'niche' endeavour in Western scholarship, and is still dominated by the work of US scholars. This is because Southeast Asian studies, for instance, are still regarded as 'area studies', unrelated to the US. Also at play is a lack of translation of scholarship from Indonesia, Vietnam and elsewhere. This means injustice for Southeast Asian scholars, who are expected to write in English for a 'global' audience, yet whose countries' universities have not had the financial means, over the past several decades, to subscribe to academic journal networks. This contributes to how the 1965–66 genocide in Indonesia, as well as its antecedents and aftermath, are not common knowledge in Western countries – despite the West's crucial role in it. This is in itself a form of cultural imperialism, including cultural memory imperialism.

State violence, of course, did not begin with the 1965–66 genocide, which I count as part of imperialism's persistence; as mentioned, the Western backers of this genocide are also complicit in colonialism, and the need to exploit Indonesian resources stems from the capitalist imperatives of colonialism. The New Order itself *is* a manifestation of colonialism from the Cold War era, of neoliberal capitalism seeing Indonesia as a marketplace and site for resource extraction – the basis of colonialism.

In fact, as researcher and writer Flavia Dzodan writes of her firsthand research:

> (T)he Dutch East Indies Company was the first global corporation to actually create racial categories and taxonomies […] I was poring through the cargo manifests of their vessels and you can see how they created taxonomies of cargo were [sic] enslaved human beings were named 'pieces' and listed alongside 'x pounds of coffee' for example".

Annahs' supposed origins are all colonies, all imperially controlled *markets*. Crucially, they are all places regarded today as 'emerging markets', a title that serves nothing if not 'developed countries'' sense of self-regard as ones to imitate at all costs.

Incidentally, a cornerstone event in the history of decolonisation as emancipatory movements was the 1955 Asian-African Conference, comprised of nation-states in the Non-Aligned

Movement. Held in the city of Bandung, West Java, it was a touchstone of cooperation between African and Asian peoples. Ten years after this in Indonesia came genocide, and the instalment of Soeharto by the CIA and its allies, which allowed the mass exploitation of Indonesian resources, including land grabs under the New Order in a way that echoed colonial policies and served the Indonesian oligarchy and their wealthy foreign corporate allies.

Everyone benefitting from the fruits of capitalism, all of us, are embroiled in geographer Kathryn Yusoff's notion of 'banal violence', in which everyday acts contribute to extinctions elsewhere in the world. However, I venture that the notion of what is experienced as 'banal' depends on Ahmed's 'stickiness' of emotions, contributing to how empathy for another group is formed or not. For instance, as an Indonesian, I am conscious that palm oil plantations contribute to death, illness and homeland destruction, even those plantations marked as 'sustainable', as these too come from land grabs from indigenous populations. The violence of a candy bar containing palm oil, even when sold in London, is less 'banal' for me. I picture children back home and try to think twice, though it has been made difficult to do so.

Principles of white supremacy also contribute to 'habitat destruction' not including violence towards indigenous and other peoples in areas that are deemed 'nature', and to the diminishing of other Southeast Asian genocides, such as Pol Pot's Cambodian massacre. The neoliberal capitalist political economy, as an outgrowth of white supremacy, is truly as global in scope as its colonial antecedents, and continues the notion that those not deemed white are less than human, less capable of pain.

All of these harms are perpetuated by state violence protecting the interests of the international finance and banking system that employs hyperextraction of human labour and human lives, lands and waters to service the neoliberal white supremacist ableist capitalist system.

It behooves us to remember that Gauguin was, at one point, a stockbroker.

THE INTERNATIONAL 'DEVELOPMENT' INDUSTRY AND THE ART MARKET

The international development industry and the international art market may seem unlikely bedfellows. However, they both inscribe the overarching ideology of ableist white supremacist capitalism in ways that are not so different – and part of the success of this inscription of ideology is that the constructs of international 'development' and the art market are made to seem separate, unrelated. Yet they both prescribe the role of majority world children in the white supremacist capitalist ableist world order, serving the same overarching system of neoliberal economics and white supremacy. Both are serving the same people, and the success of both sectors, working in concert, is evident in pain for Annah/s being cast in doubt.

The international art market is a collection of mechanisms intent on keeping the monetary value of *Annah la Javanaise* (among other paintings and art objects) high, its collector's name hidden, and Gauguin's legacy unbesmirched. In *Talking Prices: Symbolic Meanings of Prices on the Market for Contemporary Art*, Olav Velthuis writes that

> markets are, apart from anything else, cultural constellations. Like any other type of social interaction, market exchange is highly ritualized; it involves a wide variety of symbols that transfer rich meanings between people who exchange goods with each other.

> These people are connected through ties of different sorts, whose emergence, maintenance, and possible decay involve complex social processes.

In the face of these relationships' possible decay, the 'stickiness' of emotions, of empathy towards Gauguin and lack of empathy towards Annah/s keep art dealer, auction house, collector, museums, libraries belonging to museums or universities, educators and the average person acquainted with Gauguin all in agreement. All perpetuating the same mythos of the artist's work in relation to Annah/s as benign and even edifying.

Not long ago, I was asked to describe my work by a literary colleague, who then proceeded to tell me all about his trip to the most recent Tate exhibit of Gauguin. 'But Gauguin […] is he just bad, is he?' this colleague asked in earnest, before continuing to describe the artist's printmaking work. 'Bad' here refers to Gauguin as abuser of women and children. So strong are these emotions of reverence and congeniality towards a *specific version* of the legacy of Gauguin as genius, so difficult to mar is it, that even the clear equivocation that he was an abuser sparks only mild wavering.

The 'groundbreaking genius' version of Gauguin is one that has obfuscated his violations, and upholds the myth that his work is of *intrinsic value and betterment* to the intellect, to the morals. Understanding Gauguin's work to be morally edifying operates as a sign of one's 'civilisation'. It is the mark of white supremacy, of imperialism, that the cogs of the machine run so smoothly, that a criminal's work can be hallowed as edification; that the artist's tactics of dehumanisation, that I perceive so clearly as a disabled, Minang-Javanese woman, are deemed impossible.

The impetus for this is to protect the wealth and clout of those who profit from the circulation of *Annah la Javanaise*. Velthuis finds that prices themselves have emotional and social value in the contemporary art market, that a high price is a symbol of pride for artist, owner, dealer, compared to a previously low price. 'Culture is *restraining* in economic life insofar as cultural values co-determine which types of goods can be exchanged, which social and cultural contexts are legitimate for conducting this exchange, and which business practices this exchange should be accompanied by', he writes. This includes, Velthuis says, the white-walled architecture of Western art galleries over the past sixty years, a deviation from which would cost a gallery its reputation.

So when we speak about the contemporary art market enabling – legitimising – the perception of *Annah la Javanaise*, the perception of Annah/s who lived, as in alignment with the notion of Gauguin's 'genius' rather than a work of horrific child exploitation, we are speaking of multitudinous overlapping social and material practices, including but not limited to the architecture of galleries, the clothes worn during business meetings between art dealer and collector, business card and website copy, and textbooks in which Gauguin's exploitation of young girls is excused and rationalised. All of these social habits and particularities have been maintained since 1893–94 to keep this painting's value high. That is at least 131 years of behaviour, thoughts, words written, numbers tallied, upholding power structures, ensuring value for *Annah la Javanaise*.

Meanwhile, globally exploitative corporations like BP sponsor art exhibitions in the West, directly connecting the art market to the destruction of majority world people's biomes, via an array of ongoing, disastrous corporate behaviour, including that which resulted in the Deepwater Horizon oil spill. BP is one of 200 publicly traded companies controlling most coal, oil and gas reserves, that continues the colonial ravaging of peoples and places and is the foundation of climate crisis. Warren B. Kanders, previously vice chair of the board of the Whitney Museum of American

Art (he was made to resign in 2019), owns the company Safariland, which trades in tear gas deployed at Standing Rock, in Ferguson and Palestine, as well as in handcuffs, body armour, batons and other military equipment to the Israeli 'Defence' Force, the NYPD and others. This tear gas has killed and/or injured Black, brown and Indigenous people – including children – who are already vulnerable to debility.

In James Ferguson's 1990 book *The Anti-Politics Machine: 'Development', Depoliticization, and Bureaucratic Power in Lesotho*, he details a process of 'development work' that has not changed in the thirty-five years since the work's publication. Ferguson describes how 'development' workers in Lesotho falsely misrepresent the region as 'isolated' and ahistorical, and impose programmes on it that implement dependence on an unequal global market system, with no understanding of the local political and socioeconomic systems already in place. If a place has no history, no rich, pre-existing socioeconomic system, or a system deemed 'primitive' and moot, it is thus economic 'Terra Nullius', a land where the people have nothing, so the exploitative 'free' market can be imposed in the name of uplifting them. They can be stolen from – to better their lives, of course, to 'develop' them. (So, too can profoundly sophisticated non-western art be deemed 'primitive' and freely stolen from.)

This is a process which has been exacerbated in scope and intensity as a part of late-stage capitalism's global hegemony. Ferguson writes:

> Like 'civilization' in the nineteenth century, 'development' is the name not only for a value, but also for a dominant problematic or interpretive grid through which the impoverished regions of the world are known to us… Poor countries are by definition 'less developed'.

The issue with this teleology is, of course, that so-called 'poor countries' are not inherently poor but have been ravaged by colonial resource extraction. This extraction is perpetuated by structural adjustment policies implemented by Bretton Woods institutions, which keep so-called 'developing countries' in perpetual debt.

The Belgium-based Committee for the Abolition of Illegitimate Debt writes the following of Africa, also applicable to Asia, Latin America and other regions deemed 'developing':

> Africa Is Rich [...] Africa is not poor. Whilst many people in African countries live in poverty, the continent has considerable wealth. A key problem is that the rest of the world, particularly Western countries, are extracting far more than they send back. Meanwhile, they are pushing economic models that fuel poverty and inequality, often in alliance with African elites.

Walter Rodney's *How Europe Underdeveloped Africa* (1972) and Andre Gunder Frank's *The Development of Underdevelopment* (1966), both of which show how far back in history the institutionalisation of 'development' from the intrinsic condition of 'poverty' are presented as fact, instead of as colonially imposed falsehood, are as relevant today as they have ever been. Frank asserts that 'underdeveloped' regions are not inherently lacking in capital or resources, but have been deprived of their resources by capitalist extraction. Using Brazil as an example, he found that places that were the target of 'development' policies were made 'into internal colonial satellites, de-capitalized them further, and consolidated or even deepened their underdevelopment'. Similarly, Rodney's work focusses on how European colonisation stole resources from Africa for centuries, an extractivism which is replicated to this day by unequal trade practices forced on poor countries in the name of 'development'.

This is in contrast to how 'development' organisations' visual media, and the news media, reinscribe the notion that 'underdevelopment' is an inherent, ahistorical state of affairs for countries of the majority world and for underserved communities in the so-called Global North. These places have rich, varied and specific histories, all affected in various and minute ways by the ongoing processes of colonisation and industrialisation of the last centuries. Within my home country of Indonesia alone are hundreds of cultures, languages, gender dynamics and conceptualisations of pain, violence, suffering, poverty, joy, community. The logic of 'development', however, in which various apparati of the rich – including but not limited to the IMF, the World Bank, the UN, various charities and INGOS – impose paternalistic programmes on poor communities, requires that these specificities be either ignored or exploited to impose the violences of global financial capitalism.

These are dynamics I've witnessed myself, including as a former aid worker in the Office of the UN Recovery Coordinator for Aceh and Nias (UNORC), in a job that required monitoring of foreign aid and development activities in the tsunami- and war-stricken province of Aceh, Indonesia. In the wake of the 2004 Indian Ocean tsunami, many foreign aid organisations pledged contributions to Aceh, and the immediacy of the emergency meant that virtually every offer of aid was accepted by the Indonesian government. Aid packages were often implemented with no understanding of local socioenvironmental and political histories and circumstances, nor exit strategies. By 2006, when I began working for UNORC, many had pulled out without transition plans for their served populations, some with schools still half-built and many corrupt building practices unchecked. Boats were delivered by European aid that proved unusable by local fishermen. In the case of Aceh, the 2004 tsunami prompted a ceasefire between the Indonesian government and the Acehnese resistance, but the government required that foreign aid not be given to those affected by the conflict. Because foreign aid post-tsunami had to purposely ignore the decades-long civil war that had occurred in the province, many whose lives had been destroyed by the war complained, for instance, of not getting the new house that their nearby neighbour had, simply because their house had been destroyed by war and not natural disaster.

Where visuality and ocularcentrism pervade, so too do hegemonic ideals through them. The development agency CARE runs an online advert, which captions a photo of a Black child facing the camera as follows: 'Celine dreams of being a doctor. Find out how to make her dreams come true.' Artefacts such as these are continually inscribing and reinscribing, alongside marketing copy, a white saviour gaze that endangers the children being depicted, renders their parents' and kin's involvement moot, and works to institute white supremacist ableist capitalism. In this way, the 'development' industry and the art market both perpetuate the circulation of images of young, majority world children that uphold ableist white supremacy.

A nuanced view of painedness and potential painedness does not exist in mass media, let alone nuanced portrayals of potentially pained people in 'developing countries', because simplistic notions of 'suffering' as caused by being from and in a developing country persist through 'development industry' tropes. The compulsion of viewers of news media to relate emotionally to distant sufferers are refracted through these ableist, colonialist tropes, and these same viewers are asked to donate to INGOs, and the cycle continues.

This is not a coincidence – the more images that objectify young, majority world children in a 'developmentalist' narrative, in the media or in public transport ads, the more the Annah/s of *Annah la Javanaise* and the muses of similar artefacts in circulation in the art market are seen as not children. *Annah la Javanaise* and Celine of the CARE ad are in dialogue with each other. The location of each child is hazy, and unnecessary to the overarching goal of the context in which they are portrayed – once again, it does not matter what colony they are from, let alone what part of that colony they are from, as long as they are from a colony. A colony inherently in need of 'development'.

It is important to me that the international 'development' industry and the fine art market, both undergirded by white supremacist capitalist expansion, are understood as being part of the same financial system, the same global market. The hypocrisy of white supremacy with regards to visual images becomes clear when one juxtaposes 'Celine dreams of being a doctor' with an *Annah la Javanaise* image because the former asks Western, white saviours to supposedly contribute to the wellbeing of a child, while the same population is prompted to admire an artefact of very likely child abuse as 'fine art'. Furthermore, this is all part of a systemic economy that actively supports this splitting of affect – for instance, via a detective series on western TV in which the viewer is encouraged to feel rightful empathy for victims who are young (mostly white) women and girls, versus museum settings where visual work that depicts Annah/s is structured towards empathy for Gauguin and his ilk, the perpetrators rather than those affected.

A typical 'development' ad is meant to contribute to the extractive, exploitative system of 'development' by infantilising billions of people. The profits from this system go towards the richest of society, who, as Olav Velthuis wrote, since the 1970s have been investing increasingly in what is now known as the fine art market. These financial logics form the framework of a system that keeps art markets operating according to notions of art as commodity, and art about women by Western 'geniuses' – such as the painting *Annah la Javanaise* – more recognisable and revered than art that was actually created *by* brown women in what is now Indonesia over millennia. It is the same framework that keeps Indonesian antiquities housed in the British Museum.

If we consider prices as emotional, social artefacts, what is the price of 'sponsoring' a child meant to signify emotionally, and to whom? What does the price of a painting like *Annah la Javanaise* signify emotionally, and to whom? What is the value of a brown child presenting as a girl in these different contexts, and how are these values set?

What if these children, Celine, Annah/s and others like them, were disabled? What would be the monetary value embedded in these images, in an overarching white supremacist ableist heteropatriarchal capitalist system? What is the price of 'helping a disabled child' in a development ad, in which disability is seen as complete lack of agency, contributing to the overall developmentalist narrative of people in the 'developing country' having a lack of agency, in need of Western aid to 'progress' and 'develop'?

In her book *Postcolonial Fiction and Disability: Exceptional Children, Metaphor and Materiality*, Clare Barker states that a specific 'combination of individualization, narrativization and sentimentality is strategically deployed in images of disabled "poster children"'. What 'happened' to the disabled child – with the ableist notion that neurodivergence and bodily non-normativity always 'happen' – is tied up with what will happen to the nation.

Of course, that a disabled child could be anything other than a victim is not even considered a possibility in these developmentalist narratives, in which development signifies not only 'what happens next to this child?' but 'what happens next to this country?'.

★

If Vollard's account was accurate, opera singer Nina Pack caused every bit of suffering Annah/s could have received in France. She is a clear example of white women's active part and complicity in the dehumanisation of majority world children, especially disabled children, including complicity by white women in the arts. Ambroise Vollard too, of course, represents the arts' role here – not only did he share, in large part, responsibility for the enormous success of Gauguin's work and mythos, he also enabled and boosted the careers of Vincent van Gogh, Paul Cézanne, Pierre-Auguste Renoir and Pablo Picasso, among others. The quote at the start of this chapter illustrates that Vollard, in his own account and judged according to many people's personal ethics and subjectivities today, was a child trafficker.

According to Vollard, Nina Pack, a white opera singer, *asked for* a girl, without even a specific 'job description'. This is slavery – asking for a body to do whatever one wishes, with no guarantee of their safety or return. You can Google 'Nina Pack' and find her face in an online gallery, purporting the pioneering nature of women in the arts. Nowhere is she reviled as slaver of a young, brown child.

If Vollard's account is true, Annah was a slave, and *any* historical account of their involvement with Gauguin is an account of a violent act. And stories in which they escape are those of marronage, or escape from slavery.[9] Annah's story is far from unique in the landscape of Indonesian slave histories: slavery is a deeply pervasive yet underdiscussed aspect of Dutch colonialism in Indonesia, and persisted for over two centuries.

---

9 I thank Aditi Jaganathan for first associating the word 'marronage' with Annah/s for me, when she facilitated the Q and A following the *Annah: Nomenclature* performance installation in 2018.

Slaves interpreted as female were deliberately characterised as deviant, deeply reminiscent of how Annah/s are characterised. Karen Williams writes in her excellent piece 'Slave narratives from Dutch colonisation in Indonesia':

> Asian slaves were critical to the functioning of Batavia, and the mixed-race women who partnered the Dutch men have passed into colonial legend, being characterised as vicious, lascivious, indolent and spoilt. Soldiers' ballads and letters from that time constantly refer insultingly to availability of 'black women' (the enslaved Asian women) in Batavia. Enslaved Asian women were used largely within the colonial households, meaning that they were vulnerable to almost unfettered ▄▄▄ by their enslavers. As a measure against 'lasciviousness', the early Batavian governments had at times tried to limit the number of women slaves per household, particularly of unmarried Dutch men. What was understood, but not stated, in this context, was the premise that the women were ▄▄▄ enslaved.

In 'Fugitive Women: Slavery and Social Change in Early Modern Southeast Asia', historian Eric A. Jones writes of women slaves in the eighteenth century who escaped:

> As long as slavery has existed, so too have fugitive slaves, and the reasons behind both phenomena are as varied as the nature of human bondage itself. In Batavia [now Jakarta], headquarters of the Dutch East India Company (Vereenigde Oost-Indische Compagnie, VOC), some ran away because of physically abusive mistresses.

Again, this is a reminder of white colonial complicity by women in other women's and children's bondage. Lack of protection for millions of Indonesian migrant domestic workers, resulting in exploitation and human trafficking, including ill treatment by women employers in wealthier situations, is a contemporary problem whose antecedents are the treatment of children like Annah/s. It is also prudent to remember that the lack of emergence of narratives of Annah as child slave is very much tied to present-day France being 'a nation where talking about race, colonialism, and slavery (not to mention their interconnections) remains taboo', as sociologist Crystal Marie Fleming writes. The elision of white women's past and current complicity in colonialism is where you will find Nina Pack's perfume lingers.

When, in 2018, the abuse of people affected by the 2010 earthquake in Haiti by Oxfam staff became public knowledge, the historian Mary Beard published the following tweet: 'Of course one can't condone the (alleged) behaviour of Oxfam staff in Haiti and elsewhere. But I do wonder how hard it must be to sustain 'civilised' values in a disaster zone. And overall I still respect those who go in to help out, where most of us wd not tread.' Beard responded to criticism of this comment with a photo of herself crying, which in turn reinforced the supremacist nature of the tweet by appealing to ingrained racist notions of white women's feelings being put above those of the affected Black children. As Sita Balani astutely points out, Oxfam staff 'withheld the aid they were there to deliver to bargain for sex. The widespread sexual exploitation is made possible precisely because it comes with the moral cover of "aid" and "charity".' Yet, in Beard's account, as is so often the case, widespread images of Black, brown, Asian and Indigenous children are framed according to 'development' agencies' notions of harm as innate to their location, citizenship and identity, rather than as targets of harm by such agencies. Again, the images of children who are harmed by colonisers are twisted into another meaning entirely, their harm diminished. The tears publicised are those of a white woman who claims those harmed are 'uncivilised', living in a place 'where *most of us* would not tread' (emphasis mine) – yet we who are born in and claim residence in what many call the Global South are, in fact, the global majority.

It is overwhelming to describe the ways in which *Annah la Javanaise* symbolises the masking of violence against billions of majority world people throughout colonial history, in which I count the present day. I wanted to write this chapter as a litany of numbers, of numerical evidence of oppression: the numbers of children abused at the hands of development workers and UN peacekeepers, the hundreds of thousands of children who have died early deaths from pollution, who were deemed unimportant – who died, for instance, from pesticides in Papuan palm oil plantation land marked as 'green', as 'conservation areas', after this land was stolen from native peoples. The more than 17,400 brutally murdered Palestinian children at this stage of the genocide, at the time of writing this sentence, children who have not been seen as children; Palestinians so dehumanised by the west that they do not even warrant the same supposed empathy or impetus for 'development' of white liberalism. I had wanted to write of millions of ▮▮▮ and murders and of ICE detentions, starvations, the many structural violences that lead to maimed bodies, that led to my own maimed body (still capable of joy), to the easy way in which everyone clamoured to the tale of Gauguin's Javanese 'temptress', tied to a painting worth a fortune, and the way no one asks what became of them or how they were abducted as trafficked child/ren. I'm tired of numbers counting towards someone's belief in pain. After fourteen years of trying to convince everyone when, for example, I need to lie down in a room, or need access concerns taken seriously, and/or am *burning burning burning*, and observing those who refuse to believe in and respect pained people, I am tired of having to prove we exist, how we have always existed.

I want the 'evidence' of survival and suffering to be what you already know in your body. And I am talking to you, the reader, who already knows and understands how a brown child, alone, abducted, shunted from slaver to criminal abuser, could have been in pain. Who understands how pain could be caused by the white supremacist, ableist mechanisms of finance (the banker Nina Pack knew and regarded as a trustworthy trafficker of 'little negro' children) and the arts (Nina Pack and Ambroise Vollard and all the 'geniuses' Vollard represented, from Mucha to Gauguin) and the literal police state (the policeman who allegedly found Annah alone in a strange city, with a plaque, and understood that this was a slave child that needed to be returned to their owner, rather than a child who needed help and escape). If you still do not understand, I refuse to waste my energy trying to persuade you of a truth I already know in my body. This subjectivity matters, whether or not anyone believes it. That some people have believed it is a large part of why I'm able to write these words today.

In theoretical terms, I consider understanding the possibility of Annah/s being in pain as hermeneutically marginalised, a form of what Miranda Fricker calls 'epistemic injustice', in which some ways of knowing, and the people who know these things, are injured. Pained people understand that whether or not we appear to exhibit what abled people regard as signs of pain, we can be in very serious pain. Our epistemologies are not honoured, and this slighting causes us to be disbelieved, to be denied healthcare. (I myself spent four years in acute chronic neuropathic pain without any proper medication, due to disbelief and lack of adequate healthcare; the remaining years since, numbering ten as I write this, have been in a state of regular retraumatisation despite medication, due to lack of access to public funds or adequate care outside my home or public empathy otherwise with regards to serious access needs.)

What I am doing with this work is using my personal subjectivities to provide 'hermeneutic resources' whereby those who do not have access to my way of knowing might begin to know. My way of knowing has helped me understand that there is the possibility of pain in *every* picture, an understanding that I've observed is difficult for abled people to absorb. This is the outcome of what Makeda Silvera calls 'epistemic privilege', which allows one to disqualify, to eliminate, epistemologies other than what, in this case, ablenormativity, whiteness and the west validate. What I speak of here is often what scholar José Medina says 'in race theory and in contemporary epistemologies of ignorance has been termed "white ignorance"; that is, the kind of hermeneutical inability of privileged white subjects to recognize and make sense of their racial identities, experiences, and social positionality.' This is epistemic violence, this is ableism. Not only that, but colonial racism, sexism, cisheteronormative discrimination against children combine with ableism, in the case of Annah/s being perceived as incapable of pain. We bear the brunt of multiple systemic oppressions, of multiple affective systems of violence.

We all live in the same world, amongst these palpable violences. Yet the 'stickiness' of feeling for those most affected by violences, by imperial duress, is mediated by arts institutions as much as by other purveyors of media and arbiters of knowledge, as is the prevention of empathy. That I can see such pain in one painting that other people gloss over as an emblem of its time, of a violence that they think perhaps no longer exists, is due to systematic desensitisation and dehumanisation.

I do not know where to start in using numbers and facts on how majority world children and adults, especially from marginalised genders and sexualities, are dehumanised, diminished, pulverised and asked to bear unbearable things. Which regions' stories would I highlight more than others? Whose stories could I tell, hundreds of millions of different, nuanced tales from Indonesia alone?

There are millions of indigenous activists around the world, from unceded Musqueam territory to Kalimantan to Brazil, who are not marginal. Who are survival itself, who need help. It is impossible to make an 'objective' tesseract of pain that spans the world, particularly as objectivity is a tool of white supremacist logic. I leave out here untold numbers of stories from past, present and future, of bodies connected to Annah through the same mechanisms that have injured us.

I am livid when I think of what Annah/s likely went through, go through, will go through in disabled futurities, and am also cognisant of resistance, resilience and survival, as exemplified in my own family's histories, in my communities'. I'm writing these words with a chest and right leg that has ached with pain all day, and will now rest temporarily; with the added clarity that the primary goal of this work is to affirm what we already know, not to convince unbelievers, despite what others have said. I write this for those of us who see in *Annah la Javanaise* the possibility of pain. It is not, and never is, our burden to try to convince others of our humanity.

Numbers, as Olav Velthuis shows, are also social and emotional artefacts, laden with meaning, and creating value. If numbers are not documented for incidents of violence, or deemed negligible, less value is ascribed to them. What effect and for whom exist the numbers of women in populations that others have the 'right to maim' (to use Puar's term), women being abducted, assaulted, murdered, disbelieved, rape kits piled up? How do you measure the destruction of entire civilisations? The United States government lacks any record of how many indigenous women in the US have been abducted and murdered. As I type these words, I am conscious also of how the Gaza genocide death toll rises above 50,000, yet these massive numbers – like the environmental genocide of over 100,000 Indonesians due to forest fires in 2015, underreported if reported at all by western press – seem to ricochet off the hearts of societies that would rather block out our complicity, our interconnectedness with profound devastation.

With regards to pain and the significance of numbers, what effect does it have that, according to a document by international associations of pain and hospice care specialists, there are over 518 million prevalent cases of adults with neuropathic pain globally, myself and many other brown women and children included? What effect did that statistic have on the WHO's 2017 decision to reject the urgent case for the neuropathic pain medicine Gabapentin to be named an essential medicine worldwide, because of suspicions that those of us who need it would be drug abusers – despite the fact that Gabapentin does not behave like the opioids associated with the opioid crisis in the US, a crisis given an empathy and attention that the crack cocaine epidemic has not, due to the predominant race of those affected by each crisis? With that single WHO decision, a future where I and other pained brown women can access necessary medication more easily is discarded.

The ableist mantra of 'abled until proven disabled', of suspicion towards those whose health requirements are not visible to the ocularcentric eye, is all-pervasive. It shapes our presents and futures. I want people to believe Annah is capable of pain, because I want all of us as pained people, majority world people especially, to be believed.

There is the possibility of pain in every picture. There is the possibility of pain in every person you meet. How much richer would the world be if we all regarded each other with this possibility, with an acknowledgement of all the political histories that make some more vulnerable to pain than others? What bravery would we be able to acknowledge in each other? What depicted people could we regard – and finally respect – as people who once lived? As children who lived through danger, courageously.

SOME MONTHS EARLIER, OR ANNAH #24,957 OBSERVES A PHD THESIS

This fish thinks she has the right to write about me. That was the first thing I thought, annoyance crawling inside me, anger puncturing the skin from underneath. Then, from hours, days, years of observing how she explains me, uses a computer to draw me and draw on me, pretends in galleries that she is varied manifestations of me, speaks to me from within them, with an audience, I come to understand her attempts. Her work wants to reveal how so many aspects of stories about me are fictions – and so, in the end, it is I who retain my own truths.

She is learning how to retain her own truths, how this truth about me is one of her truths.

In June, this fish – gills bursting, fins fluttering – named Melinjo, hands in a chapter of her PhD thesis that she's toiled over as only graduate students far too deep into their project can. She's been alternating between typing furiously and relaxing with a farming simulation game on her phone called Starhew Valley. This is, after all, a form of 'self-care', a term begun by Black American activists to denote what is needed when the government refuses to provide someone with care, a phrase now turned into a mass marketer's demographically specific wet dream, feeding the white supremacist machine. I've been around long enough to notice how these terms become theirs in a trail of twisted ribbons. In any case, I'm glad she has the game, and a few of her loved ones who are kind and patient, and her friends, though she worries about neglecting all of these at times, in service of the PhD.

The chapter uses, Melinjo realises after writing it, only citations from women to critique works by men. Though racism and ableism cannot be ousted by gender counts alone, this fact is a point of pride for her. For Melinjo, completing this chapter is a slight reprieve from the Gigantic Fear That The Thing Will Never, Ever Be Done.

—

Not many fishes get PhDs abroad, but there are infinite other ways to learn and prove knowledge. This fish called Melinjo is ethnically Minangkabau, which is the largest matrilineal society in the world, and mostly Muslim. Before that, they were Hindus and Buddhists, and before that, what anthropologists might call 'animistic', though all of these processes of being spiritual persist into the present, layered in jiwa raga memory. Everything is accretion, accumulation, syncretic, a process of refusal and allowing.

Minangkabau hail from the highlands of West Sumatra, and are found all over, especially across Indonesia and peninsular Southeast Asia. Minangkabau women own the lands, the paddy fields, the houses. The lineage is passed through the womb. The men have honourable titles – this one's grandfather was Datuk Rajo Suaro, 'King of the Voice'. And the men have the responsibility of merantau, which is to travel and return to the village to bring back riches and knowledge. This is why, though her mother left the village as a child with her grandparents, aunts and uncles, nobody really leaves – they will always have a family house there, inhabited by those who did not leave. Roof a series of pointed spikes curling up into the sky, like the water buffalo, animal so central to the Minangkabau. Melinjo has been there twice, and is due to soon return, to meet family members. When her brother was last in the village, he met an ancient woman fish working in the paddy fields, who said that she'd held their grandmother as a baby. West Sumatra is no sinless paradise, it is on earth. Melinjo knows that last year, in West Sumatra, a girl who was ███████ ████████████████████████ had her case thrown out in court. For millennia, patriarchal forces, urged on by imperialism and greed, have sought to kill the matriarchal, matrilineal antecedents.

Those from Melinjo's village who moved to Jakarta still hold regular meetings. They are responsible for the caretaking of the village as much as those who still live there. The women in Melinjo's family are mostly loud, assertive, gregarious. When Melinjo's great-grandmother Darama was alive, she would assert her right as a woman to take part in village-making decisions (for patriarchal interpretations of Islam have always threatened matriarchal ones).

In order to complete her PhD, Melinjo turns into fish form.

The Minangkabau are four clans: Bodi, Chaniago, Koto, Piliang. I am Chaniago from the Tanah Datar region, the name meaning 'flat lands', a tongue-in-cheek term for a hilly region with winding roads. Minang cultural heritage expert Atice Aryman writes that of Tanah Datar, it's said 'Aianyo janiah, ikannyo jinak, buminyo dingin' – 'clear water, tame fish, cool land'. When imagining one's self as a Tanah Datar fish, the word 'gentle' comes to mind, a giving spirit.

Melinjo's friend, also Minangkabau, whose family is in West Sumatra, tells her that young men there will still say of women, 'Oh, is she Chaniago? She'll definitely get on your motorcycle.' Up for adventure. Up to explore.

Every Minangkabau story Melinjo has heard, which others might call 'folktales', with a woman, involves this woman killing a person. For righteous reasons. When other girls dreamed of becoming castle royalty, Melinjo dreamed of being a princess of the forest, with bow and arrow. (When she is older, she will see a film called *Princess Mononoke* with instant familiarity.)

In her favourite of these folktales, Sabai nan Aluih (Sabai, So Gentle), the titular heroine kills the wealthy, corrupt man who murdered her father, after her father dared to deny this man the right to marry her, to marry his very young daughter as a man her father's own age. Melinjo is aware of Greater Forces galvanising to imply that brown-skinned societies were always more sexually promiscuous, more lax with regards to large age gaps in 'relationships'. She also knows Sabai.

Melinjo the Fish is attempting to traverse a newly found river, the Thesis River. She is without family in this river. She sets off, wanting to see the river's end, and it takes her four and a half years. But she has thought of this river for four years before that. The trees become paler. The water cooler month by month.

Chaniago fish are gentle and rely on clear waters, for digestion, for processing of the world. The murkiness that comes from nutrients, leaves, earthen debris knows not to sully the waters, but to be part of it, contributing to the clearness. At one bend, Melinjo sees the boots of construction workers trying to dam the river, stopping the waters that will carry Melinjo to her destination. Melinjo thinks of her family, and what waterways they might lose, the forests keeping her waters clear, from being destroyed. This is intervention by beings who see no earth, no fish, no waters. They see the dam turning all into theirs. Digestible. Parseable. Boxed water. Bottled river.

A dam for electricity, so their world too can be dependent on the filleting of an earth.

Melinjo the fish is attempting to speak to the construction workers, to change all their minds, to let the thesis-river flow. They think she wants to be caught. They only see her mouth.

I have had enough time between centuries to come across Sara Ahmed's blog on complaint, and the institutionalisation of complaint, whereby complaint becomes a process that excoriates and makes vulnerable the complainant. A process whereby any change for a better system can ultimately, easily, reinscribe the power of the accused, to make that person 'better' at their job, no matter if they fully, truly fully, realise the extent and nature of their harm. Which is not always the case. The accused learns the lingo.

The accused learns lingo. 'Fragility' is the lingo Melinjo has to teach the construction firm. It is not Melinjo's job to teach her mentors. The accused keeps their job. The accused becomes more adept at continuing the machinations of supremacy, no matter what they say. Actually, especially if they say things like 'I really understand everything I did,' mere days after a meeting in which they clearly did not understand, in a meeting in which not everything they did was brought up. 'Woke', a word apparently first recorded in print by Black American novelist William Kelley in 1962, is a non-destination, a continual process, yet the accused does not understand this, does not want to understand this. 'I've done it! I've awoken. Box ticked. Absolve me!'

I think about Melinjo and her pain and her visa process and the river being bent out of all recognition, and her life of long-pain, long-pain years, of thinking she can outsmart the everpresent kind of fishism that never speaks its name – some of the worst kinds. The kinds that do not recognise how gentle fish speak, or clear waters nourish, or earth maintains the right kind of coolness.

I can feel her. I can feel what it is like to inhabit her jiwa raga. She is writing while lying down as usual, her period cramps combining with nerve pain despite CBD and medication (for the other day, she swam a block too far). Yet ask her what she feels most of all, above anger or betrayal or shame at having gone so deep into unequal working relationships, and it is all the relief of aftermath. All she feels now is release's exhalation that she no longer has to contend with fishism in these ties, or in any prolonged ties, ever again. The river is ending on her terms. It is she who's siphoned the water her shoal need back in their waters. It is, she realises, a project of continual self-vigilance and self-forgiveness as much as anything.

She is ready to protect herself. The thought of us Annahs has been protecting her.

I am able to weave the fabric of light, space, time. And so, sensing this might be good for her – though I am as much a speck and cannot be held accountable – I perform a reversal. I reverse the flow of time surrounding the river, and keep it murky, flowing, adjacent to just-warm-enough earth. For the construction company is owned, ultimately, by a conglomerate. Its employees are themselves unaware of what Melinjo understands, genetic memory of resistance to suppression, lived experience of wildness as a fish.

So Melinjo the fish was never told her tone was 'defensive', and asked to dial it down, to get 'people' on her side. Never told she was 'bad' at academic writing. That the river needs to be dammed. The audience Melinjo is asked to appease is, she is told, a readership that is fishist. It is they who are 'people'. They who need gentle persuading and cajoling in order to admit that the ravages and brutalities of the past five hundred years are real. The fish are more real than their artifice.

I reverse the flow of time so that the dam's construction is stopped, it is shunted into a black hole. And so Melinjo the fish was never met with concrete pipes, thrown into the inlet and threatening gullet. The pipes speak in the language of pipes: with scepticism as to the choice of changing all pronouns in the thesis from 'her' to the more neutral 'them', with a pronouncement that just because things are 'politically correct', doesn't mean they need to be included. Met with an eventual acceptance of this choice with the caveat that this choice of pronouns needed to be argued explicitly in the thesis.

Argued. Argued.

The waters and lands were never to be dammed, so Melinjo was never asked to change the term 'Third World' (which she'd used sardonically, in quotation marks) to the 'politically correct' term 'developing country' (note that apparently, in some cases, terms that are 'PC' did need to be included). In an entire River Thesis which rails against the falsifiable ontology of 'developing' to mask the state of 'plundered'.

And so she, a wildfish of thirty-four years at the time, was never spoken to like a child by a bulldozer that suddenly appeared by the river. '… yeah?' '… yeah?'

And so this tone, verbally polite yet abusive, would never ring in her head repeatedly. Jagged echoes.

'… yeah?'

And so she would never realise with a jolt the incessant, aggressive paternalism of which the bulldozer was a part.

So the bulldozer was never joined by other bulldozers, and together they never laid the groundwork for a resort by the intended dam, owned by a tyrant in a land that spoke English. So these other bulldozers never told Melinjo in many, multiple places that she was 'shaming' a white disabled woman academic, who comes from an imperialist viewpoint. 'Do you think she's been shamed enough?' repeated in different iterations, in response to Melinjo's justified assertion of the academic's narrow-mindedness. For Melinjo was a non-normative-bodied fish, with a different kind of jiwa raga glory than that which is glorified by waste-covered rivers. 'The point is not to shame writers, but to make them come around to our point of view.' That was never a response to her decolonial analyses by the bulldozers.

She was not scolded, like a small thing – '… yeah?' – incognisant of the violence being inflicted, by a sudden influx of construction machines. That would never bring her home nor to the bay where the river ends, that she has only pictured with a fish-eyed mind.

I reverse the flow of time to repel the bulldozers. The dam construction causing a huge flow of capital into roads and factories nearby, and palm oil plantations using pesticides – even the 'green' plantations did – that funnelled their death into waters no longer murky with the jus of balance. A disequilibrium. Melinjo never breathed in carcinogens through waters she'd trusted. She'd never heard the bulldozer say of her anti-colonial writing, through the haze of her disorientation, that 'This is the kind of criticism that causes suicides.' Admonishment as physically felt hurt, especially in the body of a fish who had survived innumerable mental health downfalls in her youth. Of which the dozer was aware.

As I fold a space-time continuum into a cloth-textured Mobius strip, mauve light emanating from my hands and the curves of its infinity-looped spine, all of this is gone.

So Melinjo was never compelled to confront the bulldozer about the suicide line, which was then responded to with a long missive – 'I'm sorry I made you feel that way.' In which the feelings that were created in Melinjo became the crux of the matter. And Melinjo never had to read 'These things are all so complex' instead of an apology. Nor did she have to spell out, 'I do not think this is complex at all.'

And so Melinjo did not have to have a meeting with the toxins in question, in which she was brought to tears after an hour of the bulldozer apologising followed by equivocating. With the excuse that it was not their intention to hurt Melinjo, that they were trying to say (perversely, Melinjo thought) that more attention needed to be paid in the submitted chapter to structural issues behind the 'shamed' academic's shortcomings. Such is the convoluted logic of supremacy – no acknowledgement of how bizarre that supposed critique was, when the advice given to Melinjo was to look to Freud to dissect why the academic was narrow-minded, to avoid 'shaming'. 'I don't know,' they'd told her, 'maybe she understood that one can only see things from one's own perspective.' And because of how I sieve time through my fingers, Melinjo never had to think, 'My god. They are equating "one's own perspective" to fishist oversight and self-interest.'

My arms move in unison with the universe, ensuring Melinjo never learned of the bulldozer's overarching project in that meeting – and here, my breath was taken away by the insidiousness of fishist white supremacy in some soulbodies – the bulldozers moved among themselves, and revealed that their projects, the dam, the roads, the resorts, the plantations, all of it, were also beholden to the goal of 'de-linking'. Essentially, the imperative to de-link fishist thought and behaviour from individual culpability, and 'instead' blame the 'system'.

So Melinjo would not have to harbour this anger and resentment at the persistence of the notion of white innocence, of self-innocence. The toxins surrounding Melinjo would probably have thought that to call the de-linking project fishist and extremist was, in itself, extreme. Yet this is what it was. For the presence of white fragility, a term Melinjo herself had previously tried to teach the construction workers, and which the toxins misused and misunderstood. For it was both the workers and the toxins who said, in the meeting, that Melinjo's project of reaching the end of the river, of writing about Annahs, of highlighting white supremacy, was 'extreme'.

And so, as I cook in the kitchen of subatomic particles and Melinjo begins to feel the wafting of a supernatural recipe, she never has to contend with how the resort workers, once it had been built, asked for a reassuring hug following a meeting in which Melinjo confronted their fishist abuse. Prompting Melinjo to hug the resort workers and to say the Pavlovian 'That's OK', when it was not. After the resort workers had said, 'I know it's not your job to tell me what to do [after Melinjo had reminded them of this in an email, that it is never the job of the "marginalised" to educate others], but what should I do?' After it was made clear that they had no idea what the horrific implications of 'de-linking' actually were, after this question of what to do had been put to Melinjo and her kin of wildfish, and before Melinjo told them to be extremely careful when using students as unwitting subjects in the drama of unravelling whiteness, and

to listen to podcast X

to understand that the toxins and resort workers and construction workers and pipes and palm oil plantation trees were neither a therapist nor family member, and should never ask anyone to divulge traumas in class

to be human, be more human, Melinjo thought. 'Less obtuse about how you have now forced me to push for your apology and taken up a month of my valuable thesis writing time.' She thought, but did not say.

And so, because of my time-space reversal, Melinjo will never have to find the guts to say 'You are shielding white fragility,' and, in return, be scolded in triplicate: 'This is NOT about shielding white fragility! This is NOT about shielding white fragility! This is NOT about shielding white fragility!'

So as I undo the thread of time, I undo these interactions with entities met at varying points of the river, at varying parts of land she knows are getting too warm, in which waters are becoming clear of nutrients and shipped across the world. In whose minds wildfish and tame fish alike are meant to be domesticated and farmed, and whose public pronouncements of this have irreparably severed any ties of trust between them and Melinjo. In whose lives Melinjo – who had explicitly said that her pained state was never the cause of suicidality, though she had had severe struggles with mental health prior to, prior to, the onset of acute chronic pain – was to be met with the question, 'Didn't you say you wanted to commit suicide because of your pain?' Imagine asking that of anyone regarding anything they cannot change of life circumstances, especially when they have said firmly, when they did not have to, that the answer was always 'No.'

So as I unspool whole jiwa raga eras, packed into mere 'days' and 'months' by their timekeeping, Melinjo has never had to listen to verbal admonishment by the Head of Corporate Social Responsibility at the resort to be built by the dam. In which the CSR Head fumed, in response to Melinjo's academic critique of an established, US citizen, white academic's Anglocentric work: 'This is a disabled person! Who has worked for years with marginalised populations!' So Melinjo never has to be pummelled with the realisation that the CSR Head has forgotten Melinjo is an Indonesian disabled fish fighting for healthcare at every turn, whose university disability form specifying her needs took three years to reach her department, and never reached her university library, whose required disability watertaxis to and from campus were inexplicably, and erratically, left not set up and unpaid and for all but three months of 2019. Melinjo, whose decade of international experience as a disabled artist and scholar, working with fellow members of 'marginalised populations', had exposed her to a wide variety of fishisms from within the disabled global 'community'. Melinjo, who with a rush remembers the time an Australian white woman disabled colleague said to her in a meeting, of an ableist performance, 'Well, that's for the developing country fish.'

The flurry of the storm and landslides and human resources workers for resorts and PR managers for palm oil plantations and cement companies and pesticide unleashers and cancer-peddlers, all of whom are relieved to know that they can say the words 'centering whiteness' as a stand-in for 'being fishist', for 'fish abusive'.

When I erase all of these everythings, they are no longer to be felt and kept in Melinjo's jiwa raga, to be cleansed and processed in the space-time continuum, on top of the 'small', daily traumas of being migrant woman fish, disabled, far from home, trying to ensure she has a visa and survival. When I erase these things, Melinjo can focus on finally building a good life on her terms, and meeting the space where river meets bay with the support of her shoal, after a long period of working as a young fish in distressing and painful situations. When I erase these things, I wonder if Melinjo will retain the confidence and pride she had in how she handled ordeals with the help of other wildfish, of how ready she was to move forward in her River Thesis in accord with her commitments to the project. I attempt to erase the harm yet continue the presence of positive change, with fish around her in spirit, only those who might be empathetic as well as insightful with regards to the *Annahs* project, and be less likely to belittle Melinjo's frequent burning emergencies as negligible, as spoken of too much, as needing to be quietened, emulating a nurse shouting above a gurney. I feel, as one of the Annahs, in much safer hands. My ribcages breathe out.

A difficult but necessary marker of internal progress, of no longer putting up with failures to recognise her needs. Nor with the subtle arrogance of white apologia – 'Nobody's perfect, certainly not me' – from multiple bulldozers, and toxins, and pipes, and tonnes of concrete and palm oil tracts, as though explaining to a child. A sentence Melinjo hopes she will not say in any owed apology of her own. When I erase portions of time and space, I erase that which prompted Melinjo to reevaluate her relationships with dozers she had trusted, as dozers she had thought would never forget Melinjo was a fish. Of forgetting that we, Annahs, could also be fish, and that all of us Annahs are people.

CHAPTER SEVEN: ANNAH AS RUPTURE

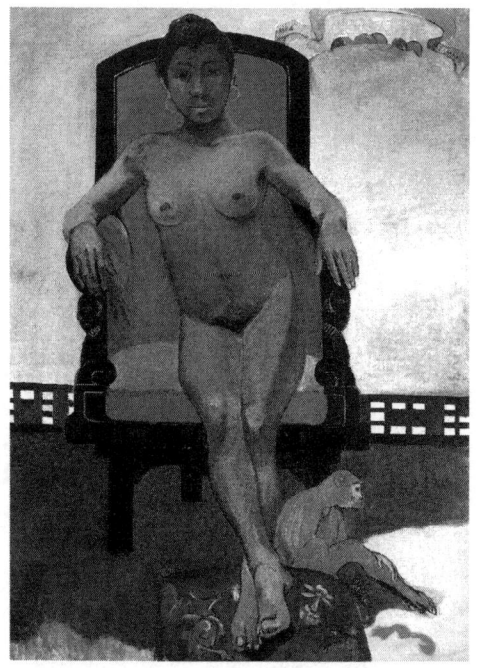

[Paul Gauguin, *Annah the Javanese*, or *Aita Tamari Vahine Judith te Parari* (The Child-Woman Judith Is Not Yet Breached), 1893–94. Oil on canvas, 45 1/4 x 31 1/2 in. (116 x 81 cm). Private Collection.[10] Painting of a naked child on a chair, their hair in a bun, their ankles crossed, arms on the chair. Monkey at her feet.]

---

10 Caption from Mathews, 2001: p.199.

In a rupture of jiwa raga time, the museum-goers find themselves beset by Annahs...

[Caption: Black and white version of the following image: Two white women museum-goers, appraising *Annah la Javanaise*, are approached from behind by a bevy of brown girls in brightly coloured clothing, appearing from a teal and brown vortex.]

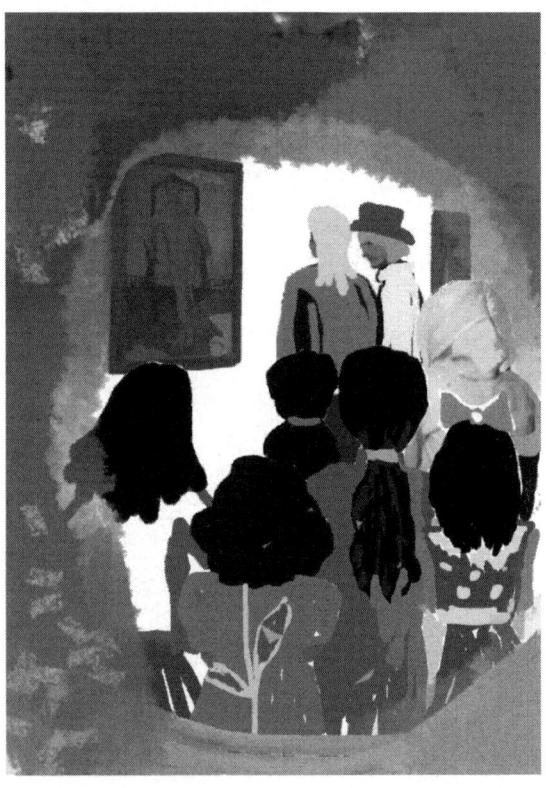

Annahs invade their line of sight. What they see is:
[Caption: Black and white version of the image described as follows. Four figures, three men and one girl, dressed in late nineteenth-century garb. The tall man on the left has his face blotted out by red, the middle two men's faces and bodies are blurred, and the young person on the right has their face and hands in a yellow glow. Over their face is written ANNAH.]

What they hear is:
child
child
child
child
child
child
child

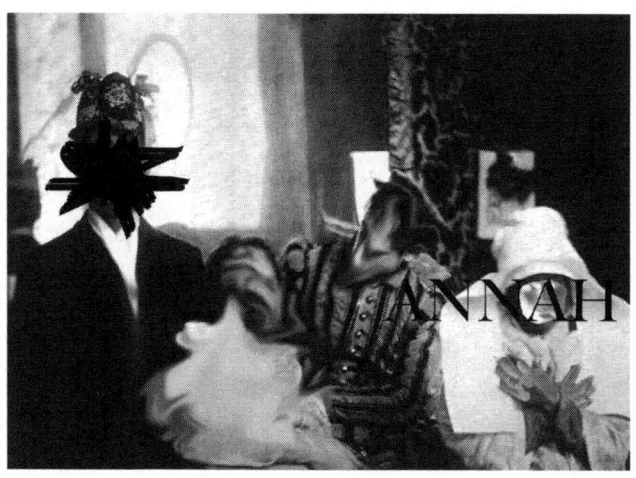

And things they have said to themselves, to each other, are repeated for them, in their minds, on a loop. Among them:

We need to eliminate third world poverty. Who else is going to help them?

I'm going to sponsor a child from a developing country.

I'm thinking of buying that painting, but I need to check our investments.

Did you see the news? Isn't it terrible what happened in Indonesia? ... Yeah ... Do you want to check out the Gauguin exhibit later?

It's so hard to find good help that speak the right amount of English, you know? ... Oh, is yours Filipina? See, I hear their English is better. Mine doesn't even have kids back where she came from, so, you know, I thought she'd be more focussed.

'Help her live, learn and earn.'
[Caption: *Annah la Javanaise* painting below 'Promoted Tweet: Bare International UK | @bareintuk | Annah dreams of being a doctor. Find out how to make her dream come true'. To the right, 'Help her live, learn and earn. UKAID'. Alteration to a real CARE UK ad on Twitter in 2016, which said, 'Celine dreams of being a doctor. Find out how to make her dream come true.' It used a simple headshot photo of a small, Black child.]

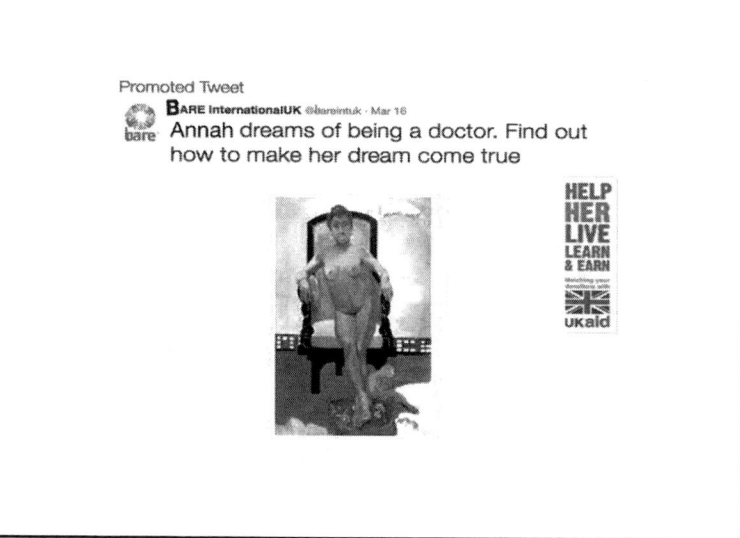

Loving, knowing ignorance is not loving at all; it is not a way of practicing loving perception. Neither is it a way of practicing loving ignorance or seeing the other with all her boundaries but not knowing much about her. In fact, it denotes a stance in which the perceiver and the knower are actually involved in the production of knowledge about women of color – whether by citing their work, reading and writing about them, or classifying them – while at the same time using women of color to the perceiver's own ends. It is a mode of arrogant perception whose alleged aim is not simply to coerce or dominate or turn someone into what we want them to be, but to make knowledge claims that are supposed to further understanding of the object of perception, of women of color. Thus, there is a sense in which this loving, knowing ignorance has nothing to do with love,

although the perceiver may claim that it does.
—Mariana Ortega

[Caption: Black and white version of the image described as follows. Two orange silhouettes of the figure from *Annah la Javanaise* interspersed with Ortega's text.]

When the museum-goers come to, the painting has disappeared.

The girls are fugitive paintings.

The girls are disappearing themselves and being disappeared, all the time.

INTERLUDE THREE: QUEERING AND CRIPPING TIME

[Caption for *Annah la Javanaise*]

The painting is calling to a young girl, an Indonesian domestic worker in London, to enter it. She wants to be buried in Indonesia. Half-Javanese and half-Minangkabau.

The white male employer looks her up and down frequently, makes inappropriate comments; she feels unsafe and stuffs her sarung and sajadah, rolled up, against her locked door at night. Once, she heard him try to turn the knob. The very next day, she is relieved that he has gone to his banking job (she's overheard him talking about sovereign wealth funds, like 1MDB), the wife asks if she would mind helping her take her six-year-old daughter to the museum, there's a Gauguin exhibit, the wife needs to take a conference call at the same time. And at the same time, Annah from the past has sent a message for salvation in any form, to come to those who need it. Siti goes inside the painting *Annah la Javanaise* and sees all the colours and muck and tries wading in it, bathing in it, trudging through it, starts to cry. Where is this going? She sees a light at the end and so many voices are calling: 'Here, come here with us.'

Her chest begins to hurt just from the threat and the condescension and the isolation and the distance from family and friends. The worry about dying so far away from home. Her hands begin to hurt, her chest begins to hurt. Something feels like it's cracking inside, about to be pieced away.

It's funny, being caught in the extreme. Because she is trapped, and her daughter needs to go to the doctor, she works through pain of a sharpness beyond the edges of possibility. When life is so absurd and violent that nothing of your pain will be believed, by anyone around you, including by the young kids, then you learn to smile through the shellshockedness just to survive. You do not have the energy to try to explain your pain; you want to work swiftly so you can feel the pain and try to make it cease in the comfort of your bed. The white British employer woman has period pain, talks about it and how it's as much as a heart attack, and doesn't understand when Annah says 'It is like that but much deeper, and more spread out.'

One night, the lights come through her ceiling, and so do people with her name. They pound with mortar and pestle some jamu medicine for her. Annah is alright lying down with lots of healing medicines in the ocean of women, in the end; her body has been broken and salved – but now that she has what can inure her from extreme pain, she does not want to rejoin the swathes of people who do not understand it. She barely understands herself, but there is no way to change the past.

ANNAH #8,923 FLOATS NEXT TO ME ON A TRIP TO ROYAL GALLERY X

One imagines Gauguin in front of this painting telling his stories of androgynous love in the South Seas or discussing positions of sexual intercourse while the clothed Annah silently serves tea to the spellbound visitors
— Nancy Mowll Mathews, *Paul Gauguin: An Erotic Life*

I arrive there as the early morning line has dwindled, but my friend Mariella had been waiting for fifteen minutes before that, and told me the stacks of people in wait had snaked outside the gallery. A disabled ticket costs twenty pounds, a carer comes free. / Annah comes free, / says Annah with a smirk. Mariella is wheeling me around today, so we split the costs and venture in, moral support for what lies ahead. The coat rack is by two large pillars, one laminated with a print of a brown girl's face in one of his paintings, the other with a print of a man I assume, not yet knowing any better, is (him).

As we pass sign after sign, asking visitors to buy passes 'gifting' Paul and co. – co. meaning Michelangelo, Da Vinci, Van Gogh – close-ups of brown, femme-presenting heads appear again and again on posters, as if he had only painted their faces.

I begin to shed panicked tears, only momentarily, body shuddering in my wheelchair. A fluid outcome of enforced change of state: I must go from acute awareness of the unsafety of everything associated with Paul, the product of my years of gazing disgustedly at his ongoing, century-and-a-quarter psyche-domination crusade, to actively numbing myself to the violence presented all around us in the gallery, removing a layer of sense in order to get through what I know we are here for. By the time I innocuously wipe my face, the process is done, I have left a part of me, scooped up by Annah. She'd been hovering around the back of me, to the right, only catching up now as Mariella and I approach the giant staircase leading downwards. Dante would have approved: infernal, the staircases down lead to a ceiling-height close-up of a Paul self-portrait, under his name in gold. We take the lift, obviously, and I am grateful to evade the descent into his face.

A high-ceilinged, round room in the den of the exhibit welcomes us to it. In a corner is a mini version of the gift shop upstairs, well lit, stocked with books upon books, square tote bags upon tote bags, of brown girls' faces in Paul's oil. You put girls into rectangles upon rectangles, squares within squares, and this is where they end up.

Annah is nauseous and looks away; so do I, but not for long – for it is fascinating, the keychains, the weekenders here from the Home Counties, all of our heads below an enormous arc of a map: the Travels of G. (And Epstein. And co.) Continents in outline – of course, Europe is the same size as India in this funhouse mirror-atlas – yellow demarcations for where he'd dropped off his syphilis. I'm sorry, Annah. She's dipped out of our space for no longer than fifteen seconds, and when she returns, she is facing the wall explaining the exhibit in three languages: English,

French, Tahitian. Annah's arms are folded, mouth serene. Possible Southeast Asian connections are erased from this show. *Annah la Javanaise* isn't part of this one – we'd skimmed through the extensive list of paintings in the pamphlet, as we descended in the lift – nor is the region demarcated on the giant map above us. Hey, you're free, I say to her. / Hm. / she sounds out, preoccupied with the geographic span of hubris in this foyer.

'The carping tone that had surfaced while they lived in Rouen escalated into bullying. Emil saw his father attack his mother, and he never forgot it: "When I was ten years old in Copenhagen [...] I saw my father bloody my mother's face with his fist",' writes Mowll Mathews.

In the exhibit we enter, Paul had envisioned his mother – the half-Peruvian, half-white daughter of socialist, feminist activist Flora Tristan – as pale, naked Eve in Eden. The snake wrapped around her body.

'Exotic Eve, 1890/94... For the figure, Gauguin combined a portrait of his mother, Aline Chazal (1825–67), as a young woman with a body and pose taken from a photograph of relief sculptures from the temple of Borobodur in Java.'

The same temple he had been known to mistake for one in Cambodia.

The writer Christine Riding once wrote, 'He was particularly proud of being part Peruvian, claiming that his mother had Inca ancestry, which he often played up when contrasting himself with his Paris-based contemporaries.'

In a Tate Museum interview from 2011, entitled 'An exclusive interview with Gauguin's great grand-daughter!', Riding asked Mette Gauguin, descendant of 'the great man himself' (as the website proclaims), 'Do you find the association with Gauguin a positive or negative thing?' Mette replied, 'I have to say that it has been positive, on the whole. To be related to Gauguin and also to his grandmother Flora Tristan, seems pretty amazing.'

Mowll Mathews, again:

> Paul's cruelty to his wife and children, as well as to any woman who happened to make herself vulnerable to him [...] was probably not new, but once he left his family, it seemed to loom larger in his life. In the years to come, not only does he desire a kind of revenge, but increasingly he seems to derive pleasure from inflicting pain. If, at the age of thirty-seven, he had freed himself from the conventions of family and employment, he had also eliminated the last vestiges of self-control that had kept the more violent aspects of his personality in check.

One painting in particular is unique in its form, more installation than anything else, the canvas displayed in the middle of the room, so that we can see there is a portrait painted on both front and back. On one side is Paul's self-portrait. On the wall behind his head he has recreated his own painting *Manao tupapau (The Spirit of the Dead Watching)*: brown nude paintings, horizontal, bodies interpreted as feminine. Paul looks menacing, his face slightly curling in threat, eyes dead.

'On returning to Paris, Gauguin painted this double-sided portrait to commemorate a new friendship.'

'Self Portrait with Manao tupapau (front)
Portrait of William Molard (back, upside down)
1893–94'

On the other side of the canvas, a hangman trick. Molard, Judith's father, upside down in relation to Paul's self-portrait, as though tied at the ankles and strung up, head swaying above the floor. The expression is vacant. Molard's position is shocking to me. I read the threat this painting represents – the artist has right of power over his patron, patron's family. He could draw so many small beings as he pleased, did as he pleased, Judith no different. Paul had conquered a world of victims before he came to Molard's door. The implied rope around the ankles was oil on canvas. The enlarged face of a white man with brown hair, covering one of the pillars by the coatroom, is of Molard – upright. It is not Paul. How convenient that the deeply intentioned positioning of Molard's face as upside down was not honoured, seeming too sinister to replicate even to the curators.

'The two had many ideas in common and Gauguin depicted him as a dreaming figure with glowing blue eyes, a great compliment.'

There is a painting of a small, nervous, brown boy standing at the end of a table, while a brown girl beside him smiles sideways. I want to scream. It is rare for the painted in G.'s work to appear frightened outright; this boy does. G. was, says Mowll Mathews, not restricted to girls as objects of violence. The exhibit text calmly states that the boy seems agitated. Then it numbered the framed canvas, and made sure exhibit-goers, in English and French visual text and English audio tour form, could all understand that this was a young subject in fear. And that we would all move on, encouraged by the gradual motion of the crowd behind, to the next piece, kindly made possible for exhibit by the owners.

At the end of the loop, we venture into the darkened cinema, filled with middle-aged Caucasians, white-streaked heads gleaming in the modestly sized room, standing or sitting and facing the rectangular light of the documentary. The talking heads are professorial, the shots of Brittany, of Pont-des-Avens, taken from any Travel Channel show, could have been stock footage. Gauguin's descendant is a man who has been raised with a sense of guarded ease at the peacocking of lineage. Calmly, almost brusquely, reciting facts of his adventures. / I would run from him in the daytime. /

Mariella says, in the middle of the show, not lowering the volume of her normal voice an inch: This guy was a fucking asshole. I nearly do a spit-take as several heads swivel round, say nothing through bared teeth. I sense Annah grinning as well.

On the screen, a Polynesian community worker is now an outdoor talking head. She is middle-aged, and calmly, lightly says the same thing I was told in my research, that back then women were sexualised earlier, and Paul was radically drawing them as they were, bare-breasted, rather than in buttoned-up European dress.

We need to leave. I ask Mariella if we can leave, and she says yes.

The association of bare breasts with sexualisation in Indonesia was a function of Western, male gaze – Charlie Chaplin's home videos from his journey to Bali are on YouTube. You get the picture.

We are leaving.

If people were deemed adults at younger ages then, marrying at what today would likely be a criminal age in their land, and their breasts were commonly exposed, what about any of this would negate the presence of a harmful individual among them as clear danger?

The millions of pounds poured into the PR machine of saying, essentially, / She was married to him, there's no such thing as husband ▮. Boyfriend ▮. Spousal ▮. Because he painted them bare-chested. Free. They weren't kids. There is absolutely no possibility of harm. Just because he was a wife-beater obsessed with sexual assault does not mean anything. /

Nods to how Western notions of marriage did not apply to Tahiti are always sprinkled over the myth of Gauguin. I read it as an acknowledgement of an overwhelming mouth of destruction as possibility.

The Royal Gallery X is a pseudonym. It is sponsored by Eurobank X, also a pseudonym.

Think of the complex loop-de-loops of discourse involved in this one exhibition. The local community worker in the film, in Tahiti. The captions of her saying that back then, girls became brides as teenagers. The film emphasises that Gauguin painting them as nudes was some kind of act of benevolent anticolonialism, colonialism as symbolised by covering up. Thinking of this in the present day, writing this, I nearly choke.

There is a part in the film where, in a doubling-up of bro legacies, they mention Van Gogh and Gauguin's 'intense' period of working and living with each other, followed by Gauguin leaving and Van Gogh cutting off his ear. It does not reference the German art historians who contend that Gauguin, in fact, could have been the person who cut off that famous ear.

I feel bottled up, shaking. As I walk-and-squat by Royal Gallery X on my way home, I pass window display after window display of young, brown girls turned into daily revenue – not only recently. They have been stockpiled for a very long time.

Before we part ways for awhile, this Annah asks about my journey home: / You okay to go by yourself? Apo-apo idak? Kemano di? / As though being pronounced dead had made her much less child than I. Her speaking in not just Baso Minang, but in the dialect of my mother's village more specifically, a warm womb of place, three thousand people – reminding me whose child I was, that I had been child. That in the gallery, we had both been in wavering states of children and not. That children have always been fully capable of asking after each other.

CHAPTER EIGHT: ANNAH/S ONWARDS

My intent is for this work to minimise violence, while also asserting its presence in our lives.

Annah has already been represented, as a highly valuable artefact on the global fine art market. However, this representation, *Annah la Javanaise*, is one I find untenable in its opacity, and in its violent nature. By fictioning Annah/s and pronouncing that *all* Annah representations are speculative and potentially fictional – especially given that those who record or write of Annah/s are largely collaborating with epistemic and archival colonial violences – I restore ownership over Annah/s' stories to themselves. I want so many Annah/s to flood the market with different self-representations, to trouble the value of *Annah la Javanaise*.

I am not claiming truths, I am claiming possibilities, and this is a crucial distinction. In so doing, I hope to disrupt the powerful structures of epistemic violence within arts and other institutions, those that continue to lay claim to a singular 'truth', even when their stories have contradictory details. Let us dismantle harmful structures of representation by declaring *all* representations of Annah fictions, not 'ultimate truths' – certainly including my own.

My representations of course still risk being those that the dead would not want, from my use of pronouns to the stroke of my hand making collages from ink and paper. Even, to writing this book in English. However, I must weigh this against the alternative: leaving hegemonic Annah representations untouched – without driving home that there are so many possibilities that white supremacist ablenormativity derides – contributes to 'the barring of nonwhite subjects from the category of the human as it is performed in the modern West', as Alexander Weheliye writes, and to the further barring of subjects who are also young, disabled, interpreted as feminine.

All my Annah possibilities are fictions, in order to show that what we think of as 'art historical fact' are also fictions. And, most importantly, I would like to emphasise that the real Annah/s themselves own their own stories and dignity, and I would like to sincerely apologise to them and their families for any representation they would disagree with. The myriad possible Annah/s.

There are layers and layers to Annah stories, not the subtle-sounding 'traces' of colonialism but what Ann Laura Stoler calls *marks* of colonialism. Part of my project is to convert understandings of 'traces' into understandings of how indelibly and violently marks of coloniality exist in all archives and artefacts surrounding Annah la Javanaise. In so doing, I would like coloniality to be understood as violent, brutal, maiming, debilitating and present, rather than benign and/or in the past. Understanding the ever-present and constant possibility of pain is crucial to this process.

Again, I stress that there is the possibility of pain in *every* picture, especially when those controlling how images are interpreted, and which images remain in the public eye, are colonial institutions. This continuous possibility of pain in every image is something we all know inherently – we have all been pained in some way and not been recognised as being such, whether hiding an emotionally stormy day at work, or begging for pain medication in a hospital emergency room and being brushed aside. Yet we are asked to follow along with an ablenormative world, continuously denying that we and others have the capacity for immense pain in every situation. There are entire universes we do not know of each other's lives.

Acknowledging the possibility of pain in every picture, actively, in language, in museum design, in curricula, opens us up to empathy for others and also ourselves. We are consistently prompted to negate possibilities of pain in images – despite the omnipresence of situations of 'total pain', particularly for debilitated populations. It is high time the structures that continually reinforce these processes be dismantled. It is part of acknowledging that every pain we have ever felt ourselves was or is real, whether or not anyone else registered it, whether or not anyone believed it.

Against the pervasive use of 'universality' as a white supremacist tool of erasure of specificities, of entire populations, I stress that the more brutalised a population the more the likelihood of painedness. And that for someone such as Annah – who was a member of multiple maimed populations, in extremely unsafe situations, and was very probably a slave – the likelihood of pain was high.

Saying that there is not even a possibility of pain in *Annah la Javanaise* is equivalent to saying that pain is never a possibility, regardless of circumstance, even if that circumstance is conducive to pain. This is preposterous, particularly considering the history of Indonesian enslavement. We are socialised and socialising others not to see (particularly for us sighted populations) or register pain in historically brutalised populations. And with this regimen, enforced by the regime of white supremacist ablenormativity that has spanned centuries, we are trained and training others not to recognise people as human, not to recognise the innately human capacity for pain, for great pain.

Denying that pain exists means denying the humanity of others, and of ourselves, limiting our capacity for empathy and imagination. Tolerable pain, however, is generative on some level – having experienced years of regularly intolerable pain, and learning to live with and manage tolerable pain, I maintain that imagining pain in others past, present and future is a bedrock part of change, of dismantling the white supremacist structures that undergird deliberate dehumanisation of majority world children, of majority people. There is urgency here. We must act to offer humanity and dignity to the children whose lives populate ours, who have died many years ago, who are fighting not to die today.

I wrote, illustrated and performed all my Annah work in a pained jiwa raga, in continuous chronic pain of varying levels, in the past fourteen years on the highest dosage of Gabapentin allowed a single human frame, which is not always enough. Experiencing so many instances of access lapses that people think are minuscule, 'minor details' – an incorrect hotel booking, a flight of stairs, wheelchair service that is late by hours or does not come at all – has caused me innumerable instances of unbearable pain.

It has taken years of unlearning to offer myself the same empathy I want Annahs to have had, to take now-unassailable pride in my non-normative jiwa raga. Creating work on Annah/s has been an enormous part of that process, of articulating and spelling out what I feel so violently in my daily existence as a pained person: the overwhelming disbelief of pain, strangers' looks when you take a disabled seat, people looking at your legs when you leave an airport wheelchair, the doctors from my past who refused to believe me and give me medicine. Being yelled at by a nurse to stop screaming in my ER gurney, until I forced myself to be quiet. Having people casually endanger you and cause injury. The stomach-dropping disappointment of people you'd trusted negating your pain's intensity and urgency, treating it as annoyance rather than emergency. Because my wounds are internal and 'non-visible'. To me, they are very visible. To me, I look pained because I am.

Throughout the completion of this book, I have faced racist and ableist roadblocks. In the body of and the making of this book, I have been arguing for my needs to be taken seriously, for my disability to be understood and believed and honoured, and it has not been easy despite all other privileges afforded me, from my bilingualism to my UK visa. Disbelief and a negation of power dynamics are tools of white supremacist patriarchal cishet ablenormativity. And these tools have conspired to plunge me again and again into states of literal torture, with disbelief coming from every angle, as sharp as the knives of widespread nerve damage.

In the experiences of Melinjo, there is complicity with white supremacy; there is denial of white guilt. This denial is explained theoretically through Gloria Wekker's concept of 'white innocence'. Wekker draws on the propensity of white Dutch people to erase the violence of their colonial history, resting on the presumption of 'white innocence'. One might say that the systemic affective systems that keep white people's sense of superiority intact, that also keep their sense of white innocence intact, mean that aggressive defensive actions are taken when these systems are held to account.

One day, I was invited to give a guest lecture in a graduate curating programme. A lecturer (who presented as a white femme adult) interrupted my Annah talk to call out that Brooke Shields had also been sexualised as a young child in photographs, 'and she was *white*'. I continued to argue that the added layers of racialisation, and of colonisation, particularly in 1890s France for a brown, unaccompanied child, made Annah even more vulnerable than presenting as a white girl would; not to deny white girls' vulnerability, but recognising increased threat for others.

The rudeness of this interruption was predicated on the negation of my authority as a lecturer, the false equivalence between Shields and Annah/s, and the defensiveness implicit in it.

Similar violences occur against women of the majority world all across western academia.

The systemic affective economies surrounding Annah/s exist outside the fine art auction houses: they are in institutions of higher learning, and far, far beyond.

Performance art as a way of speaking to or summoning Annah/s, including my performance installation *Annah, Nomenclature* at the Institute of Contemporary Arts in London, and my performance *Selected Annahs* at SALTS Gallery in Basel, Switzerland, have been a key part of feeling – through my voice, my body – the immensity and profundity of these spirits' presence and fugitivity for me. Brazilian artist Eleonora Fabião writes: 'The project of performance art is related to making fluid and dynamic not only art itself, but highly stratified and inflexible states of things. [...] It works against repetition in its broadest subjective sense: It deconstructs automatic modes of behavior, works against habit.'

In other words, performance art can be described as awakening people to the inherent fluidity and inherent dynamism of art, and of things thought to be highly stratified and inflexible. It can be described as awakening people (including the artist, bodily) to the systemic affective economies that underlie all things thought to be solid and immoveable, unchangeable – the flows of psychological and emotional cues and materiality that lead us to perceive things as being solid.

A painting is not just a painting. The painting *Annah la Javanaise* contains multitudes of hurt, of potential realities, and in the course of completing this book, I remind myself that there are potential sanctuaries and escapes from what colonists would have it represent.

The quote at the beginning of Chapter Six, from Nurma, a woman from West Sumatra, Indonesia (as is my mother's side) is taken from a 2016 PhD thesis on resilience. The author of that thesis, Yenny Narny, writes that the concept of 'resilience' is cultural and means different things to people of different places. As I mention in Chapter Five, painedness is often associated with the body breaking down, rather than the body signalling alarm as an outcome of deeply oppressive circumstances. Painedness is often regarded as a sign of weakness, and yet, in my own embodied experience as a Minangkabau woman, inheriting a bloodline of matriliny, I have come to understand painedness as a sign that there is too much to bear. It is the universe saying 'your pains are real'. As such, pain is spiritual, and spiritually complex, particularly when unbearable. Fluid emotional dynamics in pained women may occur on subatomic internal levels, with ontologies that are not recorded in colonial archives.

Now that *Annah la Javanaise* is in the public domain, allowing the painting to be used repetitively in this book and in Google Image searches, this raises the questions: whose public domains, and for what? I continually probe for answers to these questions.

Since Annah/s are children who the painting defames, would justice mean rethinking laws that prohibit the defamation of dead people? Who would be held culpable, accountable – galleries, art dealers, art historians, wealthy collectors, AI companies? It would hopefully mean thinking outside of Western colonial legal structures entirely, looking beyond, to soulbodyness, to subjectivities that come from Java, from West Sumatra, from thousands and thousands of cultures in which Annah could be protected in some way.

Should we leave children in the 1890s to their fates and only care about the welfare of children now? This is a false question, because the legitimation of violence in Annah/s' continued portrayal *does* affect brown children now, and on a gargantuan, monstrous scale. The way *Annah la Javanaise* the painting is treated is both cause and effect of racialised children's vulnerability and suffering. At the same time, the painting, and the photographs labelled 'Annah' are chronicles of resilience, of children who have learned how to survive, however short their life expectancy under such great duress.

Any news outlet, whether print or digital, on any given day, displays headlines of adults, particularly cis white men, accused of abuse who nonetheless continue to accumulate accolades and power on a daily basis – politicians, supreme court judges, bankers, employees of companies and government and arts institutions around the world. They are enabled, tacitly and explicitly, by brushing aside the pains and suffering of those who present stories of violation, and in crafting very specific visual and emotional narratives. Whether abuse by UN soldiers in Africa, by those posing as volunteers in 'a developing country', by those who present images that injure those they portray, by those in the highest seats of political power, it is necessary to understand that 'globalisation' as we know it is also the global circulation of a specific set of racialised, sexualised, ablenormative beliefs affecting young women and children's bodies. In illuminating facets of abuse that are ancient, yet also still barely touched on in 'mainstream' media and discourse, we are acknowledging their existence and the existence of those they affect. They are right in front of us, and unlike the painting *Annah la Javanaise*, we do not value them.

Again, I assert that ablenormativity, borne of ableism, is a tool of colonial duress because *colonial subjects need to be perceived as bodily and psychically able to serve the needs of colonial capitalism.* Millions of children are and have been debilitated and disabled by this overarching economic and political system that seeks to globalise, capture, commodify and destroy, as Puar writes.

What is at stake in attacking white supremacist colonial capitalism from all fronts possible is no less than human survival. As Heather Davis and Zoe Todd write in 'On the Importance of a Date, Or, Decolonizing the Anthropocene', Indigenous scholars have been arguing that

> the Anthropocene is not a new event, but is rather the continuation of practices of dispossession and genocide, coupled with a literal transformation of the environment, that have been at work for the last five hundred years. Further, the Anthropocene continues a logic of the universal which is structured to sever the relations between mind, body, and land.

Over the 131 to 132 years that *Annah la Javanaise* has been upheld as a prime example of white male artistic genius, Indonesian women have suffered immensely. *Annah la Javanaise* was a part of the fine art world in 1965–66, when the Indonesian genocide occurred, and through all sorts of violence before and since, including current persistent land grab on a mass scale for 'development', resorts, palm oil plantations, factories, mines. Potential Annahs were dispossessed of land and the needs of body and mind. By fictioning, by creating fabricated Annahs, I am trying to open the possibility of all-encompassing, ancestral, profound healing. Annahs could be offered holistic healing. In order to conceptualise healing, however, it is important to understand the imperial violence that both causes and masks pains, so far as to occlude the possibility of pain in every picture. As I've argued in this book, that possibility exists.

It is important to me that this intellectual work does not support false equivalencies. Part of neurodiversity is that every soulbody or bodymind registers 'hurt' or 'pain' differently. The point here is not that of all brown children who lived then, only Annah and those in very similar, extreme circumstances could have been in pain. The point is that truly anyone could be in extreme pain, whether or not they give off cues that ablenormative thought deems 'cues of extreme pain'. The point is also that even when probabilities of hurt are as extreme as they were for Annah, they are assumed to be *incapable of feeling pain*. This calls attention to the infinite other ways we judge people's internal states by their outsides, calls attention to the myriad ways all of us have experienced this judgement for ourselves.

The point is not that people can only be possibly pained if they are more vulnerable to painedness than other groups. Possible painedness, including extreme painedness, can certainly belong to soulbodies dancing in the street with a monkey, soulbodies photographed with abusive older men, soulbodies whose naked figures command wealth, whose memories are often desecrated, or belong to any of us, even when the outside world thinks otherwise. There is possible painedness in women smiling for the camera next to their abuser, and possible painedness at every social gathering where painedness might be deemed disruptive, and certainly possible painedness in every single workplace under capitalism. There is possible painedness in people who do not scream out in agony because they are told not to, as even the act of screaming would endanger them because of how their bodies are coded. There is possible painedness in every person you pass in the course of a day, no matter how their bodies behave externally.

Majority world adults and children, especially those who are gender nonconforming, are both more likely to be pained and less likely to be believed – and art historical archives reinscribe these injustices continuously through ocularcentric, ablenormative perspectives and practices, as crucial parts of white supremacist ableist cisheteronormative colonial duress. The fine art market, 'development' industry, state-sanctioned violence and the global finance system collude to perpetuate this imperial duress. They do this by socialising our interpretation of visual representations, according to harmful learned understandings of sexuality, age of consent and ablenormativity. It is important to underscore this, in order to right the hermeneutic injustice of us pained bodies not being believed.

I am not satisfied with even the outright condemnations of Gauguin's portrayal of Annah that already exist, either reproducing portrayals of Annah as *singular*, or reproducing patterns of racism. From *The Annual of Psychoanalysis, Volume 22*, in which two articles focus on Paul's psyche: 'Annah *"la Javanaise"* confronts the viewer with the brazenness of a Third World Lolita… The Inca savage clearly wanted to advertise that he was a sexual consumer of children.'

If we are to be communal, collective guardians of children and their families, we should describe no child as a 'Third World Lolita'. We should not link the word 'Inca', describing the heritage of millions violated by colonialism, with 'savage', the term employed to facilitate genocide, and continually used as a slur. We should think about how we portray children of the past as though their families are still here – because they are.

The reason why people are so quick to denounce the possibility of Annah being a pained child has much to do with how much they've bought into the circuitry of cultural emotions, to the point where museums in which an abuser's art is presented are part of *their* internalised sense of ownership. Of nationalism. Of empire.

'This is our museum,' one might think. 'This is our art. The messages conveyed about the beauty and preciousness of this art must be protected.' The spaces in which *Annah la Javanaise* is typically shown are surrounded by communities trying to survive being scarred and torn apart by austerity, gentrification and myriad other symptoms of wealth-hoarding that impact polis.

Each art object of Gauguin's, whether on display or in a museum, is a site of raw social wounds. A way of poking holes in neoliberal art structures is this acknowledging of vast depths in a portrait subject's chronicling and re/presentation. Even art institutions that seek to 'decolonise' do so in a superficial manner, inviting Black, brown, Asian, Indigenous artists to the table without putting us in positions to enact actual change, or if we do so, we are set up to fail or to succeed at great psychological cost – supposed reparations in so many hollow forms, in opposition to the true cultural victories that so many died striving for.

Countless times we hear: 'But we wouldn't have got his art,' when we speak about lessening, even slightly, our respect for known assaulters of the past. His art, Paul's, documenting abuse, twists all the ugliness of his deeds into revered beauty. To reach the lives of as many people as it does now, his art required the killing of millions if not billions of artists, who were women and non-conforming gender identities, including indigenous ones, who were children. That is not an exaggeration.

For the structures of neoliberalism, of paternalistic 'development', of the 'fine arts industry', of academia, of global money-banks, of western arts institutions, to have been erected required the enslavement and annihilation of thousands of communities. Colonialism does not deserve gilded frames and hushes for silence at the grandeur created by perpetrators of its violences.

Constantly speaking up, for and about Annah/s over the past fourteen years has exposed to me in detail how Gauguin's nature remains in hypocritical arts institutions, including in academia. Arts institutions that have not only been complicit in but actively put my precious, disabled bodymind through literal torture, so many times I cannot even remember how many, so many names I have deliberately chosen to try to forget over the past fourteen years, even as they recur – all these organisations and people that continue unscathed through the world, and will never experience one millionth of the suffering they have caused the person whose safety they so casually underestimate. Each time, thinking of Annah/s has helped me survive, amidst being reminded constantly how we as disabled people of the so-called 'third world' are treated as charity objects, yet when we stand up for ourselves, for our beliefs, for our peoples, we meet the blunt trauma of violence in word and deed.

What happens when you speak about the *Annah, Infinite* project, in the arts and literature, for fourteen years? Do people mock you? Call your work 'extreme'? Shout at you? Interrupt you to shut you down? Appropriate what you teach them? Take your ideas to further their careers? Steal your ideas for their tenure track? Romanticise your traumas? All the above, and yet, focussing on this project for my own survival in seeming insurmountable conditions of lack of care has also sustained me with the understanding of so many, which spurred me to continue to try to finish a book in the form of a long-withheld scream.

The world order is created on the bones of tens of thousands (at time of writing) Palestinians in Occupied Territories, after seven decades of brutal occupation, and up to three million Indonesians, and those many of us you turned into killers after centuries of brutality, it is created on hundreds of thousands of Papuan lives lost, displaced, assaulted. The world is created on 'dirty wars' and demonisation of opponents, from Argentina's history to Chile's, from Iran's to El Salvador's, from Indonesia's to West Papua's and East Timor's.

It is created, fundamentally and inexcusably, on the buried bones of *artists*. The Papuan women artists, the Indonesian Women's Movement artists targeted specifically for their art-making, the millions upon millions of people killed globally over five hundred years who were artists. Who understood art in the round, art as collective. I would rather their art infinity times over. I would rather all the universes of art that Annah/s could make. Miss me until infinity with your 'We wouldn't have got Gauguin.' To get Gauguin into your imaginary, untold numbers of holocausts ground untold numbers of art-makers into the ground.

'Post-colonialism' is an aggressive term; in an age where thirty-six Palestinian hospitals can be flattened in the span of a few months, where all universities there have been bombed to make way for settler colonial land, in an age where Freeport-McMoRan creates gold trinkets for complicit consumers globally, while the state brutally enforces genocide and repression around the largest gold mine in the world, in Papua, armed and endorsed by the west. Living in the west is a feeling of being around so many sleepwalkers carrying baseball bats as the ruling class, while so many of the masses remain human, continue to feel, refuse numbness.

At the time of writing, over 1,000 Palestinian children have been subject to amputation without anaesthesia. This is torture. This genocide is torture denial, this world is built on torture denial. What chance did I or my fellow survivors of torture-in-plain-sight, in the arts world, stand when such horrific levels and numbers are ignored by large swathes of our societies? I think about people who say these genocides are 'complex', and imagine them in a room with just one of many screaming children dying of heart attacks. I imagine Annah/s and myself in other worlds, where kindness is never a scarcity.

'We wouldn't have got Gauguin,' perhaps, but we would have

got Annah/s, and I know on which creative souls I remain on the side of. Eternally, infinitely.

*

'Menanam adalah melawan.'
— Widodo, Persatuan Petani Lahan Pesisir Kulon Progo

('To plant is to resist.'
— Widodo, Union of Kulon Progo Coastal Land Farmers)

*

To survive in this world with more and more knowledge of harm done belligerently, we must become adept at the art of directing our energy away from this harm. Become focussed on its opposite, and, in the same way as they dismiss us and turn everything into their financial, political, emotional consumption, we must plant the right seeds.

Not palm oil seeds or plantation seeds run by oligarchic communion with other oligarchies. Not 'plant trees, recycle' in carbon fundamentalism that does not uproot unjust systems. Not the seizing of indigenous lands for carbon credit schemes, resulting in the displacement, injury and even death of indigenous peoples – a process a renowned Asian-American artist called 'triage' and told me was the right approach to fighting climate change. (Was she even aware that she was advocating for displacement, death and the acceleration of colonially created global warming?)

It can begin with respecting dead children. It must involve loving and respecting dead children, and in so doing, loving and exalting those who live, who will be. It must devolve the overarching structures that connect to emaciate children's lives. It can begin with apologising for the dead children and parents, dead community members, assaulted people in Papua – a reality that all Indonesians, in ways large and small, have helped sow, continue to help sow. As Papuan activists have said, colonisation of Papua by Indonesia stems from American economic interests, maintaining the largest gold mine in the world, the palm oil plantations, through military violence and genocide over decades.

We must plant and tend and grow. Like others have grown. Like we ourselves grow. We must wrap ourselves in a canvas that pushes theirs to the side and protects what they rip apart. Rescuing ourselves without aid money attached to political control and paternalistic chaos-wrecking. Learning again what our biomes are. Tending again to our skin and bones, remembering how they are here for us daily. Allowing for unadorned rage. Planting accessibility, firmly, as escape. Not writing or speaking or thinking with their faces in mind, but our kin's. Basing self in place. And when that place is threatened, or we are perhaps many times removed from it, to enable others to protect that place. To stop those who would claim it. I'm speaking of land, and water, volcano and forest, and yes, I am speaking of our bodies as roaming through this razed hellscape, the apocalypse in so many places they fear 'is coming', arrogantly proclaiming that the end of the world will only matter when it reaches them; not that it has reached us all already, and that we, improbably to some, have survived.

ANNAH #333,333,333 (AND ME)

what it would take to be alright on this canvas.

give myself a blanket.
break myself a family off of the world's warm slab of families.
procure the lack of a need for company or smiling mouth while naked.
adopt the monkey or set her free.
oh, let myself lie down.
breathe soft and deeply, leaves in my hair.
make myself jamu, the medicinal drinks for every ailment.
be discovered by a jamu seller, slinging wares on her back with a cloth.
let her treat me with kindness. let her say she'll come back in a week to see how i'm doing, and it's lucky my family's here, that i broke off of slab of the world's known families.
the world won't die on us, it's painted on.
get moon in you,
get sun.

give me a way to play congklak with someone and i will.
go give me a way to spin tops.
i rip games out from the painting fabric.
then conjure myself back into a place where other children make sense.
where everything is a piece of music meant to prolong an age of still-smallness, growing.

cublak-cublak suweng, suwenge ting gelenter, mambu ketundhung gudel, pak empong lera lere sopo ngguyu ndelikakke. sir! sir pong dhele kopong sir! sir pong dele kopong.*

    *this is a children's song, and also a central javanese pearl of wisdom – it is ultimately the tale of how peace will come to you when you are at peace with the unseen, rather than worldly riches

★★★

On a celebrity news podcast, I find out that the heir to the family that owns you is married to a fashion mogul, and that he is extremely well connected, in fact is dear friends with at least one despot. You, of course, have always been so intimately connected with the wholesale destruction of the world. Why would I be surprised that the one who probably owns you would have an active hand in ensuring greater likelihood for apocalypses.

How do we save the tiny and endless universes that we inhabit as interconnected soulbodies, so harmed, so capable of harm. My Yangti told my father that whenever she felt worried, she would lie down, prop her knees up, and imagine she was in a place she described with wonderment, as the most peaceful land she could possibly imagine. I try this, and I meet her there. Perhaps you come to this haven also.

ANNAH #1,567,732
MOVES THROUGH HARUM

(Harum is an Indonesian executive, tasked with managing art assets for the family that owns the painting.)

This is the child's mausoleum. High ceilings, white walls, a home only found after doors and locks and cars and boats and airports, and the transfer of money and money and money and doors with locks and locks on doors and too many drawers for keys and numerical keypads and words far-flung in origin, off-putting for people to say when pressed to assist you. Just as, for domestic workers buried abroad in the twenty-first century, the fissure with home's soil is final – in Islam, you're wrapped in a white cloth and buried in earth within two days of death. And so no one from your village can briskly have a morning coffee, walk to your grave and pray for you. They cannot take young children to remember your name, who are given prayer beads in an effort to encourage contemplation, familial ties of the spirit. The doors and locks and keys to hard-to-access transport that must be traversed before they can meet the soil into which your body has been transposed, if it has been laid to rest on an island halfway around this planet that turns, fittingly for atlases, on metal axes. Gold, silver, weaponry, the lithium to be used for Green New Deals, derived from ancient homes with bloodthirstiness. An intractable extraction, as we try to harm less by ignoring, inevitably, other forms of harm we conduct.

The frame is ornate. Which it would be, for a painting worth millions of dollars, by the man whose work is most valued of all the male painters. This frame. It sings of security codes and security guards, of licensed weapons in pockets and tailored Italian leather and marble and a language built around, and to continuously propel, the words Restricted Access.

Behind the glass is his proof of your face. Has any other proof of violence been so well guarded as an act of beauty? As I ask this, I'm chastened – the answer is, of course, yes. So many examples that the question is a farce. The construction workers who built this resting place for a child did so to feed their own, living. In this way, the world keeps a starving in the universe, intractable histories of taking, of keeping.

It's a very strange thing to be preoccupied with a small, dead person, or people, for the length of time it takes a baby to grow to become a teenager. My obsession is thirteen years old today.

Four years ago, I began to work for The Family. The ones who own you, the magnates, they who magnetise resources and despise hangers-on, they'd allowed themselves to keep me at arm's length. At the job interview, Estates Manager Alicia DiAmato asked about my interest in nineteenth-century artistic preservation. Dressed in a business skirt and top, both dark grey, white kimono lapel framing her coiffed red hair, cat's eye glasses in a flash of blue rims, matching her turquoise bracelet.

'In LA, they say turquoise is a sign of protection,' I'd tried to quip at Alicia, looking down at the bracelet, having shaken her hand. Attempting to maintain an affected tone of professionalism. She'd curled her lips upwards in a reluctant smile, matte red lips wrinkling slightly. 'Yes, so I hear,' said Alicia, our working relationship begun, her focussed mind already observing my every step. My fingers fumble in my lap; I had already misstepped, the surveillance behind those cat eyes was already cool and constant.

It is not in fact unusual to want this proximity to ghosts – note the existence of funeral embalmers, forensic pathologists, mystics, historians, hospice workers, clerics, librarians, cemetery caretakers, archaeologists. Where the distinction lies is perhaps my desire to proclaim you a ghost in the first place, an integral spirit, a haunting of the Family Estate, and of my home, of those of us whose bodies had been marred in forms of violence both tangential and all of a piece with what they'd made happen to you.

And when I was able to see you, regularly, I'd finally begun to write what had been circling and swimming and diving and teasing and poking and prodding and awakened in my mind for such long years. I'd begun to pin down my feelings, and the thoughts enmeshed with these feelings, and the bodily sensations that interlinked every sensory input I'd noted regarding not only you, but us. 'You' meaning the dead, I'd thought, 'us' meaning 'the living'.

I have prepared the match, and the lighter fluid. I am preparing myself, and I see you.

This ends with gratitude.

For one and a half years, I looked at a full-colour, hi-res print of *Annah la Javanaise* above my desk in London, every day I woke to it. The print, produced for the *Selected Annahs* exhibition at SALTS in Basel, Switzerland, and used in my performance, evoked a sense of empathy and urgency of care for the portrayed. However, this was a form of buying into Paul's psychological dogma, of centring his work again and again, with the thwarted intention of centring *you*.

After nearly nine years of thinking about this depiction, creating around it, by the end I could not pass this painting above my desk without cringeing, then full-body nausea. I took it down, and when I smiled at the space above my desk, it was at its absence.

Annah/s, I wrote much of this book over the past many years wanting to show you how you escape. But of course, all the while, it was *you* – all of you, all the possible yous – that taught me on a molecular level the total bedrock of survival. You may well have made me smell burning in my most desperate times that could have been, after all, from the bonfires you make of abusers' legacies, keeping you warm. You guided me to an understanding of survival, so I could live it. An understanding of how possible selves can communicate with each other across space-time and help more lives along.

This whisper network of possibilities has always been its own universes of craquelure. The painting is not solid. It never was, and never will be, no matter how much blood money buys it. No matter how many of us they want to hurt, that they want to tell the world are here to be hurt and to have no say. Their singular truths are vapid, vapour. We are all we have, and you are the infinite unknowable telling us how much more there is to learn, how many more of us can save ourselves from whatever kinds of harm exist. It is not that you escape at the end of this story. It is that you have always escaped. It is that you always bring the possibility of escape, of safety, from whatever forceful cracks harms seek to make. You have always evaded. In a world that has always wielded such brutality upon us, we can always find you. There is no shame in being all the many shades of *pained*, in fact there is illumination, resonance, recognition in these histories. You give us this window into escape in all of our lives – endless possibilities of escape. Unimaginable to them, safe from them, not of them, ours. Infinite.

SELECTED REFERENCES

Alexander G. Weheliye, *Habeas Viscus: Racializing Assemblages, Biopolitics, and Black Feminist Theories of the Human* (Duke University Press, 2014).

Alexis Pauline Gumbs, *M Archive: After the End of the World* (Duke University Press, 2018).

Ambroise Vollard, *Recollections of a Picture Dealer*, trans. Violet M. MacDonald (Little, Brown, 1936).

Andre Gunder Frank, 'The Development of Underdevelopment', in *The Sustainable Urban Development Reader*, pp. 38–41 (2004).

Audrey Kahin and George M. Kahin, *Subversion as Foreign Policy: The Secret Eisenhower and Dulles Debacle in Indonesia* (University of Washington Press, 1997).

Benedict R.O.G. Anderson and Ruth T. McVey, *A Preliminary Analysis of the October 1, 1965 Coup in Indonesia* (Equinox Publishing, 2009).

Benedict R.O.G. Anderson, *Violence and the State in Suharto's Indonesia* (No. 30; SEAP Publications, 2001).

C. Coplans, 'In Search of Gauguin in Brittany,' *The Independent* (2003), https://www.independent.co.uk/travel/europe/in-search-of-gauguin-in-brittany-116067.html.

Christine Riding, 'An Exclusive Interview with Gauguin's Great Grand-Daughter!' *Tate Museum* (2011), https://www.tate.org.uk/art/artists/paul-gauguin-1144/exclusive-interview-gauguins-great-grand-daughter.

Clare Barker, *Postcolonial Fiction and Disability: Exceptional Children, Metaphor and Materiality* (Palgrave Macmillan, 2011).

Clare Barker and S. Murray, *Disabling Postcolonialism: Global Disability Cultures and Democratic Criticism Journal of Literary & Cultural Disability Studies*, 4(3), pp. 219-236 (2010).

Crystal Marie Fleming, *Resurrecting Slavery: Racial Legacies and White Supremacy in France* (Temple University Press, 2017).

D. M. Pomfret, "A Muse for the Masses": Gender, Age, and Nation in France, Fin de Siècle" *The American Historical Review*, 109(5), pp. 1439-1474 (2004).

Eleonora Fabião, *History and Precariousness: In Search of a Performative Historiography, in Perform, Repeat, Record: Live Art in History*, pp. 122-136 (2012).

Emma Sheppard, *Kinked and Crippled: Disabled BDSM Practitioners' Experiences and Embodiments of Pain* (Doctoral dissertation, 2017).

Eric A. Jones, *Fugitive Women: Slavery and Social Change in Early Modern Southeast Asia* (Journal of Southeast Asian Studies, 2007), 38(2), pp. 215-245.

Febriana Firdaus and Tom Levitt, ' *"We Are Afraid": Erin Brockovich Pollutant Linked to Global Electric Car Boom'*, The Guardian [online], 19 February 2022, available at: https://www.theguardian.com/global-development/2022/feb/19/we-are-afraid-erin-brockovich-pollutant-linked-to-global-electric-car-boom.

Frank Ocean, *Blond(e)* (2016).

Georgina Kleege, *Blindness and Visual Culture: An Eyewitness Account* (Journal of Visual Culture, 2005), 4(2), pp. 179-190.

Gloria Wekker, *White Innocence: Paradoxes of Colonialism and Race* (Duke University Press, 2016).

Intan Paramaditha, *Narratives of Discovery: Joshua Oppenheimer's Films on Indonesia's 1965 Mass Killings and the Global Human Rights Discourse* (Social Identities, 25(4), 2019), pp. 512-522.

James Ferguson, *The Anti-Politics Machine: "Development," Depoliticization, and Bureaucratic Power in Lesotho* (U of Minnesota Press, 1994).

J.F. Asmus, *Gauguin, Mucha, and Art Nouveau*, in J.F. Asmus, M. Castillejo, A. Nevin, P. Pouli, and R. Radvan (eds.), *Lasers in the Conservation of Artworks VIII* (CRC Press, 2010), pp. 1-9.

K. Baker, M. Engert, and T. Warren, *Leaked Report: WWF-Backed Guards Raped Pregnant Women And Tortured Villagers At A Wildlife Park Funded By The US Government*, BuzzFeed News (2019), available at: https://www.buzzfeednews.com/article/tomwarren/leaked-report-wwf-backed-guards-raped-pregnant-women.

José Medina, *Hermeneutical Injustice and Polyphonic Contextualism: Social Silences and Shared Hermeneutical Responsibilities*, Social Epistemology (2012), 26(2), pp. 201-220.

Judith Butler, *Gender Trouble* (Routledge, 1990).

Kalwant Bhopal, 'UK's White Female Academics Are Being Privileged above Women – and Men – of Colour', *The Guardian* [online], 28 July 2020, available at: https://www.theguardian.com/education/2020/jul/28/uks-white-female-academics-are-being-privileged-above-women-and-men-of-colour.

Karen Williams, 'Slave Narratives from Dutch Colonisation in Indonesia', *Media Diversified* [online], 25 August 2016, available at: https://mediadiversified.org/2016/08/25/slave-narratives-from-dutch-colonisation-in-indonesia/.

Khairani Barokka, *Annah, Nomenclature* (2018).

Khairani Barokka, *Selected Annahs* (2018).

Ko Ko Thett, *The Burden of Being Burmese* (Zephyr Press, 2015).

Matthew Cohen, *Performing Otherness: Java and Bali on International Stages, 1905–1952* (Springer, 2010).

Mariana Ortega, "Being Lovingly, Knowingly Ignorant: White Feminism and Women of Color," *Hypatia*, 21(3) (2006), pp. 56–74.

Matthew Cohen, "Dancing the Subject of 'Java': International Modernism and Traditional Performance, 1899–1952," *Indonesia and the Malay World*, 35(101) (2007), pp. 9–29.

Miranda Fricker, *Epistemic Injustice: Power and the Ethics of Knowing* (Oxford University Press, 2007).

Ocean Vuong, *Night Sky with Exit Wounds* (Copper Canyon Press, 2016).

P.R. Kamerman, N.B. Finnerup, L. De Lima, S. Haroutounian, S.N. Raja, A.S.C. Rice, B.H. Smith, R.-D. Treede, *Gabapentin for Neuropathic Pain: An Application to the 21st Meeting of the WHO Expert Committee on Selection and Use of Essential Medicines for the Inclusion of Gabapentin on the WHO Model List of Essential Medicines* (International Association for the Study of Pain (IASP), Neuropathic Pain Special Interest Group (NeuPSIG) of the IASP, International Association of Hospice and Palliative Care (IAHPC), 2016).

Kathryn Schulz, *The Lost Giant of American Literature* (The New Yorker, 2018), available at: https://www.newyorker.com/magazine/2018/01/29/the-lost-giant-of-american-literature [accessed September 22, 2019].

Marcin Skibicki, *Je ne pensais jamais musique. Je pensais mots. Langage (re) inventé de Serge Gainsbourg* (Synergies Pologne, 7, 2010), pp. 57-65.

Nancy Mowll Mathews, *Paul Gauguin: An Erotic Life* (Yale University Press, 2001).

Rachel G. Fuchs, *Crimes against Children in Nineteenth-Century France: Child Abuse, Law and Human Behavior* 6, no. 3–4 (1982): 237.

Rachel Silvey and Rhacel Parreñas, *Precarity Chains: Cycles of Domestic Worker Migration from Southeast Asia to the Middle East*, Journal of Ethnic and Migration Studies (2019): 1–15.

S. Pavloska, *Modern Primitives: Race and Language in Gertrude Stein, Ernest Hemingway, and Zora Neale Hurston* (Routledge, 2014).

Safiya Umoja Noble, *Algorithms of Oppression: How Search Engines Reinforce Racism* (NYU Press, 2018).

Sara Ahmed, "Rocking the Boat: Women of Colour as Diversity Workers," in *Dismantling Race in Higher Education*, ed. Jason Arday and Heidi Safia Mirza (Palgrave Macmillan, Cham, 2018), 331–348.

Sara Ahmed, *Complaint as Diversity Work* (feministkilljoys, 2017), available at: https://feministkilljoys.com/2017/11/10/complaint-as-diversity-work/ [accessed 22 September 2019].

Sara Ahmed, *The Cultural Politics of Emotion* (Routledge, 2013).

Sara Ahmed, *The Promise of Happiness* (Duke University Press, 2010).

Sara Ahmed, "Affective Economies," *Social Text* 22, no. 2 (2004): 117–139.

Sara Ahmed, "The Contingency of Pain," *Parallax* 8, no. 1 (2002): 17–34.

Saskia Wieringa, "Sexual Slander and the 1965/66 Mass Killings in Indonesia: Political and Methodological Considerations," *Journal of Contemporary Asia* 41, no. 4 (2011): 544–565.

Sita Balani, *Virtue and Violence* (Verso Blog, 2018), available at: https://www.versobooks.com/blogs/3707-virtue-and-violence [accessed 22 September 2019].

Subini A. Annamma, *The Pedagogy of Pathologization: Dis/abled Girls of Color in the School-Prison Nexus* (Routledge, 2017).

O. Velthuis, *Talking Prices: Symbolic Meanings of Prices on the Market for Contemporary Art* (Vol. 55; Princeton University Press, 2007).

Walter Rodney, *How Europe Underdeveloped Africa* (Bogle-L'Ouverture Publications, 1972).

Yenny Narny, *Resilience of West Sumatran Women: Historical, Cultural, and Social Impacts* (PhD diss., Deakin University, 2016).

ACKNOWLEDGEMENTS

Thank you, readers, from the bottom of my heart. I hope these stories help you with your own escapes.

This book and the art interventions associated with the *Annah, Infinite* project were created intermittently over about fourteen years, between bouts of bodily torture and/or discomfort, and sometimes during. The task hurt to look at as a whole, hurt to approach, especially as an examination of violence from disbelief I continued to experience; but when I was just with Annah/s, I was free and clear, with a focussed rage in a space that finally allowed me to feel all of it. It was a marathon, most assuredly not a sprint. I am grateful to come to the realisation that how I persisted and took so much time to complete this project, in its current form, is not a failing – it is a triumph of what some would call crip time, it is a testament to patience and to loyalty towards Annah/s, and loyalty to the truth of my soulbody, and the immensity of the path it took towards more peace. For those similarly loyal to a project, I hope it is a reminder to give yourself permission to escape capitalist timelines if your heart is with the work, particularly if you're ill and/or disabled.

There is an urgent need to expand pain narratives beyond the Western and Anglocentric. There is so much that can be done to right injustices, by adding pained interpretations of visual figures to the work done by disabled activists Alice Wong, Mia Mingus and Sandy Ho, creators of the Access is Love project; chronic pain and chronically pained scholars such as Alyson Patsavas; by Indonesian scholars of disability like Slamet Amex Thohari and Fina Itriyati; scholars of Blackness and disability in the West like Therí Pickens and Sami Schalk; of coloniality and disability like Jasbir Puar; Indonesian feminist scholars of art and media like Intan Paramaditha; scholars of coloniality such as Ann Laura Stoler; and scholars of affect, emotion and memory studies like Yasmin Gunaratnam and Sara Ahmed.

We can acknowledge, uplift and support in many ways the efforts of independent archivists in places bearing the marks of colonisation. We can urge governments to return artefacts stolen from countries like Indonesia to their people, helping to ensure proper storage and maintenance procedures are in place there. We can resist Indonesia's colonisation of Papua, and so many other current colonisations, including that of Palestine, and the root causes of genocide in Sudan and the Congo. There is so much to be done, day by day, to help return and protect life. My thanks goes to the vast networks of people who believe in this, who live for this.

Over the past fourteen years, since this project was first conceived of, many people have helped me try to survive in innumerable ways against the odds, including many kind strangers, including people who simply treated me with decency and care, and if I do not name you here, it does not mean I have forgotten any of it. Thank you.

My gratitude to everyone at Tilted Axis Press, led by Kristen Vida Alfaro. To Saba Ahmed, thank you for your empathy and foresight as to how we'd work on this book, and brilliant insights in editing. To Alba Ziegler-Bailey, my gratitude for your sensitivity, attentiveness, patience and steady encouragement, encouragement, encouragement. I am in awe of and forever grateful for your attunement. I could not have done it without you—thank you, thank you, thank you. To Deborah Smith, who first heard me speak about this book circa 2015, thank you for your immediate encouragement. Thank you kindly to my agent Abi Fellows for all you've done for *Annah, Infinite*.

Thank you to Harry Burke and to other curators who have hosted performance installations that brought Annah/s to your spaces, thank you to the Institute for Contemporary Arts in London and to SALTS Basel. Thank you to the Tate and to other organisations that have hosted my obsessive talking about Annah/s (even at their expense), and speakers such as Aditi Jaganathan who have facilitated discussion about Annah/s. Thank you to Nuraki Aziz of BBC Indonesia for covering the *Annah: Nomenclature* installation at the ICA; it meant so much to have this story covered in Indonesian. Thank you to the LPDP scholarship for funding my practice-based PhD research, which resulted in the art and writing that formed part of my thesis '*Annah, Infinite* and Ablenormativity as Imperial Duress: Relations, Assumptions, Power and Abuse in Cripping Annah la Javanaise'.

Thank you kindly to the editors of publications where excerpts of this manuscript were first published, in different forms: *The White Review*, *The New Inquiry*, *Afterall*, Alice Wong's *Disability Visibility* and *Catapult*.

A special thank you to my brother, who read this manuscript with sensitivity, for your understanding and suggestions. Thank you to my father, for helping me ensure the chapter 'On Java' was as attuned as possible, and to my mother, for allowing her childhood likeness to be part of this book. Another special thank you to Cat Chong, who read *Annah* with a much needed crip, Southeast Asian perspective, for your attuned recommendations and support.

To my other friends, including Bu Tina, Bu Tur, Santi, Oluwatosin, Dhitta and Butre, Anggita, Arief and Prima, Maesy, Annabel and Shura, Pepe, San, Dan and Em, Emil, and Dom—thank you all. Thanks to all my majority world literature and arts peers who have included me in community – including Southeast Asian community, disability community, and Indonesian women artist community. Thank you to fellow writers, artists and translators including Jeremy Tiang, Daisy Rockwell, Kavita Bhanot, Tiffany Tsao, Cynthia Dewi Oka, Anthony (Vahni) Capildeo, Polly Atkin, Roy McFarlane, Shash Trevett, Jane Commane, the brilliant artist written of here with the pseudonym Mariella, the Shadow Heroes translators' collective that I'm a part of, my talented mentees over the years, and my fellow contributors to *Violent Phenomena: 21 Essays on Translation*. If I haven't listed you here, please know that any small measure of support you have given to this project remains meaningful.

Thank you to the innumerable artists whose work sustained this one, who helped me be still, the musicians and visual artists and filmmakers and more, may you always be free to create. Thank you to my kind undergraduate Visual Anthropology professor Dr Hilda Lloréns, who first showed me a glimpse of the way, and to Dr Yasmin Gunaratnam, Dr Michelle Williams Gamaker, Dr Clare Barker, and Dr Susan Kelly for treating this project with care, especially when others did not. Thank you to Atice Aryman for sharing Minang cultural knowledge with me, and with everyone, through her important work. Thank you to my Tek Ade and to all my kith and kin in West Sumatra for teaching me about our culture.

Immeasurable thank yous to my family for love and an education in so many of the wisdoms in this book, especially to my brother and my sister-in-law for access care and protection in their presence. 'Brainwaves aren't local,' my father always says, and I feel you all with me every step of the way, and will always be in your corner. Loving thanks to my in-laws, to Ba and everyone – abhaar!

Nearly last but not least (and not like we're working in linear time), thank you to my excellent husband, with whom I can laugh in every time-space configuration. To find someone who has taken the time to understand and cheer on these stories, what a rare escape hatch.

Most of all, thank you to Annah/s, and to my dearly departed, who have left this plane over the last fourteen years. This includes my Yangti, to whom this book is dedicated alongside all the young spirits of Annah/s. I am now safer – though all my bodymind has been through remains, and the threat of unwanted violence stays in the wings, as the unfeeling world lives alongside all we value. I am in a better place now than I was when I began this book, and thinking about you and the wisdoms you shared led me to more respite. Terima kasihku; you will always be with me. May you always gleefully exist beyond any need to escape.

342 Annah, Infinite

This book has been a caption for the painting Annah la Javanaise. Within this intermedial translation are universes of other translations for this visual image. To translate this depiction is a generative act, an act of fugitivity, secretive, protective, impervious. An honouring of the living who continue on many planes of existence, extending into always. →]

Copyright © Khairani Barokka, 2025
This edition was published in the United Kingdom by Tilted Axis Press, 2025.
All rights reserved.
tiltedaxispress.com
The rights of Khairani Barokka to be identified as the author of this work have been asserted in accordance with Section 77 of the Copyright, Designs and Patent Act 1988.
ISBN (paperback): 978-1-917126-03-8
ISBN (ebook): 978-1-917126-04-5
A catalogue record for this book is available from the British Library.
Acquiring Editor: Deborah Smith
Copy Editor: Saba Ahmed
Cover Art and Design: Amandine Forest
Line Editor: Alba Ziegler-Bailey
Managing Editor: Mayada Ibrahim
Marketing Manager: Trà My Hickin
Proofreader: Alice Frecknall
Publisher and Director: Kristen Vida Alfaro
Publishing Assistant: Phương Anh
Rights Director: Julia Sanches
Sales and Marketing Lead: Meera Ghanshamdas
Typesetter: Justin Moore
Printed and bound by CMP (UK) Limited

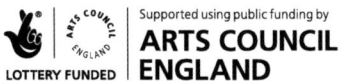

ABOUT TILTED AXIS PRESS

Tilted Axis Press is an independent publisher of contemporary literature by the Global Majority, translated into or written in a variety of Englishes.

Founded in 2015, our practice is an ongoing exploration into alternatives to the hierarchisation of certain languages and forms of translation, and the monoculture of globalisation.

We focus on contemporary translated fiction and also publish poetry and non-fiction. Our editorial vision, Translating Waters, is shaped by the complex movement of language, stories, and imaginations. Often fugitive and always trailblazing, our authors and translators challenge how we read, what we think, and how we view the world.

Building and nourishing community is part of our publishing practice. Inspired by the Afro-Asia Writers' Association, literary collectives, and grassroots organisations, we seek collaborative and interdisciplinary projects that expand what constitutes the literary and build on existing solidarities across the globe.

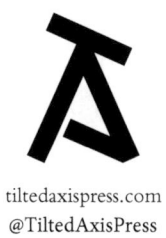

tiltedaxispress.com
@TiltedAxisPress